The Psychosocial Development of Puerto Rican Women

THE PSYCHOSOCIAL DEVELOPMENT OF PUERTO RICAN WOMEN

EDITED BY

Cynthia T. García Coll & María de Lourdes Mattei

PRAEGER

New York
Westport, Connecticut
London

Copyright Acknowledgment

The editors and publisher are grateful to the estate of
Julia de Burgos for permission to quote from the following:
Julia de Burgos: Obra Poética, Istituto de Cultura Puertorri-
queña, 1961. Primera Edicion.
Y. Jiménez de Baez, Julia de Burgo: Vida y poesia,
Editorial Coquí, 1966.

Library of Congress Cataloging-in-Publication Data

The Psychosocial development of Puerto Rican women /edited
   by Cynthia T. García Coll and María de Lourdes Mattei.
      p.   cm.
   Bibliography: p.
   Includes index.
   ISBN 0-275-92345-2 (alk. paper)
   1. Women--Puerto Rico--Psychology. 2. Puerto Rican women--
Psychology. I. García Coll, Cynthia T. II. Mattei, María
de Lourdes.
HQ1206.P78 1989
155.6'33'097295--dc 19   88-26047

Library of Congress Catalog Card Number: 88-26047
ISBN: 0-275-92345-2

First published in 1989

Praeger Publishers, One Madison Avenue, New York, NY 10010
A division of Greenwood Press, Inc.

Printed in the United States of America
∞™
The paper used in this book complies with the Permanent
Paper Standard issued by the National Information Standards
Organization (Z39.48 -1984).

10 9 8 7 6 5 4 3 2 1

Dedicado a mi compañero Andrés
MLM

A las niñas Puertorriqueñas . . . para que sepan
de donde vienen . . . y hacia donde van
CGC

Contents

Tables

Preface

María de Lourdes Mattei
Cynthia T. García Coll

Y me veo, me veo, me veo
de frente y para siempre:
aquí, hoy, humana,
poeta, borincana
y Una

"Veo, veo," Iris M. Landrón, 1976

Wet, dew-covered feet quickly pace down the mud path to the river. It is early morning on a clear, radiantly lush December day in the countryside of Puerto Rico. Rosa, the oldest of 10, washes the family's clothes while her mother begins preparing the meals for the day. "Will 'papi' come home today? . . . I hope I can go back to school soon . . . maybe. . . ." Her thoughts swirl and twirl as she wrings the white cotton. Racing questions cloud her forehead with warm salty drops. Ay Bendito!

Twenty years later Rosa sees her five-year-old daughter to school as she drives to her job as a bilingual receptionist in a human services agency in a small city in Massachusetts. "The heating here is making my asthma worse," comments Rosa in a dry whisper as she takes her bulky magenta coat off and straightens the short-sleeved dress she bought on her last trip to the city. All in one life course. . . .

How will Rosa raise her daughter? She grew up in a big family; she is alone in a two-bedroom apartment. Rosa completed her G.E.D. (graduate equivalency diploma) when her aunt sent for her; her mother could not read or write; Rosa's daughter will learn computers. Rosa hardly spanks her daughter, and she fears the girl will not respect her; Rosa still remembers her father's dark whipping belt. Her mother never left her hometown; her family made up her circle of friends. In a very different land, thousands of miles from where she was born, Rosa has two close friends—a workmate and her upstairs neighbor. Rosa's mother died after her eleventh labor. Alone at night, after her only child falls asleep, Rosa wonders who will take care of her after she retires.

Characterized by dramatic political and economic transformations, this century has witnessed significant changes in every sphere of Puerto Rican culture and society. Like many other Latin American countries, the closing of the nineteenth century found Puerto Rico an agricultural society with poverty rampant throughout the insular landscape. Four centuries under the imperial reign of Spain had seen the decimation of the Island's indigenous population, the acquisition of slaves from Africa, and the arrival of numerous white settlers from Spain and other Mediterranean lands, as well as others who sought to escape liberation struggles in other Spanish colonies. The forging of a Puerto Rican national identity and the development of an autonomous culture surged to encounter a new century and a new imperial power, the United States.[1]

Today Puerto Rico is an industrial, consumer-oriented society. As a colonial satellite of the United States, the Puerto Rican cultural orbit has two geographical foci, San Juan and New York City. Massive migratory waves commenced in the 1930s and gave momentum to the circular flux between the Island and the United States. This geographical oscillation continues to pulse today (see History Task Force 1979; Morales 1986). The 1980 U.S. Census figures estimate the Island population at more than 3 million (Census 1980); another 2.3 million reside in the United States (Census 1987). Moreover, Puerto Ricans in the United States are a part of the fastest growing minority population, the Hispanics.

For Puerto Ricans, no aspect of social life has remained unchanged. Women's position is no exception.

Traditionally relegated to a predominantly domestic sphere of influence and activity, Puerto Rican women currently participate and shape family and work modes unimaginable to our grandmothers (e.g., single heads of households, factory and professional occupations). However, as Rosa exemplifies, the social, political, and economic changes have brought about complex dilemmas for Puerto Rican women throughout their lifespan.

In a spirited effort to contribute to the sparse but growing body of literature on Puerto Rican women,[2] this book presents a diversity of dilemmas faced by a variety of Puerto Rican women at various periods in their life cycle. The psychosocial issues discussed through a wide range of methodologies and perspectives are organized following major developmental stages: Childhood and Adolescence, Adulthood, and Growing Old. This developmental approach adds a dynamic angle to the study of gender: It reflects the interplay of psychosocial factors as they impact throughout a woman's lifespan (e.g., Rossi 1985; Levinson 1978; Erickson 1982).

In Chapter 1 Zavala-Martínez delves into the life and work of one of our most significant poets, Julia de Burgos. Julia's life experiences illustrate the multiple transitions and traumatic translocations endured by many Puerto Ricans. Beginning in rural, poverty-stricken, insular surroundings, Julia's life ends in the inner-city extremes of New York City. The ghosts of past losses are shadowed in the cherished and lost landscape of her verse. Zavala-Martínez insightfully examines the parallels between the tragic elements of the sociocultural context and Julia's personal development as a woman-poet. Her analysis offers us a biographical, vivid metaphor of a Puerto Rican woman's struggle to transcend the calamitous conditions of her individual existence through creative activity. Thus, Julia de Burgos, transcending her personal tragedy, leaves us with a culturally affirming legacy, one that endows and elevates our collective history.

Continuing to draw on Puerto Rican women's literature, Vélez uses literary analysis of short stories in order to portray cultural contradictions inherent in the constructions of "a woman's place." Vélez highlights the dialectical tension engendered by universal as well as cultural-specific themes of growth and development, drawing on psychoanalytic and cultural constructs. Exploring the symbolism and allegories reflected in the plots, Vélez exposes the ambivalence and internal struggles manifested in the characters' attempts to integrate their individual drives and desires with the societal expectations prescribed by their place in traditional Puerto Rican culture.

The developmental periods represented in our next section, Childhood and Adolescence, have received minimal attention in the literature on Puerto Rican women. Addressing a significant childhood experience encountered by many Puerto Rican girls in the United States, Vázquez-Nuttall and Romero-García examine the clash of demands in the transition from home to school. The conflicts, discontinuities, and discriminations encountered in the move from a Puerto Rican family milieu to a school environment in the United States, are discussed. Particular attention is paid to the contrast between the traditional socialization patterns of our culture and the school's values and expectations. The authors conclude with valuable recommendations pertinent to all interested in the pedagogical development of Puerto Rican children.

A topic that has generated considerable public and academic attention is the subject of our chapter on Adolescence. Two generations earlier, adolescent pregnancy was the norm rather than the exception in Puerto Rico—as in many agricultural societies. With the socioeconomic upheavals of this century (e.g., industrialization, increase in literacy, and participation of women in a changing labor force), a proportion of Puerto Rican women has delayed childbearing to later stages. At the same time, pregnancy during the adolescent years continues to be prevalent among certain segments of this population. In Chapter 4 García Coll and her associates analyze the consequences of pregnancy and childbearing for a low socioeconomic, urban group of women in Puerto Rico. Their study compares the reported experiences of young and older adolescents with adult women during pregnancy and the post-partum period. Their findings challenge commonly held assumptions about the unidimensionally negative consequences of adolescent pregnancy.

A variety of psychosocial dilemmas are examined in the next section on Adulthood and Growing Old. Each chapter touches on an important issue handled during the adult period. Focusing on the relational world of a group of professional women on the Island, Margarida Juliá employs a phenomenological approach to explore the developmental and sociocultural themes voiced through their inter-

views. According to this author, these themes are suggestive of the woman's developmental position as reflected in
her definition of self and in relation to others, but they
are expressed within a cultural context where continuities
of family attachments, loyalties, and responsibilities are
emphasized.

Starting with a historical perspective, Santos Ortiz
and Muñoz Vázquez explore female adult sexuality in Chapter 6. The authors contrast reported expressions of sexuality in two groups of Puerto Rican women on the Island.
Their findings and discussion suggest the significance of
socioeconomic factors in the experience and expression of
adult female sexuality.

The following chapter makes us consider the psychological consequences of migration. Considered one of the
most stressful psychological events in an individual life
(Pacheco et al. 1979), Comas-Díaz provides a framework to
understand the impact of migration at various developmental stages. Furthermore, the author discusses the mental
health implications of contemporary migration patterns,
taking into account gender as well as race. In her conclusions, Comas-Díaz provides culturally specific guidelines
for assessment and psychotherapeutic interventions to ameliorate the detrimental psychological consequences of cross-
cultural transitions.

Considering the alarming rise of households headed
by Puerto Rican women (43 percent) in the United States
(Census 1987), Borrás analyzes the dilemmas involved in
child discipline. In traditional Puerto Rican culture the
father typically exercises the disciplinarian function;
mothers provide the nurturance. When a husband is not
present (or is inconsistently available), women find themselves having to fulfill both roles. Borrás discusses the
conflicts experienced by these women as they confront the
increasing demands of their new situation. Case examples
are used to illustrate the issues as well as to suggest
psychotherapeutic interventions designed to address this
problem.

The erosion of traditional social structures can set
the stage for new complexities and confusing difficulties,
as well as unimagined possibilities for growth and development. In Chapter 9 Mattei explores the social networks
of urban, working Puerto Rican women in the United States.
The literature amply documents the significant functions
that women play in the Puerto Rican family. Emphasizing

the contradictory aspects of traditional relational ties, the author discusses characteristics of social networks that may enhance and/or impede Puerto Rican women's autonomy.

In our concluding chapter attention is drawn to one of the most neglected and invisible groups of Puerto Rican women--the elderly. Mahard presents some early sociodemographic findings from a recent large-scale survey conducted in New York City. Focusing on migration and acculturation processes, the author elaborates on the high risk elements encountered by Puerto Rican women in this period of their lifespan.

We hope that the psychosocial issues discussed in this book inspire further explorations and studies of Puerto Rican women at all stages . . . everywhere.[3]

NOTES

1. For comprehensive accounts of Puerto Rican history see Morales Carrión (1972), Maldonado-Dennis (1972),and Quintero Rivera (1976, 1988). In addition, an insightful and thought-provoking commentary on Puerto Rican cultural life and heritage can be found in Gonzáles (1980, 1986). For a perspective on economic development, see Dietz (1986).

2. Among the authors who have carved a place in the literature for expanding our knowledge of Puerto Rican women's history, we thank Azize (1985, 1987), Picó (1980), Rivera Quintero (1980), and Silvestrini (1980). On psychosocial issues we note Rivera Ramos (1985) and especially Acosta-Belén (1980, 1986).

3. We would like to acknowledge the support of Maureen McElroy, Gloria DeCorral, and Dr. George Zimmar of Praeger Publishers in the preparation of this manuscript.

REFERENCES

Acosta-Belén, E., ed. 1980. La Mujer en la Sociedad Puertorriqueña. Río Piedras: Editorial Huracán.

_____. 1986. The Puerto Rican Woman: Perspectives on Culture, History and Society, 2nd edition. New York: Praeger.

Azize, Y. 1985. La Mujer en la Lucha. Río Piedras: Editorial Cultural.

Azize, Y., ed. 1987. La Mujer en Puerto Rico: Ensayos en Investigación. Río Piedras: Huracán.

Dietz, J. L. 1986. Economic History of Puerto Rico. Institutional Change and Capitalist Development. Princeton, N.J.: Princeton Univ. Press.

Erickson, E. 1982. The Life Cycle Completed. New York: W. Norton.

González, J. L. 1980. El País de Cuatro Pisos, y Otros Ensayos. Río Piedras: Editorial Huracán.

_____. 1986. Nueva Visita al Cuarto Piso. Santurce: Puerto Rico: Colección Del Flamboyán.

History Task Force. 1979. Centro Estudios Puertorriqueños. Labor Migration Under Capitalism: The Puerto Rican Experience. New York: Monthly Review Press.

Landrón, I. 1976. Veo, Veo. En Poemario de la Mujer Puertorriqueña. Limc 1, vol. 1. San Juan: Instituto de Cultura Puertorriqueña.

Levinson, D. J., with C. N. Darrow, E. B. Klein, M. H. Levinson, and M. McKee. 1978. The Seasons of a Man's Life. New York: Knopf.

Maldonado-Dennis, M. 1972. Puerto Rico: A Socio-Historic Interpretation. New York: Vintage.

Morales Carrión, A. 1972. Albores Históricos del Capitalismo en Puerto Rico. Río Piedras: Editorial Universitaria.

Morales, J. 1986. Puerto Rican Poverty and Migration: We Just Had to Try Elsewhere. New York: Praeger.

Pacheco, A. M., S. Wapner, and N. Lucca. 1979. La migración como una transición crítica para la persona en su ambiente: Una interpretación organísmico--evolutiva. Revista de Ciencias Sociales, 21 (1-2), 123-55.

Picó, I. 1980. Apuntes Preliminares para el Estudio de la Mujer Puertorriqueña y su Participación en las

Luchas Sociales de Principios del Siglo XX. In E. Acosta-Belén, ed., La Mujer en la Sociedad Puertorriqueña. Río Piedras: Editorial Huracán, pp. 23-40.

Quintero Rivera, A. G. 1976. Conflicto de Clase y Politico en Puerto Rico. Río Piedras: Editorial Huracán.

Rivera Quintero, A. 1988. Patricios y Plebeyos: Burgueses, Hacendados, Artesanos y Obreros. Río Piedras: Huracán.

Rivera Quintero, M. 1980. Incorporación de las Mujeres al Mercado de Trabajo en el Desarrollo del Capitalismo. In E. Acosta-Belén, ed., La Mujer en la Sociedad Puertorriqueña. Río Piedras: Editorial Huracán, pp. 41-66.

Rivera Ramos, A. N. 1985. La Mujer Puertorriqueña: Investigaciones Psico-Sociales. Centro para el Estudio y Desarrollo de la Personalidad Puertorriqueña.

Rossi, A., ed. 1985. Gender and the Life Course. New York: Aldine.

Silvestrini, B. G. 1980. La Mujer Puertorriqueña y el Movimiento Obrero en la Década de 1930. In E. Acosta-Belén, ed., La Mujer en la Sociedad Puertorriqueña. Río Piedras: Editorial Huracán, pp. 67-90.

U.S. Census Bureau. Department of Commerce. 1987, August. The Hispanic Population in the United States: March 1986 and 1987. Advanced Report.

_____. Department of Commerce. 1980. Puerto Rico.

The Psychosocial
Development of
Puerto Rican
Women

1

A Critical Inquiry
into the Life and Work
of Julia de Burgos

Iris Zavala-Martínez, Ph.D.

INTRODUCTION

"Y fui toda en mí como fue en mí la vida" (I was all in
me as life had been with me).

On the night of July 5, 1953, at the corner of 105th
Street and Fifth Avenue, in what is known as El Barrio or
Spanish Harlem in New York City, a woman was found unconscious. Name and address unknown. She was taken to
Harlem Hospital where she died the following morning without ever regaining consciousness. That woman was Julia
de Burgos.

To retrace the steps and forces that converged on a
solitary street is to pay homage and demonstrate solidarity
with Puerto Rico's best-known poetess. This chapter contributes to a growing body of literature about Julia de
Burgos from a perspective that critically examines the
dialectic of her life and work, to fully comprehend how
she was "all in me as life had been with me." ·

To name her or to quote her poetry evokes a strange
identification and bonding feeling for many Puerto Ricans,

All translations of Julia de Burgos' poetry are the author's
unless otherwise indicated. All quotations of poetry are
from de Burgos, Obra Poética. All references to letters of
Julia de Burgos relate to letters she wrote to her younger
sister, Consuelo, and which are quoted in Jiménez de Báez
(1966). I quote a direct translation into English and cite
place and date to facilitate the English text.

a phenomenon that has been recognized by numerous writers. Julia appears to represent a significant psychohistorical element for Puerto Ricans and to embody crucial strivings of women. The sense of identification and the feeling of intimacy that her life and work provoke are not incidental; these are the social and historical constructions of subjective meaning associated with her legacy. Julia's life and work incorporated dimensions of Puerto Rican reality that reverberate on the chords of national identity. She exalted and transformed the natural landscape of Puerto Rican countryside, forever imprinting it in her poems. She wrote of love and loss of love with a fragile openness and passion that released yearnings from stultifying social norms. She denounced oppressive social realities and affirmed the legitimacy of a people's emancipatory strivings. She experienced immigration, and forecasted the struggle for survival, identity, and legitimation that future generations of Puerto Rican migrants would live in the United States. She was a historical premonition (Barradas 1985) and an embodiment of the forces seeking historical, social, and personal liberation.

Julia's life struggles and poetic work also convey critical aspects of the experience of many women (Margarida 1984; Rivera Lassén 1975; Solá 1985; Vázquez Ramírez 1987). This inquiry attends to the compelling feminist[1] thrust in her work and its significance for Puerto Rican women. Julia's poetry gives voice to a search for authenticity, legitimization, self-definition, and determination; to questioning sex role socialization and traditional roles; to expressing social concerns about oppression and injustice; and to articulating the dialectics of love, disillusionment, pain, and loss. Julia was able to wrest from her life experience the complexities of multiple feelings and to convey these through exquisite verse. In doing so she constructed an irrevocable intimate presence of the Puerto Rican national self and consciousness. As Dávila (1984) well put it, "Intima figura nacional metida en el álbum de la familia." (An intimate national figure inserted in the family album.)

This retrospective analysis focuses on Julia's poetry and life events in order to grasp the significant developmental elements that have contributed to and influenced our collective and individual female psyche, and that have created a mystique about her. But the intent is to demystify, so it is crucial to reexamine her life and poetry within a framework that can bring into full focus the complex psychohistorical contours of her subjective experience. Such an effort necessitates an analysis integrating principles of the dialectical and ideological experience of an individual in his or her context. The unfolding of the dialectical relationship of social, cultural, and historical conditions structures a reality that can render intelligible individual experience and behavior (see Zavala-Martínez 1981). From a critical perspective, this work attempts to uncover the interactive forces and contradictions in her experience and how these are mediated by socially dominant ideologies. Julia's subjectivity and the representation of her interiorized understanding of reality both were bound as a "project and product"[2] to the prevailing socioeconomic structure.

This analysis also implies incorporating a feminist psychological perspective to discover ways women negotiate their emancipatory strivings within a social context formed by oppressive and colonialistic experiences. This orientation makes it crucial to resort to more recent psychological discourse on women's development (Gilligan 1982; Miller 1976) and to relevant psychodynamic concepts that facilitate our understanding of individual subjectivity. Given these propositions, this discourse attempts to articulate the dialectics of the poetic praxis of Julia de Burgos.

This work, however, is not literary criticism as it is known. The task here is one of thematic exploration—to uncover the relationship between life events, poetic discourse, and the personal self.

Julia's life and work have been examined by various writers to whom this work is indebted. The works of Yvette Jiménez de Báez (1966) and José Emilio González (1961, 1976) were most invaluable, as were the works of Solá (1985, 1986), Barradas (1985) and others (see references). For example, Umpierre's (1987) comments regarding the limitations of reductionist approaches to understand Julia's work have been examined, as have other insightful observation made by others. This work also expands upon the psychological analysis of Margarida (1984), which seminally elaborates upon the significance of loss in Julia's life, among other crucial issues.

The historiography of Puerto Rican women has been a critical project of the decades of the 1970s and 1980s. A conscientious feminist mandate has propelled a reexamination and reanalysis of women's lives. These efforts have also been part of a critical endeavor by Puerto Rican scholars, overall, to discover and reclaim Puerto Rican social history and experience through cogent critical analysis.[3] This work contributes to these efforts and to the growing literature that militates against oppressive, mystified, or a-historical representations of Puerto Rican people and their expressions. This project is in solidarity with Julia's voice of creativity as a liberating praxis.

> Y me siento invencible,
> porque mi ahora es fuerte columna de avanzada
> en la aurora que apunta. . .
>
> El hombre y mi alma
>
> (I feel invincible,
> because my present is a strong column of the
> vanguard in the dawn that breaks. . .)

THE SOCIOHISTORICAL CONTEXT

One main theoretical assumption here relates to contextualizing individual life events and processes within concrete social and historical conditions and forces. Julia is not simply Julia with arbitrary themes and "natural" tendencies toward certain themes. Julia is part of Puerto Rico's overall historical and collective psychosocial development. As such, one needs to identify the sociohistorical context of her times to be able later to interrelate the subjective factors of her life history.

Julia was born in 1914 in a Puerto Rico that had become a possession of the United States just 16 years earlier. The turn of the century saw the change of colonial domination from Spanish to U.S. hands, which in turn produced profound and conflictual economic, cultural, and political transformations (Figueroa 1983; Fernández-Méndez 1970). Coffee production, which was central to the nineteenth-century Puerto Rican economy, was being supplanted by large sugar cane and tobacco industries. Small farms and communal agricultural systems were being threatened and forced to sell out to large landowners. A working class was emerging that would organize itself to reclaim its rights (Quintero 1971). Women began to acquire a new role in the island's economy, a role that was to have political, cultural, and personal ramifications for all

Puerto Ricans. Women started to work in small-market industries such as needlework, tobacco stripping, and straw hat making (Rivera Quintero 1979). By 1920 women's labor force participation was 22 percent and by 1930 it was 26.1 percent (Picó 1979). Women also assumed a high percentage of teaching, nursing, and clerical positions by the 1930s. As women joined the labor force, they also began to participate in women's groups within the unions, particularly in the Free Federation of Labor, and were militants for social and economic justice in the working-class struggles of this time (Azize 1979). The growing participation of women in the island's economy prepared the terrain for an increasing consciousness about women's exploitation and the impact of patriarchy on all levels of women's lives. Puerto Rican women engaged "en la lucha" for their multiple legitimate rights (Zavala-Martínez 1986).

As women developed consciousness about their changing roles, a parallel political movement was developing that accentuated the political and economic realities of the island (Pagán 1959; Quintero 1971). The economic policies dictated by colonialist interests were in crisis and opposed by different sectors of Puerto Rican society. Sugar cane workers and others went on strike, while students and anticolonialists organized politically. Puerto Rican Nationalists intensely militated against organized colonial domination, becoming the focus of severe repression during the 1930s (People Press of Puerto Rico Project 1977).

These events in Puerto Rico were preceded or paralleled on the international scene by World War I in 1914, the Bolshevik Revolution of 1917, the stock market crash of 1929, and the Great Depression of the 1930s. The effects of the depression in the United States were felt even stronger in Puerto Rico, where unemployment and hunger were widespread by the end of the decade. As the economic focus began to shift from agrarian to industrial work opportunities in urban areas, the impact was felt by poor agricultural families who were forced to leave the rural areas for the cities. These socioeconomic forces set the stage in Puerto Rico for the island to grapple with economic and psychic survival.

During this period Puerto Rico was struggling with an unstable economic base; with the emergence of a working class, anticolonist, and feminist consciousness; and was grappling with a threatened national identity. Julia's family also struggled for economic survival and was a part of this conflicted era. This was the context wherein Julia's life history unfolds; it was a time of great social, economic, and cultural upheavals. It was the historical period before, during, and after the Spanish Civil War and World War II, which was marked by contesting ideological strivings.

THE DEVELOPMENTAL CONTEXT AND LIFE HISTORY

"Yo fui estallido fuerte de la selva y el río"
(I was a strong outburst of the jungle and the river)

Julia Constanza Burgos García was born on February 17, 1914, in Barrio Santa Cruz of Carolina to a part-German father, Francisco Burgos Hans, and a Puerto Rican mother, Paula García. She was the first of 13 siblings, of which only six survived, and was witness to these tragic family losses. Her father, Francisco, apparently considered himself the town's "wise man." He had a vivid imagination and a great interest in literature, thus influencing his first born. He stimulated Julia's imagination by narrating to her the stories of Don Quixote, Marco Polo, Bolívar, and Napoleón, all of them adventurers, discoverers, searchers, and possible role models, ego ideals, and fantasies for this man. Julia and her father often rode horseback through their rural surroundings, inventing fanciful stories on the way. These early experiences appear to have nurtured Julia's intellectual and poetic interest in discovering new meanings in her surroundings and in transforming these into unique verses. More important, the countryside and nature later emerge as key elements in her poetry; with these she delved into her past and the significance of the land. Nature also helped her to adapt and to cope with harsh realities. Natural elements became the vehicles for sublimating pain and for mediating the initial dialectic between her life events and her poetic praxis.

Paula García, Julia's mother, had a distinct personality that was in contrast to her husband's adventurous kindred form. She was a pivotal source of inspiration and encouragement to her daughter. Paula was a caring, affectionate, and sensitive mulatta woman who encouraged Julia's educational pursuits and influenced Julia's love and identification with nature, especially of the river. Paula introduced the Loíza River to Julia, and the river

theme was later to become one of the most enduring symbols in her poetry (Jiménez de Báez 1966). In her best
known poem, "Río Grande de Loíza," she reveals its intimate childhood significance.

The Burgos family was caught, as were many rural
families, in the throes of economic forces they did not
control but that, nonetheless, extracted their human toll.
The family endured a poverty that was to persist well into
Julia's adulthood, as was revealed in a letter to her sister, Consuelo, years later: "That damned environment of
our childhood, how it follows us!" (New York, August 12,
1946). Julia's early experience of unrelenting poverty and
of losses structured a key dimension of her childhood.
Seven of her 13 siblings died of malnutrition and hunger.
The impact of these deaths upon her parents was surely
devastating, but the impact of these deaths upon Julia,
who survived, was to be seen. Jiménez de Báez (1966)
identifies these early painful experiences as forming in
Julia a profound tendency to explore the themes of pain,
sorrow, and grief through her poetry. Julia does, repeatedly, resort to the metaphor of "dolor" (pain, sorrow) to
either describe herself or her circumstances. She says
for example: "Soy diluvio de duelos" (I am a deluge of
sorrow/grief), or "Ese es mi destino: La sombra al lado
de la luz, el dolor junto a la felicidad." (That is my
destiny: shadows next to light, pain next to happiness.)
Julia's life history, in fact, documents her multiple painful experiences.

Margarida (1984) analyzed the impact of the experience of loss in Julia's life. She observed that the internalization of losses due to socioeconomic inequities contributed to the gestation of a profound sensitivity to loss
and an anxiety about loss, and that Julia seemed to have
contained the anger at those unseen forces that victimized
her family. Further, as Julia was the oldest and a sur-
vivor, she was to help her mother with household tasks
and also be a source of comfort to her mother as the death
toll of her siblings mounted. These events forced Julia
early on to assume a caretaking role, becoming parentified
through this process (Margarida 1984). This author relates this to the psychological literature on family functioning that has described this role when a child takes on
parenting responsibilities, both physically and psychologically, to meet some otherwise unmet needs and functions
(Boszormenyi-Nagy and Spark 1965). Julia was also the

one who fetched her father when he would disappear after
a drinking bout. Margarida pointed out the impact of
their father's drinking on the family and on Julia, which
can be surmised from what is known about the effects of
alcoholism on family structure (Kritzberg 1988). Her
father's periodic absence supports the hypothesis that Julia
assumed certain parenting functions for both parents, for
her siblings, a reality that continued into her adulthood.

It is important to discuss the etiological factors that
could have contributed to her father's drinking. Francisco Burgos Hans appeared to be seeking control over and
relief from his unbearable feelings of rage, sadness, and
powerlessness resulting from the deaths of his children
(Margarida 1984), and from the gradual loss of his farm,
which was a source of identification and autonomy. He
was unable to provide sufficiently for his family and thus
to fulfill the socialized responsibility of men of his time,
although he also worked with the National Guard. Victimized by forces he did not control, he turned to the alcoholic solution, which led to abdication of his role as a
father and provider.

Margarida summarized the experience of loss as related to family dynamics and socioeconomic deprivations as
follows:

> it is not hard to see how the socio-economic
> background from which she came structured
> . . . the inherent difficulty in the process of
> healthy mourning. Being the oldest of six
> within an alcoholic family system, Julia's role
> can be stipulated to have been one full of
> responsibilities in tending to the care of both
> parents; a depressed mother, mourning the
> loss of her children and an alcoholic father,
> who perhaps sought to numb the pain and loss
> through his drinking. From our knowledge of
> family systems like Julia's, we know how chil-
> dren serve the function of keeping parents
> from being depressed. Children become re-
> sponsible caretakers for the emotional needs
> of parents [1984, 6].

All of these early childhood experiences left their
mark. Julia was to feel responsible for her family during
her early adulthood; she was to constantly struggle for

economic survival; she was to attempt to transcend the pain of her life through her poetry; and in her own words, she was to be "un lento agonizar entre espadas perpetuas" (a slow agony between perpetual swords). Early on Julia's life was a struggle, a duel between disparate forces. The tension between her individual developmental needs and her family's needs epitomized both her life and her poetic expression: the operation of and search for a resolution or reconciliation of contradictory or dual forces. Jiménez de Báez (1967, 9) stated that "the poet defines this way the duality that determines her whole life . . . living will be an eternal struggle to equilibrate the contrary, to find the essential unity of the person and the reality . . . to integrate oneself from the origin will be the goal of the spirit." Julia was to express this, years later to her sister, Consuelo: "This life broken in two that I live between the essence and the form, between the implacable onslaught of circumstances and the warm and gentle echo of love that beckons me" (New York, March 1, 1940). Barradas (1985) analyzed the struggle between opposites in her poetry such as the struggle between her different selves, between the past and present, between self-definition and social expectations and her attempt at reconciliation of opposites or dual elements.

These early childhood experiences contributed to a deeply rooted sorrow, to her seeking consolation through the natural environment, and to her delving into memories and fantasies of nature (Jiménez de Báez 1966). Julia's poetry, in fact, provides testimony as to the adaptive strength she forged from these difficult experiences. Julia turns to her introjected childhood landscape for her most resourceful expressive language and metaphors. She writes in "Campo-2": "Soy un niño crecido amontonando escombros de inocencias robadas" (I am a grown-up child gathering the remains of a stolen innocence); and "no es un cuento de ira lo que quiere este niño/¡Mi infancia busca infancia!" (It is not a story of rage that this child wants/My infancy seeks infancy!) But she transforms the losses and transcends the anguish, turning these into statement of protest and affirmation: "¡Oh llanto campesino. . .!/Niño venido de tan lejos con mi infancia en los brazos/Yo te regalo niño/La ofensiva despierta de mis árboles!" (Oh peasant cry/Child come from afar with my infancy in its arms/I give you child/The alert offensive of my trees!) For Julia, the trees become: "Los guardias

voluntarios de mi niñez,/. . . escopetas del tiempo mane-
jadas tan sólo por la tierra!" (The voluntary guards of
my childhood . . . rifles of time managed only by the
earth!) These guardians of her childhood could well represent symbolic caretakers of her and of the rights of the
land. Some of Julia's poems with similar imagery and
metaphors appear to recapitulate childhood experiences but
transformed into a creative act of survival, affirmation of
hope, and denunciation of injustice. However, the poverty
of her childhood was to endure and ultimately to prevail.

The influence of Julia's crucial early childhood experiences needs to be related to her adolescence and the
socialization process that provided a context for her emerging self.

"Llegó la adolescencia. Me sorprendió la vida. . ."
(Adolescence arrived. Life surprised me. . .)

Paula and Francisco Burgos understood that their
eldest daughter was intelligent: She was the hope and
pride of their poor rural family. Because of the severe
economic hardships they experienced on the rural farm,
they relocated two times to facilitate Julia's schooling.
They sold their farm and collectivized their hopes with the
help of their community to obtain money for her education.
The family moved first to Río Grande and then to developing urban Río Piedras, but their economic situation did
not improve in the city although they lost their beloved
farm land and uprooted themselves. This experience of
displacement was to be similar to that of many poor farm-
ers and their families. As the agricultural economy de-
clined and industries developed in urban centers, a rural-
urban migration was propelled that would have sociocultural implications and a psychological impact. Puerto
Ricans became socioeconomic refugees in their own country.
Years later Julia wrote in "Campo-1": "¡La esperanza
está ardiendo en el campo!/¡El hombre está ardiendo . . .
Es la tierra que se abre, quemada de injusticias" (Hope
is ablaze in the country/Man's ablaze . . . It's the land
that opens, burnt with injustice).

For Julia, these moves meant another painful life
event. She had to adjust and adapt to urban and class
conditions that were quite new to her. She experienced
humiliation at school because of her poverty, but she and
her family persisted, and Julia excelled at school. She
completed four high school years in three, graduating in

May 1931. Julia studied for two years at the University of Puerto Rico and obtained a teaching certificate as a normalista in May of 1933. She could not continue for lack of money but her hopes of finishing university studies endured. During 1934 she worked with the Puerto Rican Economic Rehabilitation Agency (PRERA), which was the colonial compensatory response to the economic and social inequities of that time. Ironically, Julia's work involved a food program for poor and hungry families and children. Her own experiences of poverty were now sublimated as she again cared for the poor, this time through a social program. For a brief period in 1935 she taught elementary school in a rural sector of Naranjito and had her first re-encounter with the rural countryside since leaving the family farm. This setting became the locale where she would reintegrate her past into her first poems.

"Me he encontrado yo misma al encontrar mi verso"
(I found myself in finding my verse)

In 1934 she married Rubén Rodríguez Beauchamp, whom she divorced three years later in 1937. This failed marriage must have left an adverse impact since such a rupture with traditional social expectations for women carries a price. Julia experienced the oppressiveness of prevailing social norms, which she later revealed in her poems conveying her assertive unconventional stance.

During the period of the mid-1930s numerous events occurred of contradictory emotional and social significance. Julia became the family breadwinner, supporting it through her writings. The once parentified child now was the main provider. When her mother was diagnosed with cancer in 1935, the family's economic needs became overwhelming. On a very different level, she met literary figures of her generation and began a lifelong friendship with the well-known Puerto Rican writer, Luis Lloréns Torres. She sought knowledge and avidly read the writing of Stefan Zweig, Nietzche, Kant, and enjoyed the music of Wagner and Beethoven. She seemed to have been seeking her German roots and seeking to discover her differentness.

Julia politicized her social and feminist consciousness and became involved with the activities of the Nationalist party. During the 1930s she wrote militant poems addressing the issues of oppression and demonstrating the need to struggle against the inequities experienced by Puerto Ricans under colonial rule. These inequities she knew well from her childhood; through her understanding of women's rights; from suffering herself the effects of political, class, race, and sexist oppression; and from experiencing the freedom and harmony of nature. Julia gave voice to these themes in her first book of poems published in 1938, Poemas en Veinte Surcos (Poems in Twenty Furrows). This book epitomizes her search for self-determination and authenticity as a person and as a woman, her remembrance and creative transformation of her impoverished rural childhood, her reliance on the river as a transcendental metaphor, and her social and political consciousness of self-determination. Julia's early poetry reveals this multiple quest, a process that has been identified in contemporary feminist psychological literature as crucial to women's development of their self and sense of being (Miller 1976). Julia puts it this way in her poem "Intima":

> Me prolongué en el rumbo de aquel camino errante
> que se abría en mi interior,
> y me llegué hasta mí, íntima.
> (I prolonged myself in the curse of that errant path
> that was opening in my interior
> and arrived toward myself, intimately).

The sale of this book was needed to help pay for family expenses, particularly for her dying mother's medical bills; and Julia traveled throughout the island selling her poetry book. This brave effort affirmed the ongoing dialectic between her socioeconomic survival and her creative survival. Paula García died in 1939. The loss was great and, ironically, was preceded by Julia meeting the man who became her great love.[4] The coexistence of contrary or opposing events became anchored in Julia's life.

Later that year, when only 25 years old, Julia obtained a literary award from the Puerto Rican Literary Institute for her second book of poetry, Canción de La Verdad Sencilla, described by José Emilio González (1976) as "the celebration of love." Her productivity, in the midst of sociopolitical turmoil and impinging personal demands, emerged as a testament of her power to struggle with contradictory forces and of her ability to overcome her reality by transforming it. "Personal creativity is a continuous process of bringing forth a changing vision of oneself, and of oneself in relation to the world" (Miller

1976, 111). Although Julia was energized by the transcendental expectation of love, her poems express uncertainties and feelings of aloneness and solitude reflecting her continual struggle in the throes of opposing forces. The constancy of this dialectic appears to drive her transforming creative impulse and emerges as a salient characteristic of her poems. She writes, "dolor y amor me llevan/ sujeta a la emoción" (Pain and love have/subjected by emotion). She has already forewarned that her destiny was shadow/light, pain/joy. But the contradictions perplex her as she reflects on her own process: "I've been involved in so many twisted circumstances of inexorable floggings, that I don't know why I still have dreams that come out in songs" (Cuba, October 2, 1940). It is precisely because she could write her "songs" that she could overcome adversities.

Julia was a woman ahead of her time. She matured and came into womanhood during the turbulent changing decade of the 1930s. She manifested and affirmed her poetic potential; she married, divorced, and lost a mother; she exercised her feminist and sociopolitical consciousness. She needed to renew her energies, rechart her course. She had experienced a painful loss and was weary of the socially limiting environment in which she found herself. As a feminist woman ahead of her time yet mediated by the social ideology of her time, she sought love and self-actualization and thought that through an amorous relationship she would realize her quest and hopes. She followed the Dominican intellectual she had met in Puerto Rico to New York City and then to Cuba. Julia saw Puerto Rico for the last time in January 1940 at 26 years of age. The journey that had started in a rural barrio and struggled through to a developing university town was to continue. Now she would experience immigration and a form of exile (Barradas 1985).

"Separarse de todo lo que existe"
(To separate from all that exists)

New York City was seen through the eyes of one in love, but also from the perspective of someone who was excruciatingly sensitive, reflective, and critical of growing alienation of "modern" life. To her, the city was "like huge military barracks" where "the houses are all alike without charm." (New York, January 30, 1940). She found that her skill with the English language was to be her "most powerful weapon besides . . . will power." But as with many immigrants, she experienced paradoxical feelings of loss, aloneness, nostalgia, and optimism (Grinberg and Grinberg 1984). And like many immigrants and future generations of Puerto Ricans, she encountered severe economic instability, a reality that replicated her past. But Julia was optimistic that her love relationship would transform her life. She stated, "He is my great pillar in life, my serenity, and at the same time my energy." (New York, February 8, 1940). Although this relationship demanded changing geographic locales at the expense of family loyalties and responsibilities, she was moved by the expectation of fulfilling her needs and desire for intimacy and affiliation.

It is important to interpret this dimension in Julia's life. Women's development and socialization is characterized by "a context of attachment and affiliation with others" (Miller 1976, 83), although these connections can also compromise individuation and a woman's autonomy. Miller affirms that women's sense of self becomes very much organized around being able to make, and then to maintain, affiliations and relationships" (p. 83). This situation can then be destructive as "the threat of disruption of an affiliation is perceived not just as a loss of a relationship but as something closer to a total loss of self." As "intimacy becomes the critical experience that brings the self back into connection with others" (Gilligan 1982, 163), then a loss of intimacy is experienced as an injury to the self. Julia pursued this longed-for intimacy and did later experience an "injury." Her need to relate and love motivated her even in the throes of the transition between wanting to affiliate and wanting to individuate. She suffered great anguish over her lover's departure for Cuba and also felt ambivalence and confusion about being "his shadow" and of the "effort to hide my self from my own conscience." (New York, April 1940). Julia experienced the tension of this conflict, which she expressed as, "Me veo equidistante del amor y el dolor" (I am equidistant from love and pain). Julia sees herself continually attempting to reconcile binary, opposing, or contradictory elements, as being caught between equidistant forces.

She resolved to follow her love to Cuba and her stay in New York lasted only six months. In this short period, she was interviewed by La Prensa and given public homage by the Association of Puerto Rican Journalists and Writers. Nonetheless, she had lived "cruel circumstances" in New York and experienced a "true crisis of complete loneliness"; further, she still was anguished by her mother's death. Evidence of her distress is revealed in her retrospective narration of suicidal ideation and of a depressive crisis en route to Florida where she would embark for Cuba:

> on the bus en route to Florida I had to be
> helped and I almost stayed in a clinic in
> Miami . . . the mental depression would have
> led me to take that step . . . but now that
> the risk has passed, I will tell you so that
> you see that there are worse ills than eco-
> nomic necessity. I've sustained a struggle
> with fate and I've triumphed. [Havana, July
> 9, 1940]

Even at such a young age (26 years), Julia's intense sensitivity to loneliness, pain, and loss reveals itself through her vulnerability to depression. Depression is frequently exhibited by women due to environmental and role stressors (Brown and Harris 1978; Chesler 1972), threats to self-esteem and identity, and a vulnerability to losses. Julia's life history contains ample evidence of environmental and role stressors, of threats to her developing self, and of multiple painful events and losses. From a sociocritical perspective, her depressive vulnerability emerges as a social construction of privatized subjectivity (Zavala-Martínez 1984). This vulnerability became more privatized and prominent in her life, and it eventually became self-destructive. As Cloward and Piven (1979) stated, "our society encourages or permits women to imagine, emulate, and act out . . . essentially privatized modes of self-destruction" (p. 660). "Stresses are refracted through an ideology which encourages women to search within their psyche and their bodies for the sources of their problems" (p. 668).

In Cuba Julia experienced the contradictions of class and color as well as the demeaning social role that patriarchal traditionality imposed on women, and she was to be subjected to economic tensions and recurrent instability of living quarters. She also experienced intensely her identity both as companion to her beloved and as an emerging literary voice.

Julia was rejected by the family of her beloved, who outrightly forbade him to marry her. She experienced the duality of a delegitimized wife while attempting to authenticate her love. She had abandoned her family and homeland for him—she had, in essence, sacrificed herself for him and had been socialized to believe that her happiness and realization as a woman were obtainable only through a relationship with a man. As she observed, "one pays a high price for love" (Cuba, July 1, 1941). Ironically, she saw these contradictions at the same time that she was victimized by them. In a letter to Consuelo, she writes that she was "maintaining her role as wife, prejudiced and prudish . . .," and begins to convey her increasing frustration: "at any time . . . unexpectedly out in the street, if _____ [lover] meets up with a friend of the family, he'll introduce me as a friend . . . I swear that it's horrible! And it makes me feel so alone, so defenseless. . . . Sometimes I just get angry!" (Cuba, July 14, 1941.) Julia reveals certain difficulty and guilt about her feeling anger, even though she was entitled to this expression, given the invalidation and frustration she experienced.

A parallel aspect of her Cuban experience between 1940 and 1942 was more rewarding and exciting. She was energized by her optimism and by finding the free Cuba of Martí to be a country that "no longer suffers the disease of dreaming" and where "effort is not lost." (Trinidad, July 2, 1940). She met numerous intellectuals, among them Juan Bosch and Raúl Roa. She continued to write and finished her third book, El Mar y Tú (The Sea and You), which was not published until 1954, and talked about a fourth book, Campo. In 1941 she was excited about studying again and took numerous courses at the University hoping to finish her degree. She participated in public demonstrations for Puerto Rican independence and for other social issues and wrote militant poems as the world was convulsed by the fascist forces of World War II. A culminating event of her Cuban experience was her meeting Pablo Neruda early in 1942, who promised to write the prologue to El Mar y Tú. This unfortunately never happened.

Her relationship was in crisis. She attempted to study and excelled in her exams, but the relationship had deteriorated substantially and ultimately interrupted her studies.

The discontinuities, the lost expectations, the socio-economic instabilities, and the deligitimation she experienced took their toll. Julia's thirst for knowledge was again frustrated and interrupted by the crucial factors that continually defined her situation: economic insufficiency and the search for actualization of her intimate, authentic, and legitimate person. As she came to terms with the demise of her relationship, and in the throes of disillusionment, she reproached herself for abandoning her family for her love and wrote to Consuelo:

> When I think that I abandoned you all at a
> difficult time to follow him . . . my heart
> wants to burst. . . . I must begin my life
> anew. It will be difficult with two enormous
> defeats already. . . . I will try to drown
> myself in the current painful situation of the
> world so that I don't feel so deeply my pro-
> found aloneness. [Havana, June 8, 1942]

Her departure from Cuba was forced precipitously upon her when her lover handed her an airplane ticket to Florida for that same day. In an already emotionally distraught state, she left Cuba in June 1942 and arrived in New York with five dollars and "profoundly alone, shattered, and bewildered" (New York, June 22, 1942). Although she returned to New York City disillusioned, she wrote that after a period she "volví a ser yo" (I returned to being myself). This was a crucial affirmation, given the emotional onslaught she experienced and a statement to her will to regain her sense of self. Though she was anguished and deeply disillusioned, she coped by displacing her anger at the man she loved generalizing her disillusionment to humanity as a whole. Margarida (1984) observed and stated that this "unexpressed anger" could also be at her father for emotionally abandoning the family through his drinking and being "inaccessible." Julia could not ventilate her rage at the object of her love, she had to deflect it. This is consistent with literature that has examined how women are socialized to repress their anger and then to turn it inwardly in self-defeating ways (Goldhor Lerner 1985; Zavala-Martínez 1984). In fact, Julia was to hurt herself in this way over the next 11 years.

"Es un dolor sentado más allá de la muerte"
(It is a pain situated beyond death)

Once again, Julia made a migratory change, but her
baggage this time was not full of amorous expectations,
but rather of recurrent painful and stressful experiences
and losses accompanied by an incipient drinking habit.
New York became "a reflection of internal conflicts," a
"metaphor of her pain" (Barradas 1985). New York also
represented a possibility of resolution, not only of her
internal conflicts, but of their external social counterparts and the dialectic between these forces. New York
represented an alternative to the two island experiences
that suffocated and distorted her emancipatory strivings.
As she wrote in "Soy un cuerpo de ahora," "¡Cómo quiere
tumbarme esta carga de siglos!" (Oh how it wants to
knock me down, this burden of centuries!)

Julia had to survive and obtained whatever employment she could. She also moved frequently from place to
place, similar to the situation in Cuba. Economic and
living instability do not bode well for emotional health;
on the contrary, they work to erode psychic well-being
and to heighten feelings of desamparo (homelessness, deso-
lation). As she wrote, "this rootlessness/exile that I find
myself in, wandering from country to country, from defeat/
failure to defeat" (New York, March 2, 1943). But she
was hopeful, productive, and still quite young (29 years
old). She met and married Armando Marín in 1943 and
wrote verses that reflected her political consciousness, her
commitment to independence and to social transformation.
She briefly worked for the newspaper Pueblos Hispánicos in
1944 and during the same period cared for her ailing
friend, Luis Lloréns Torres. In 1946, her creativity was
well highlighted when she won a journalism prize from the
Puerto Rican Institute of Culture for an essay published
in the newspaper Semanario Hispano.

In another move, she and her husband lived for a
year in Washington, D.C. and then returned to New York.
At this time she expressed a longing to return to Puerto
Rico "to work towards the total liberation of our country"
(January 22, 1945), but she did not return. Instead, her
life events began to blur as her drinking increased. Just
as the data about the ongoing role of her father had
gradually been obscured, the circumstances of her marriage and life situations during this period are also
vague. But it was clear that Julia was attempting to

treat her pain. Around 1947–48, she developed cirrhosis of the liver.

The literature on female alcoholism reveals that the "assault on the bottle represents the breaking of a more rigid taboo, the shattering of a deeply divided image of femininity" (Fraser 1981, 298), and often is related to stressful life events, loss, and separation, past alcoholism in the family--particularly by fathers--and to feeling of inadequacy (Fraser 1981). It has also been said that there is a relationship between alcoholism among women, their emancipation, and feeling of self-esteem. Litman (1978) states that "depression and alcoholism in women represent strategies which are used in an attempt to cope with social roles and cultural expectations that are narrow and inhibiting . . . both are characterized by low self-esteem and an exaggeratedly punitive self-concept" (p. 125).

Julia, the very woman who was "de pie por mi conciencia" (affirming my conscience); who was "contra todo lo injusto y lo inhumano, . . . iré . . . con la tea en la mano" (against the unjust and inhuman . . . I'll be . . . upholding the torch); who was "afirmación de alma y energía" (affirmation of soul and energy), that brave woman who struggled against the onslaught of opposing forces and contradictions harbored deep inner wounds that would not heal. Moreover, the conditions that could contribute to healing were long absent from her life, accentuating the tragedy of victimization--not just the tragedy of Julia's life, but the tragedy of a world structured to dehumanize and to mask its complicity. Julia needed a community of solidarity and the sisterhood of caring, and she needed to regain a sense of validation, self-worth, and legitimacy. But she did not obtain these during her life.

From about 1949 to 1953 Julia went in and out of numerous hospitals in New York City: Metropolitan, Mount Sinai, San Lucas, Harlem, Lincoln, Bellevue, New York, and Goldwater Memorial. She also stayed at numerous convalescent homes without improvement. In 1951, after a renewed crisis, she wrote "Poema con un solo después" (Poem with a Solo Afterword): "Yo nada más caía gota a gota a la nada" (I was but falling drop by drop into the void). Julia could reflect on herself and on her own processes, even if her own deterioration and despair were the objects of her verse. She predicted this devastating loneliness in a poem written in Cuba, "Poema con la tonada última":

> Voy a quedarme sola,
> sin canciones, ni piel
> como un túnel por dentro, donde el mismo silencio
>   se enloquece y se mata.
> (I am going to stay alone,/without songs, no skin,/
> like the inside of a tunnel,/ where silence itself
> goes mad and kills itself).

Julia stated in her last letters to her sister that
she was alone, penniless, homeless, and that her equilibrio
mental (mental stability) was damaged. Her sister, who
has been the "only active affect of my heart," had now
become "the only refuge of my desperate solitude" (April
7, 1953). And Julia, who had looked out for her sister in
the past and had been the family's mainstay years earlier,
could not provide for anyone, nor had she anything more
to sacrifice. The hurt and pain had overcome her, the
persistent survival struggle had extenuated her, the multiple disillusions had undermined her resolve, and the recurrent losses and long-standing unmet needs had disor-
ganized her. She had experienced loss of self, loss of
others, loss of meaning (Kegan 1982). Years before she
had written,

> Es un dolor sentado más allá de la muerte;
> dolor hecho de espigas y sueños desbandados.
> (It is a pain situated beyond death;
> a pain made of spikes and dispersed dreams.)
>   Poemas de la íntima agonía

In the language she mastered, she synthesized that
"all of me is loneliness in/a rebellious heart" (The Sun in
Welfare Island, April 30, 1953), and offered this gesture
of leave taking:

> It has to be from here,
>   right this instance,
> my cry into the world.
> Life was somewhere forgotten
> and sought refuge in depths of tears
>   and sorrows
> over this vast empire of solitude
>   and darkness.
>   . . . .
>   . . . .
>   . . . .

It has to be from here,
forgotten but unshaken
among comrades of silence
deep into Welfare Island
my farewell to the world.
                    Farewell to Welfare Island
                    February 1953

On July 5, 1953, four months after writing "The Sun in Welfare Island" and not long after leaving Goldwater Memorial Hospital, Julia collapsed on a street corner in El Barrio and died of lobular pneumonia. She was 39 years old. Her father, who died in the 1960s, also had an alcoholism-related death.

Without any identification on her, and while friends and family searched for her, her body remained initially unclaimed and was buried in a common grave in Potter's Field, New York, on July 21, 1953. She expressed this precognition of her death in a poem she wrote in Santiago, Cuba in July 1940:

Morir conmigo misma, abandonada y sola,
en la más densa roca de una isla desierta.
En el instante un ansia suprema de claveles,
y en el paisaje un trágico horizonte de piedra.
(To die with myself, abandoned and alone,
on the thickest rock of a deserted island.
At the moment a supreme yearning of carnations,
and in the landscape a tragic horizon of stone.)
                    Poema para mi muerte

Julia was eventually found and identified. She was honored posthumously in New York through the efforts of writers and poets. Then she was finally returned to her homeland on September 6, 1953. There she was paid the tribute she deserved and had needed for her sense of legitimacy. Julia was buried in Carolina, the childhood landscape she had left over 20 years before. The interactive forces of her social and private worlds had run its course, yet she was to prevail through her poetry.

THE DIALECTIC OF CONFLUENT FORCES:
POETRY AS PRAXIS

Julia de Burgos' poetry is a testament and legacy of intense life experiences being potentiated through literary

expression. Julia's poetry was her praxis, her life action. She conveyed and consolidated her internal subjective experience of objective social realities into a concrete
form. José Emilio González (1976) said, "there is no dis-
crepancy between the person and its expression. Reading
her poems, we know Julia. That's why she is so alive
amongst us. Julia herself was a poetic being."

The recurrent themes in Julia's poetry substantiate
the interaction and tension of confluent forces: social
history and individual life history. Julia struggled to
authenticate a woman's voice. The search for authentic
self-definition, affiliation, and intimacy is noted in the
psychological literature as a process giving meaning to
women's relational experiences. Various Puerto Rican
writers have noted the salience of this search in Julia's
poems (González 1976; Rivera Lassén 1975; Solá 1986;
Margarida 1984; Vázquez Ramírez 1987). Julia's life and
poetry embodied a struggle to legitimize a creative singu-
lar voice that could denounce social inequities and articulate her ruminations on sorrow, love, and death, and that
would give form to her repeated inquiries about her identity in relation to the world. She says of herself, "I,
Multiple/like in contradiction/tied to a sentiment without
limits/that alternatively united and disunites me/to the
world." Julia could not be as society wanted her to be,
she asserts: "I wanted to be like a man wanted to be:
an intention of life/a game of hide and seek with myself/
but I was made of the present/and my feet which touched
promising ground/would not walk backwards." And as if
conscious of what she was manifesting, she wrote, "Already
defined my present path,.I felt that I was an outpouring
of all the earth's land . . . of all peoples . . . of all
epochs." As such, Julia represented women's emancipatory
strivings, while she denounced social and political injus-
tices. She denounced hunger, colonialism, racism, fascism—
oppressive forces that she had in some way known. She
sided with human emancipation and affirmed this in a
poem: "I live in that new person that struggles in each
front/free from want and with justice of ideas." She
spoke out and said, "Let us announce the cry of the
present/We are closed fists!" Julia's consciousness had no
borders; she was transnational; she was concerned with
justice for all humanity. As Umpierre (1987) well put it,
"it is through poetry that de Burgos confronts the challenge of society, it is in poetry where she finds her

power." González (1976) observed that Julia had a "strange capacity to integrate and assimilate in her own existential sphere, all that came into contact with her" and she does this with poetic lyricism.

This analysis illustrates how the contradictions and dualities she lived were objects of her inquiry, of her verses, and how her interiorized childhood and social experiences are forged in her poems. Within these, Julia could articulate sentiments of love, disillusion, and despair. Her journey into love, as expressed by her second book, Canción de la Verdad Sencilla, exquisitely expresses these sentiments. She wrote, for example, "And here you see me stars/spread out and tender with his love upon my breast." She exalts love, the loved one, and her need to express herself: "I wanted to stay within the secret of my sorrow/but my soul can't reach the silence of a poem without words/and it jumps out through my lips made into dust of intimate throbbings." But as she could articulate love feelings, so she could express feelings of utter sorrow and despair and ruminations on death. She wrote, "I will discard paths that are burrowed within me like roots" and "I am also going to lose stars/and dew/and small streams"; and, as if foretelling her future, she asked, "Tell me, what is left of the world, what?" Julia commented on her anguish and in verses prognosticating her death, she offered us a message of how to view her, of her true meaning. She wrote, "How will I be called when the only memory is a rock on a deserted island? . . . they will call me a Poet." Julia affirms her truest identity and what gives her legitimacy; she lives in verse, her praxis is her poetry, and she left for posterity this legacy of dialogue.

A SYNTHESIS

Julia de Burgos' voice disrupted the muffled silence of her time. She spoke out, she searched, she questioned, she endeavored to care and to relate intimately. And she was triumphant, though not in her lifetime. Her poetry books reflect cycles of her life from childhood yearnings to rebellious youth, to enamored woman, to reflections on her life and death. Her life posed for her multiple challenges. Her development was besieged early on by the impact of adverse family, environmental, and social reali-

ties. Early childhood trauma appeared to contribute to
deep-rooted feelings of sorrow, aloneness, and of unmet
basic ego needs for which she compensated by meeting the
needs of others. As she grew, her intellectual development and the gratification she obtained from her excellence
provided her with sources of positive self-esteem. As a
budding young woman, she discovered that through poetry,
she could best articulate the dialectic of her inner and
external world and found comfort in the practice of her
creative expression. But as Julia matured, she was repeatedly assaulted by the struggle to survive socioeconomi-
cally, to survive as a creative woman, and to survive as
a caretaker of family members and of herself. She battled
the hypocrisy of ideas and norms, and confronted those
forces that limited her feminine self. She experienced recurrent stressful moves, transitions, and subsequent instability.

All of these aspects of her life took their toll. She
had coped through many years of difficult circumstances
and was beset for too long by too many factors. Further,
the stresses of being different, of seeking to assert her
creativity, and of rejecting a subordinate role and cultural expectation needed to be buffered by a network of
support. Her sources of support, validation, and self-
esteem, however, were not sufficiently grounded for her
well-being. The chronicity of these adverse social and
personal realities ultimately threatened and jeopardized
her psychologically.

Ironically, as Julia gave up her caretaker's role,
as she could no longer compensate for her own caring by
denying her needs, it was then that her depression and
alcoholism increased. Developmentally, she was at a stage
when women's lives are too often defined by children and
familial concerns. Julia had no children, and she appeared to be losing her family anchoring. She was excruciatingly alone and defenseless.

Further, it is crucial to note that the historical
time when she was most vulnerable was also a critical
period for Puerto Rico and for the collective Puerto Rican
psyche--a reality that embodies the confluence of and relationship between personal history and sociohistorical
events. Julia most likely felt profound pain, disillusionment, and rage by the frustrated Nationalist uprising of
1950 in Puerto Rico, by the imprisonment of its leaders,
and by the repression of ideals in which she so strongly

believed.[5] It was as if visions had been simultaneously shattered; as if the defeat of political ideals for change that had so much meaning for her were symbolic of her own process, of her demise.

It is also important to understand the contextual social reality she lived in New York City. She suffered the discrimination many Puerto Rican migrants experienced as they came in vast numbers in the early 1950s. There is an anecdote that reveals some of this quite succinctly. On a hospital admission form, Julia had written next to "occupation": writer, journalist, translator. These words were subsequently crossed out by hospital staff and replaced by "suffers from amnesia." In many ways, this incident is a metaphor of her life (García Bahne, personal communication, April 1988), as it synthesizes her struggle for legitimation in a world structured to delegitimize and invalidate her efforts at self-determination and self-definition.

In summary, multiple interactive forces operated in Julia's development and life history both as a woman and as a Puerto Rican in a historical period that sought its collective legitimacy and nationhood, and that was characterized by recurrent socioeconomic and political crisis. This context and these forces mediated and dialectically forged her response--both the creative and the destructive. It is admirable that her development and life history in the context of a woman's struggle for emancipation and creativity, and in the context of oppressive sociopolitical realities, left a national legacy that dignifies her praxis, her poetry.

There are questions still to be answered and aspects to be clarified about Julia. But it is sufficient to conclude that this courageous woman generated after her death a community of solidarity and intimacy among generations of Puerto Ricans unknown to her. Her affiliative need was realized: Julia's poetry bonds many women's experiences, and her vision energizes and legitimizes collective emancipatory strivings of many Puerto Ricans.

ACKNOWLEDGMENTS

I am greatly indebted to the excellent word processing skills of Judith Shea and Rosa María Colón; to the supportive and careful comments of the Pandoreñas of Boston and

of the editors; and to the dedicated editorial wizardry of
Dr. Richard Yensen. I am also grateful for the thoughtful
comments of Jose Parés, Mari Arce, and Dr. Betty García.
The section "The Developmental Context and Life History"
sketches biographical data mainly from the study by Yvette
Jiménez de Báez (1966). Her tremendous contribution deserves acknowledgment. A critical psychological analysis
of life events, however, is incorporated. And I am thank-
ful to that gentleman who in 1966 selflessly gave me his
copy of Julia's poetry, and to Mari Tere and all the women
and men who have experienced Julia de Burgos' poetry, as
we are linked by imperceptible but strong bonds of intimacy.

NOTES

1. Feminism is taken to mean a critical theoretical
orientation that denounces subjugation and seeks to uncover its ideological forms in women's lives. It refers to
a vision of solidarity and humanization.
2. See Barratt, unpublished manuscript. The analysis of subjectivity as a complex embodiment both of self-
representation and of ideologically rooted social formations
emerged from contemporary ramifications in critical theory.
3. See the work of the Centro de Estudios Puertorriqueños, Hunter College, for example, or those of the Centro
de Estudio de la Realidad Puertorriqueña (CEREP), P.O.
Box 22200, UPR Station, Río Piedras, Puerto Rico 00931.
4. This man's name was not made public until recent years. Yvette Jiménez de Báez states that she had
no permission to identify him. A recent publication of
edited works, however, identified him as Dr. Juan Isidro
Jiménez Grullón (Mairena 1985). I have used a generic
reference to him, as it is used originally.
5. The Nationalist Insurrection of October 1950 was
the armed uprising of Nationalists in different parts of
the island. Puerto Rico was declared under a state of
emergency and the National Guard was mobilized. On
October 30 Albizu Campos, the Nationalist leader, was
taken prisoner after a shootout and tear gassing of his
home in old San Juan. Hundreds were injured and thousands were arrested.

REFERENCES

Azize, Y. 1979. Luchas de la mujer en Puerto Rico, 1889–1919. San Juan: Litografía Metropolitana.

Barradas, E. 1985. "Entre la esencia y la forma: Sobre el momento Neoyorquino en la poesía de Julia de Burgos." In Mairena, Homenaje a Julia de Burgos, 7, 20:23–48.

Barratt, B. (Unpublished manuscript). Introductory Comments. In Barratt, B., G. Gregg, T. Sloan, and W. R. Earnest. Critical Studies on the Ideological Structure of Personality. Ann Arbor, University of Michigan.

Boszormenyi-Nagy, I., and G. Spark. 1965. Invisible Loyalties. New York: Harper & Row.

Bowlby, J. 1980. Attachment and Loss: Sadness and Depression. New York: Basic Books.

Brown, G., and T. Harris. 1978. Social Origins of Depression: A Study in Psychiatric Disorder in Women. New York: Free Press.

Chesler, P. 1972. Women and Madness. Garden City, N.Y.: Doubleday.

Cloward, R. A., and F. Fox Piven. 1979. "Hidden protest: The channeling of female innovation and resistance." Signs: Journal of Women in Culture and Society, 4:651–69.

Dávila, A. 1984. "Un clavel interpuesto (apuntes sobre la imagen de Julia de Burgos)." En Rojo (Suplemento), p. 15.

de Burgos, J. 1961. Obra Poética. San Juan: Instituto de Cultura Puertorriqueña.

Fernández-Méndez, E. 1970. Historia Cultural de Puerto Rico. San Juan: Editorial Universitaria.

Figueroa, L. 1983. Breve Historia de Puerto Rico. Río Piedras: Editorial Edil.

Fraser, J. 1981. "The female alcoholic." In E. Howell and M. Bayes, eds., Women and Mental Health, pp. 296-305. New York: Basic Books.

Gilligan, C. 1982. In a Different Voice: Psychological Theory and Women's Development. Cambridge, Mass.: Harvard University Press.

Goldhor Lerner, H. 1985. The Dance of Anger. New York: Harper & Row.

González, J. E. 1961. "La poesía de Julia de Burgos, estudio preliminar." In J. de Burgos, Obra Poética, pp. 11-59. San Juan: Instituto de Cultura Puertorriqueña.
_____. 1976. "Julia de Burgos: La mujer y la poesía." Sin Nombre, 7, 3:86-100.

Grinberg, L., and R. Grinberg. 1984. Psicoanálisis de la migración y del exilo. Madrid: Alianza Editorial.

Jiménez de Báez, Y. 1966. Julia de Burgos: Vida y Poesía. San Juan: Editorial Coquí.

Kegan, R. 1982. The Evolving Self. Problems and Process in Human Development. Cambridge, Mass.: Harvard University Press.

Kritsberg, W. 1988. The Adult Children of Alcoholics Syndrome. New York: Bantam.

Litman, G. K. 1978. "Clinical aspects of sex-role stereotyping." In J. Chatwynd and O. Hartnett, eds., The Sex Role System: Psychological and Social Perspectives. London: Routledge and Kegan Paul.

Margarida, M. T. 1984. "A psychological analysis of the life and work of Julia de Burgos." Unpublished manuscript presented at a meeting of the Massachusetts School of Professional Psychology.

Miller, J. B. 1976. Toward a New Psychology of Women. Boston: Beacon.

Pagán, B. 1959. Historia de los Partidos Políticos Puertorriqueños, 1898-1956. Barcelona, España: M. Pareja.

Peoples Press of Puerto Rico Project. 1977. Puerto Rico:
The Flame of Resistance. San Francisco: Peoples
Press.

Picó, I. 1979. "The history of women's struggle for equality in Puerto Rico." In E. Acosta-Belén, ed., The
Puerto Rican Woman. New York: Praeger.

Quintero, A. 1971. La Lucha Obrera en Puerto Rico.
San Juan: CEREP.

Rivera Lassén, A. 1975. "A Julia de Burgos." El Tacón
de la Chancleta, 8-9.

Rivera Quintero, M. 1979. "Capitalist development and
the incorporation of women to the labor force." In
E. Acosta-Belén, ed., The Puerto Rican Woman. New
York: Praeger.

Solá, M. 1985. "Desde hoy hacia Julia de Burgos."
Revista Mariena, 7, 20:13-22.

Solá, M., ed. 1986. "La poesía de Julia de Burgos:
Mujer en humana lucha." In Yo Misma Fui Mi Ruta.
Río Piedras: Editorial Huracán.

Umpierre, L. M. 1987. "Metapoetic code in Julia de
Burgos 'El Mar y Tú': Towards a revision." In E.
Rogers and T. Rogers, eds., In Retrospect: Essay on
Latin American Literature. York: South Carolina
Spanish Literature Publication Co. (pp. 85-94).

Vázquez Ramírez, D. 1987. "Julia de Burgos: Feminista."
Homines, 10, 2:482-89.

Zavala-Martínez, I. 1981. "Mental health and the Puerto
Ricans in the United States: A critical literature review. Unpublished manuscript.

_____. 1984. "Depression among women of Mexican
descent." Dissertation Abstracts International, 42 sec.
2B. University Microfilms No. 8411207.

_____. 1986. "En La Lucha: The economic and socio-emotional struggles of Puerto Rican women in the United States." In R. Lefkowitz and A. Withorn, eds., For Crying Outloud: Women and Poverty in the United States. New York: Pilgrim Press. Revised version, Women and Therapy (1988), 6, 4:3-24.

2

Cultural Constructions of Women by Contemporary Puerto Rican Women Authors

Diana L. Vélez, Ph.D.

We read short stories because they give us pleasure and because they tell us about a possible world or worlds that somehow correspond to what we know to be true. Hence literature is a window on culture, though not in a simple or direct way. Literature makes truth claims that we, the readers, validate in activating the texts as we read. There are many ways of reading a given text and there is no sure way to predict how a particular story or poem will be apprehended by a reader. But close analysis of stories written by a category of writers--Puerto Rican women, for example--does provide us with material that is marked culturally and that refers to a particular set of social circumstances. Writers must make their writing comprehensible, interesting, and pleasurable to a set of readers. In analyzing ways in which that pleasure is structured, we move closer to an understanding of the social subject in any given social formation.

Clearly, then, we are not suggesting a simple model in which the written text merely reflects the society in which it was written, since there are any numbers of mediating factors and circumstances that make possible any literary production. There are also complex processes at work in any reading activated by a reader. True, the written text is the product of a writer with a psyche and a complex subjectivity, but the text does not "belong" to this writer, for even in the act of production, the woman writer is herself inscribed in a variety of sociopolitical

and historical circumstances which make her a social subject and, as such, subject to the laws of the symbolic order that she acceded to when she became a person and
learned how to use language.

To the reader who is not versed in literary studies,
this way of looking at writing can be somewhat unsettling.
And it should be, because what has taken place in literary
studies is nothing short of a Copernican revolution. No
longer is there a concern with what the author meant nor,
strictly speaking, is there a concern with what is in the
text. Instead, the critic is concerned with the activation
of certain readings, and uses terms such as "subject position," "discourse," and "apprehending the other." These
terms are an attempt to de-essentialize human beings by
placing them in a larger context of social practices.

This does not mean humans are done away with. It
only means they are removed from their central position,
in much the same way that the earth is no longer seen to
be the center around which the solar system revolves.
Rather than viewing human beings as free-standing "individuals," this approach allows us to view humans as "subjects." This term is used to mean subject as in "subject
of a sentence," which speaks to the separation between the
"I" who speaks and the "I" that is the subject of their
enunciation. They are clearly not one and the same and
this difference has theoretical importance. The term "subject" is also used to mean "subject to certain laws," for,
unlike the Red Queen in Alice in Wonderland, we cannot
choose to have words mean only what we want them to
mean. Language is shared, systematic, the sedimentation
of years of social history and, when we learn to use it,
we learn "our place" in the world. That place is "I" as
opposed to "you" or "her." It is also, some critics argue,
a gendered place or subjectivity.

But what social significance does all this have? The
political importance of narrative becomes clear when we
realize that the stories communities--nations, classes, and
so on--tell themselves about themselves and others are
practices that influence or bring about other practices.
For example, the collective narrative of Manifest Destiny
in the nineteenth century allowed the social subjects of
that era to engage in certain practices with regard to
Native Americans that fit in with the story they were telling themselves about who they were and what they should
be doing in the world. Thus, our discourses circulate
power in particular ways that can be studied.

One of the ways in which this circulation of power can be studied is by reading texts produced by social subjects who are members of communities different from our own. But here again, I want to avoid slipping into a discourse that reinscribes universality, for I deeply distrust that story. In recent years there has been a growing dissatisfaction with the received common sense, that is, a humanistic formula that tells us we are all the same, really, and that literature, by extension, must speak to the universal values of Man. Not only is the term "Man" used to exclude women as well as non-European peoples who do not share Western values, but the discourses of universality try to erase differences by appropriating the stories of those "Others." An awareness of the pitfalls of this kind of logocentricity has been effected in some literature departments across the country and one of the results has been a questioning of the established literary canon. This questioning was brought about, in part, by feminist political movements as well as by Black and other civil rights movements. The rationale for this change is the knowledge that the society's "Others" have a story to tell that is quite different from that told by those who occupy a central position in the society's collective narrative.

Another related development is the removal of disciplinary barriers in a project that might be called "cultural studies," which acknowledges that talking across disciplines is difficult, but worthwhile and necessary. It is hoped that this chapter will contribute in some way to both projects.

METHODOLOGY

In this chapter I will analyze the narrative strategies and references found in three short stories written by three contemporary Puerto Rican women. I will examine the relationship of these texts to that cultural construction called "woman's place."

The stories analyzed herein were chosen because they problematize gender issues within the cultural context known as contemporary Puerto Rico. This complex society underwent massive social change in the years after World War II as its economy was industrialized within one generation's lifetime. The upheaval brought about by this change included--in the cultural realm--the displacement

of traditional categories, not the least of which was that
known as "woman." This socially constructed category was
and is a ground of contestation, and its parameters change
in response to shifts in the economic order.

As stated, literature must be analyzed in its social
context as a component of ideology where the ideas that
human beings have about their lives are played out in the
imaginary realm through the practice of writing. Writing
that engages in contesting restrictive cultural norms can
thus be fruitfully analyzed, producing readings that enhance our understanding of society. In producing recog-
nizable literary artifacts, women writers must use the
various codes of the same language--phallocentric though
it may be--that men use. But, that language is full of
discontinuities and gaps, though it aims to cover these
over. In writing a coherent narrative, the author must
use the syntactical and other constructions of language
that smooth over contradiction, thereby leaving out important material. But, as in dreams and everyday life, what
is blocked, what is elided is often that which holds the
key to the interpretation of events, the key to meaning.
Thus, in analyzing women's writings, the critic should
look not for the continuity or the unity of the works but
rather for their multiplicity and their contradictions. It
would be an unfortunately synthetic move to fix on the
similarities found in these texts because it is in their internal differences that the larger cultural field "speaks"
women's place. Moreover, as Catherine Belsey states,
"The object of the critic . . . is to seek not the unity of
the work, but the multiplicity and diversity of its possible
meanings, its incompleteness, the omissions which it displays but cannot describe, and above all, its contradictions."[1] Clearly the approach is not to look for authorial
intention, nor is it to see the writing as a form of "individual expression" for the critic's task is quite other: to
look for the "unconscious" of the work, a construction that
comes into existence "in the moment of its entry into literary form, in the gap between the ideological project and
the specific literary form."[2]

HISTORICAL BACKGROUND

It was not until the 1960s that Puerto Rican women
began to write short stories in significant numbers. Prior

to that women had written primarily poetry, a culturally acceptable genre, especially if the poetry dealt with the theme of love. Moreover, while such poets as Julia de Burgos had undermined the roles assigned to women in the culture, in Puerto Rico there had been little overtly feminist writing, with some important exceptions such as Luisa Capetillo's work. Ana Lydia Vega's essay, "De bípeda desplumada a escritora puertorriqueña con E y P machúsculas: textimonios autocensurados," analyzes the reasons why prose writing had been exclusively male territory in Puerto Rico until the 1960s.[3] Bringing into comic relief (pun intended) the local specificity of barriers faced by Puerto Rican women writers, Vega examines the difficulties faced by women who choose to trade in their <u>plumas</u> (feather dusters) for <u>plumas</u> (pens). Filled with double entendres and carnivalesque word plays, the essay is a hilarious Caribbean update of Virginia Woolf's <u>A Room of One's Own</u>.

The short story was the major genre chosen by Puerto Rican prose writers after World War II. Given its importance, it is noteworthy that the generation of short-story writers immediately preceding the contemporary generation of 1960 consisted exclusively of male writers. Moreover, almost without exception, the images of women found in that writing were negative stereotypes of demanding, selfish castrators who facilitated U.S. cultural domination with their demands for the manufactured products of the metropolis. In other cases, women symbolized a lost origin, a mythical past with its primal connection to the land, an organic, untroubled golden age without class distinctions.[4] René Marqués, a gifted writer who occupied a privileged position as spokesperson of his generation, went so far as to state that Puerto Rico was in danger of losing its cultural identity to a North American matriarchy![5] For Marqués, at least, the liberation of women and the maintenance of Puerto Rico's culture were mutually exclusive. (What if--asks Ana Lydia Vega--a component of that national heritage we are trying to protect should happen to be sexism? "¿Y si el machismo resulta ser uno de esos tan proclamados Valores Nacionales?")[6]

The women whose works I will study here read the cultural text into which they are inscribed in a different way. Their writing is almost exclusively feminist, and when questions of national identity do arise they are not posed in opposition to women's issues but as an integral part of the larger problem of identity.

The first tale allegorizes both Puerto Rico and women's primal connection to each other. The story's male figure brings chaos into the lives of the twin sisters by separating them and forcing them to give up the protection they had enjoyed in each other. The moral of this story might be that if leaving behind home and family with its repetitive sameness (tradition) brings only the alienation of mindless labor, it might be better to keep the safety and magic of familial bonds. On a broader level, the allegory might be read as an argument for maintaining some of Puerto Rico's traditional ways lest the rapid change and temptations of consumer goods destroy its social fabric.

The second story's adolescent protagonist is a girl caught between fundamentalist Christian doctrine and the temptations of a secular life. In this text the girl must choose between two polar opposites that are perhaps not as different as they might seem to be at first: virgin or whore. The structural impossibility of those subject positions is inscribed in the text as a final contradiction, for the story ends in a question.

The third story's protagonist is a widow facing freedom from an abusive husband who has just died. The diary is a fictive artifact in which she moves in dialogic self-reflection, arriving finally at a subject position very similar to the one she has just left behind. It is her son--not her husband--who is now her master.

It is clear from this cursory summary that, since women find it both possible and impossible to take up the subject positions prescribed for them by the culture, these texts will necessarily be constructed out of ambivalence on both the formal and thematic levels. These stories question identity and women's place in terms of self and other. Developmental transitions appear in their writing as fraught with dangers, not because of their protagonists' weaknesses but because of the difficulties women face in occupying the place society has marked out for them.

DEVELOPMENTAL ISSUES

In all three stories, developmental transitions are steps in a process that reinscribes "women's place" as a cultural category. The contradiction is that the characters in these stories find themselves forced to take part in their own oppression as they search for a way out of the social, the cultural--a search that is doomed to failure. The stories chosen are portrayals of three different developmental stages: childhood, adolescence, and adulthood. These categories allow us to examine (1) how the writers portray characters and situations that involve human beings in the process of growth and development; (2) how authors problematize obstacles to full human functioning that women face at each of these junctures; (3) how the texts can be read so that possible solutions to dilemmas are activated in the act of reading; and (4) what structural impossibilities to full humanity for women are present in the cultural text as elaborated in the narrative.

CHILDHOOD

The first story, "Pico Rico, Mandorico" by Rosario Ferré, is a fairy tale with universal implications about the transition from childhood into adulthood.[7] This story, which is a more political rewriting of Christina Rosetti's Goblin Market, also contains an embedded critique of alienated labor and traditional, that is, heterosexist values.[8] Moreover, the story problematizes the need to integrate a divided self and, by extension, the need to integrate the self into a community of others. The protagonist must overcome oral drives, selfishness, destructive individualism, and the resulting alienation before becoming whole. But the story's subversive power lies in the way it posits an all-female world of sensuality and artistic play. "Rosario Ferré . . . plantó bombas en el terreno licitísimo del cuento infantil." (Rosario Ferré placed bombs in the very acceptable terrain of children's literature.)[9]

It would not be an exaggeration to say that all of Rosario Ferré's stories are structured as fairy tales. Moreover, she would probably consider it a compliment. For rather than seeing the fairy tale as something for the exclusive consumption of children--not in itself a bad thing, though restricted in scope--she sees the enchantment of folk/fairy tales as containing important lessons for young and old alike.[10] For his part, Bruno Bettelheim, in a rich study of fairy tales and their usefulness in the growth process, states that these stories perform differently, are read differently by children--I would add "adults"--in different stages of their development.[11] That is, in our

readings of these tales, we take what we need at the
moment as we activate the texts in the act of reading.
Therefore, a critical reading of a fairy tale might involve
making informed guesses as to how it might be read by a
child, by an adolescent, and by an adult—that is, how it
might be activated differently by readers at different
points in their lives.

According to Bettelheim, as the child becomes increasingly independent of her parents, both emotionally and
physically, she also becomes painfully aware of her physical and emotional smallness when compared to the world
with which she now must cope. Fantasy makes available
to the child a possible world in which obstacles are overcome, allowing her to visualize the future with optimism.
The ability to spin fantasies, says Bettelheim, is an
achievement that makes all others possible.[12] But fairy
tales do not do this by presenting a sunny world filled
only with pleasant events. These stories portray evil
characters who are out to thwart the hero/heroine. In
fact, overcoming barriers is one of the structuring elements
of the fairy tale form, according to Vladimir Propp.[13]

In "Pico Rico, Mandorico," two sisters, Alicia and
Elisa, are warned by their mother on her deathbed that
they should always work together, and that if they do so,
no evil will befall them. The two are described as being
so alike that the townspeople have trouble telling them
apart so they simply call them "the Alisias," a combination of the two names. This, then, can be read as a
narrative about integration, about getting the warring
sides of the human personality to work in unison for the
health and well-being of the human subject, even as it
accepts the split posited by psychoanalytic theory. This
is one of the functions elaborated by Bettelheim, but he
also states that the gender of heroes in folk fairy tales
is irrelevant, for children take whatever they need from
the tale, regardless of the genders of the protagonists.
But I would argue that in this story the fact that these
are heroines and not heroes is central to the narrative.

Both their bond to each other and the work they do
are described in terms that are archetypically female: the
two were born "holding onto each other so tightly they
were 'like two halves of a shell'."[14] (Emphasis added.)
After their mother dies, they earn their living doing
needlework. But this typically female work is not innocent, for it requires that they each carry a pair of

sharpened scissors that "dangle from their waists like sharpened stars." "Cada una llevaba siempre consigo un par de tijeras gemelas que le colgaban del cinto <u>como una estrella amolada</u>."[15] (Emphasis added.) Femininity, then, is not presented here as passivity or powerlessness. It is a form of aesthetic production—like weaving—but it contains an element of danger.

The two sisters have privileged access to the aesthetic, not only in their work but also in their play. Moreover, their bond to each other contains an element of magic: When they walk past the townspeople in the heat of the summer, the people feel "as if the sound of icy xylophones were suddenly fluttering on their skin"; if one sister drinks too fast, the other feels a piercing ache in her temples; if one pricks her finger while sewing, a mysterious drop of blood suddenly appears on the other's fingertip.[16]

The two sisters spend their time sewing and playing word games that allow them to exercise their imaginations. This practice lets them escape the fate of the other townsfolk who, because they work from sunrise to sunset, have lost the ability to sleep (or to dream, to imagine—in Spanish, <u>sueño</u> has all of these meanings and more). In addition to being privileged by not being alienated, they also have access to hidden knowledge, to the arcane. In playing their innocent games they learn "the difficult art of making their souls leave their bodies."[17]

All goes well until one day a horseman appears dressed in black. The cultural encoding of black-clad horsemen harks back to a period when Puerto Rico was a Spanish colony and the Guardia Civil was a feared law enforcer. Black is also marked for mystery and evil. The horseman has a basket of fruit which he tries to sell. On his shoulder is a monkey—his helpmate, a figure that can be read as representing his animal "Other" or his unconscious drives, for the monkey does what he, the horseman, would like to do but cannot. Alicia refuses the horseman's entreaties, mocking him for his large nose—the <u>pico</u> of the title and culturally encoded for masculine power—but Elisa is tempted by the fruit. This separation marks the violation of the mother's warning and can be read variously, depending on the reader's age and developmental needs. A child might read it as a symbolic representation of forbidden oral gratification. Another reading—more likely to be activated by adult readers—would

be to see the fruit as representing sexuality or sexual
desire.

Among others, the blues tradition contains many examples of this symbolism, one of which is Robert Johnson's
famous line, "If you don't want my peaches, honey, don't
shake my tree." Fruit as sex has a long history in
Judeo-Christian symbolism beginning with the Garden of
Eden story. But here that primal story is reversed; temp-
tation is offered for female consumption by a male who
would thereby lead her into perdition. In Ferré's work,
fruits play a major role as symbols of male-female interaction and betrayal. To buy the fruit, since Elisa cannot borrow the money from her sister—who sees through
his verses and realizes that he is none other than the
local landowner—Elisa cuts off one of her braids and gives
it to him in exchange for the fruit. That is, she mutilates
herself in order to satisfy the temporary oral—or sexual—
gratification offered by the fruit. That night, Elisa, ig-
noring her sister's entreaties, eats of the fruit until she
is full. She then become ill and, like the other townspeople, is unable to coax sleep, dreams, or fantasy; she
becomes alienated, working her fingers to the bone like a
zombie, no longer able to cultivate her imagination. Thus,
she has lost an important aspect of her humanity. She
has been separated from her self; she is alienated. Alicia
is at the point of despair when she suddenly realizes that
the way to heal her sister is to get her to eat again of
the fruit as an antidote to the received poison. (Fairy
tales rarely explain how protagonists know the solution to
problems.) She starts off in search of the mysterious
horseman. Finding him asleep under a tree, she realizes
that he is, in fact, the local terrateniente, or landowner.
Wearing a hat that covers her braids, thus disguising herself as her sister, she tries to get him to sell her the
fruit but his monkey pulls off her hat, revealing her
identity. Then, in an act of encoded rape, he savagely
covers her with the fruits' poisonous juices. Alicia re-
sponds by snipping off his nose with her scissors dejándolo
tuco, leaving him with just a stump, symbolically castrat-
ing him. She then returns to her sister's room, descending
through the skylight as she had done earlier in the narrative. Her sister, delighted to see her, licks the poisonous
juices from her body and eats the fruit pulp caught in
her skirts. Elisa recovers instantly, able once more to
dream, sleep, and fantasize. The townsfolk give up their

alienating work from dawn till dusk because now that the landowner's nose is only a stump, they can recognize him even at a distance.

This story subverts a number of accepted cultural norms. First, the all-female household contradicts the usual gender balance and lesbianism is encoded throughout but especially at the end, with its oral sexuality. Second, on a purely textual level, this tale runs counter to tradition, for fairy tales with siblings always representing male and female—Hansel and Gretel, brother and sister, and so on—never two females in an all-woman world. Third, evil is traditionally represented by witches, females who have power by virtue of their knowledge of the arcane, including the knowledge of black magic. In this tale, it is the two girls who have access to "good" knowledge while the evil man's power is based only on masquerade and on the townspeople's self-denial.

Another idea questioned in the narrative is the value of hard work and self-sacrifice. Whereas hard work is portrayed as harmful, for it leads to alienation, play is the regenerative force that feeds the imagination and magically frees us from the bonds of the purely material.

Alicia, by taking what she needed, by force if necessary, violates both the property rights of the landowner and a social code that idealizes passivity in girls. Moreover, her act becomes meaningful to the whole collective, for it frees the workers from their alienation by revealing to them the truth about their oppressor.

> Y como en adelante los habitantes del pueblo
> pudieron reconocer al hacendado, a distancia
> y fácilmente, porque éste se veía condenado a
> pasearse por la comarca con la nariz tuca,
> se dieron cuenta de lo absurdo de su resigna-
> ción y de su mansedumbre y se negaron a
> trabajar para él de sol a sol, recobrando al
> punto la maravillosa facultad de conciliar el
> sueño.[19]

Through her act, she discloses, she unmasks, she makes manifest that which was hidden: the fact that his power was based solely on a fiction and on their acquiescence. While she effectively disempowers him by cutting off his source of power—his big nose, the title of the tale, the basis of his trickery—she also shows that believing in oneself is half the battle. The connection between her act and their freedom is made explicit in the narrative, and a girl reading this story might activate this reading for herself as heroine.

Another possible direction for a reading is to note that, although the title, "Pico Rico, Mandorico," refers to a Puerto Rican children's rhyme, it bears a strong resemblance to the name of that island nation. This gives the narrative an allegorical possibility wherein work and nationality intersect symbolically in the story.

As with any piece of fiction or poetry, one reading does not exhaust the tale's meaning. What this initial analysis illustrates is that in writing a story structured as a fairy tale, Rosario Ferré has indeed placed bombs in the very acceptable genre of children's literature, for she has undermined the received norms of hard work, compulsory heterosexuality, and excessive individualism while exalting the value of aesthetic pleasure.

ADOLESCENCE

"Milagros, calle Mercurio," by Carmen Lugo Filippi, begins with an epigraph about lost innocence, a reference to Little Red Riding Hood: "Ha muerto la blanca Caperucita Roja" (Little Red Riding Hood is dead—the adjective "white" cannot be added in the English without ruining the prosody).[20] Unlike our first story, and unlike fairy tales in general, this one ends in a question that leaves the reader in the grip of an irresolvable contradiction. The contradiction lies in the impossibility of occupying either of the binary opposites—virgin and whore—the two subject positions traditionally available to Puerto Rican women. But this narrative hints at broader issues, such as the place of voyeurism in female sexuality and the appropriation of the other which is involved in any act of narration. Moreover, it allows the reader to question female complicity as the protagonist prepares her ward to accept the male gaze as a condition of her subjecthood in society. She prepares her to be a woman by showing her how to guarantee being "seen" by another.

The story is told by a first person dramatized narrator, a divorced female head of household who earns her living as a beautician, despite her three years of university training in comparative literature. We learn from

her--in straightforward realist prose--that when she lived
in San Juan and worked in a fashionable salon, she had
managed to wrest for herself a position of relative power
vis-à-vis her high-class customers by virtue of her knowledge of several languages. Her skill at beauty parlor
power-plays establishes her as a capable, strong woman.
She has since moved to Puerto Rico's somewhat provincial
second city, Ponce.

One day she sees Milagros and her imagination is
sparked by the tall, impassive adolescent with her waist-
length hair. Milagros' mother, she finds out from a gossipy neighbor, will not allow Milagros to cut her hair because she is a religious fundamentalist--"aleluyas," as
they are disparagingly called in Puerto Rico.

> Fue justamente en esa época cuando ví por
> vez primera a Milagros. La recuerdo tan
> vivamente, tal como si estuviera viendo una
> pelicula española en blanco y negro, de esas
> bien sombrías que transcurren en un pueble-
> cito de mala muerte, donde la esbelta pro-
> tagonista de pelo larguísimo camina lenta-
> mente y de pronto la cámara se le acerca;
> perfecto "close-up" algo parsimonioso que
> resbala por la cara blanquísima y se regodea
> en las facciones inexpresivas, sobre todo, en
> la mirada lánguida y como ausente. (It was
> just around the time that I saw Milagros for
> the first time. I recall it vividly. It was
> as if I were watching a black and white
> Spanish movie, one of those dark ones where
> the story takes place in a one-horse town,
> where suddenly the willowy protagonist with
> her long tresses walks along slowly and sud-
> denly the camera zooms in--a perfect close-up--
> then slowly glides over her facial features,
> focusing especially on her languid, distant
> eyes.)21

The narrator apprehends her object in a peculiarly
cinematic way. Her "look" is informed by years of college
student assistance at film clubs and she refers to the
scene where Milagros walks to church with her mother and
sister as "typically Buñuelesque." But one sentence later
she undermines that distanced attitude, calling it the

cynicism of Mt. Olympus. She is ambivalent, for while she does wish her film club friends from the university could be there with her to witness the scene, she realizes it would be "para luego elaborar las teorías más abstrusas y de paso enfrascarse en animadas discusiones existencialistas. Pero solo estabas tú. (in order to make up the most abstruse theories later, getting into lively existential debates. But there was only you).[22]

While she knows she must make sense of Milagros on her own and that her university cronies' alienated discourse is inadequate, her own discourse continues to be filmic. Indeed, she inscribes Milagros in her own Buñuelesque film, her own text. It is the Buñuel of the two films, Viridiana and Belle du Jour, wherein bourgeois sexual norms and mores are undermined by the behavioral inconsistencies of the protagonists. It is a film tradition that, through irony and satire, gives sexuality its due as an insistent force in human life, one that humans have difficulty keeping within the artificially restrictive constraints of culture. Buñuel's anti-clericalism is also well known and like his stories, this one is about "fallenness" and the pitfalls of false virtue.

It is this cinematic tradition to which our narrator refers in trying to apprehend her object, but by doing so, she also appropriates Milagros in a peculiar fashion into her own desire. She wants to transform the object of her gaze. The shop owner's interest is stimulated by the subtle changes she notes in Milagros' attire as she watches her go to and from school and church daily--"un discreto escote en forma de V, una falda más ceñida que de costumbre, unas sandalias baratas pero algo pizpiretas" (a discreet v-neck, a skirt that was a little tighter than usual, cheap but somewhat flashy sandals).[23] The Pygmalion story is relevant here as the fictive narrator, taken by the very discreet object of her desire, thinks of what she could do to that head of hair if only she could. It is that very desire that is forbidden by the mother's fundamentalist beliefs. But the fictive narrator is able to introduce Milagros into "the world"--as fundamentalist Christians refer to the secular sphere--when Milagros develops scalp psoriasis and is brought into the beauty shop for treatment. It is then that the fictive narrator, by showing Milagros a new world--the world of style, beauty, makeup--appropriates Milagros into her own script.

This problematic is indexed on the formal level by changes in narrative voice. From first person narrator, suddenly there is a change in voice and we are reading an internal dialogue between the narrator--who now has a name, Marina--and her Other, a voice that contains aspects of the superego but cannot be reduced to it alone. It is the second person narrator who addresses Marina:

> Sí, porque constituía para tí un verdadero
> reto el pelo de Milagros. Incluso fantaseabas
> con los posibles cortes, verdaderas obras
> maestras dignas de figurar en Hair and Style
> o en Jours de France (Yes, because Milagros'
> hair was a real challenge to you. You even
> fantasized about possible hairdos, real works
> of art fit for the pages of Hair and Style or
> Jours de France).[24]

Marina is remembering, but her memory takes a second-person voice, distancing us thereby from what up to now had been a credible narrator. The shift from mono-logic to dialogic discourse works as a narrative strategy for it allows us to step back from the deceptively realistic mode used up until this point. We begin to question the story's own discourse for, if the narrator is herself a split subject, her motives suddenly become as suspect as those of any other character in the story, and she loses her privileged position as the "teller of the tale."

What purpose does this undermining of the fictive narrator's voice serve? I have argued elsewhere[25] that a smooth, believable narrative voice runs contrary to feminist questioning of the naming function. To question voice, speaker's position, and the completeness or adequacy of any utterance to its object--the object it is trying to apprehend--is to question "common sense," a discourse that has been oppressive to women (as well as to non-Westerners, as stated earlier). But in questioning this discourse, we must keep in mind that occupying a female subject position does not preclude complicity, nor does it preclude acceptance of the dominant ideology's placement of women. We all know there are misogynistic women who identify with men. Being biologically female is no guarantee against the acceptance of misogynistic ideology. If that were the case, all women would be feminists. Instead, women writers, like all writers, must "make sense" when they write, and to a certain extent, as Catherine Belsey reminds us, making sense means smoothing over contradiction.[26]

The narrative shifts in voice in this story serve to bring common sense discourse into relief, thus undermining it. Up to this point in the narrative the obvious problem has been the mother's religious overprotection. But as the first-person narrative voice is problematized, the issue becomes that of writing people into our scripts, our appropriation of the Other. Milagros' mother has a script for her daughter as virgin, a script that assumes physical integrity: "Me prohibió cortar uno solo de aquellos cabellos" (She forbade me to trim off even one inch of hair).[27] But the beauty shop keeper has a script for her object as well. Her discourse on Milagros is not innocent any more than is the mother's. In fact, it involves preparing Milagros for entry into society as the "seen," the "looked at" object, a position for which women are often prepared by other women, as we shall see.

When Milagros' mother brings her in for treatments, Milagros starts to familiarize herself with the way in which mass culture inscribes women. An ironic voice informs us that after her third treatment Milagros lost her shyness: "Incluso me pedía revistas y hasta fotonovelas, tipo de literatura esencial en cualquier salón de belleza." (She would even ask me for magazines and fotonovelas, essential literature in any beauty shop.)[28] The narrator plays a mediating role, arranging Milagros' hair into beautiful styles and telling her she looks like a movie star. The girl is moved by her image in the mirror and "submerges" herself in the contemplation of the magazines' images.[29] Her coming into being as an adult is accomplished through the mirror of her reflection in a false image of herself. She is prepared by Marina so that she can submit to the male gaze, so that she can become, truly, the object of another.

The story's denouement begins with the discovery that Milagros has been caught doing a striptease in a roadside joint frequented by elderly men. The reader learns this via several mediations: The narrator finds out from the gossipy neighbor, Doña Fina—ironic, for "fina" means refined—Doña Fina finds out from her nephew Rada, an undercover cop, who first learns of it from an informer. Thus, we are to understand that Milagros' name and her shameful story have passed through several voices before reaching us.

Dramatized for effect, Doña Fina's narrative is marked as literary by the narrator:

> Con suma complacencia estiraba la oración de transición, aquella que nos introduciría en el antro pecaminoso, mágica frase de pase, santo y seña que abriría el misterioso recinto para permitirnos contemplar el secreto ritual de la sacerdotisa. (She took pleasure in stretching out her transition sentence, the one that would bring us to the sinful entrance, the magical phrase, the open sesame, the sign that would allow us to see the priestess's secret ritual.)[30]

But though Doña Fina's discourse is commented on through irony, the same religious terminology and dramatization informs Marina's own voice. She gives herself over to fantasy as she imagines Rada's discovery of Milagros' secret. She spins her own imaginary tale, a cinematic tale in which she identifies with Rada, making herself into a voyeuse. She constructs an imaginary striptease, filled with erotic detail, in which Milagros, long hair in center stage, dances for a viewer (herself). The language is erotic, filled with religious terminology: The stage is an "improvisado altar" (improvised altar); the men are alternately "acólitos sexagenarios" (sexagenarian acolytes) or "sexagenarios sacerdotes" (sexagenarian priests); the dance is "el rito" (the rite). Marina's complicity in this fall from grace is hinted at by reference to "el pelo lleno de pizpiretos miosotis," for it was Marina who first made this hair adornment available to Milagros, and these were the exact words used to describe it earlier in the narrative.

Dance and music are connecting elements in the narrative. They first appear with Milagros' mother's tambourine dance and song to God in church, a religious ecstasy that Milagros observes with indifference. This scene is witnessed by Marina, whose curiosity makes her follow them there. Music appears a second time when Milagros herself dances to popular salsa while Marina is gone from the beauty parlor for a few minutes. Again, Marina is in the role of voyeuse, for she returns unexpectedly and catches Milagros dancing. She watches her in silence for a few minutes, thus violating her privacy, for it is clear from the girl's reaction that she does not enjoy being seen dancing (yet). The third and final

dance is the strip tease that Marina constructs in her
imagination, as Marina once again occupies the position
of illicit viewer. The first dance is religious, the second
purely secular, and the third is secular with an ironically religious twist. The second dance is marked by the
sexist lyrics that define woman as a disposable commodity,
for the song Milagros dances to in the beauty shop is the
popular hit, "Tu amor es un periódico de ayer" (Your love
is like yesterday's paper). Thus, in the narrative, the
"dances" or practices that are culturally approved of for
women are those of religious self-denial, secular self-
erasure, and of self-debasement. These dances can be
read as metonymic for the discourses into which women can
inscribe themselves, the point being that there is no individual exit from sexist culture's discursive inscription of
women, for in them women can either be pure or they can
be debased. Both are impossible subject positions because
no one can self-consciously be a virgin or a whore.

The day after the striptease bust, Milagros shows up
in the beauty parlor wearing tight pants and carrying a
suitcase. Brandishing a $20 bill, she asks Marina to
make her up in shocking red and to cut her hair any way
she pleases (emphasis added). Marina's desire to transform her object is thus realized, for Milagros does not
choose a hairdo, leaving it to Marina, who after all,
does have ideas about how to transform her. Milagros'
entry into the sexual has no need of those details. At
the end of the story she has freed herself from the re-
strictions imposed by her mother's code, but her sexuality
is not therefore "free." Rather, it is perhaps entering
into that peculiar form of Latino sexual repression that
Latinas themselves have described so well: "(W)hile the
chilliest Anglo-Saxon repression of sex pretends it simply
doesn't exist, Latin repression says it's a filthy fact of
life, use it for what it's worth . . . shake it in his
face, wear it as a decoy. It's all over the floor and it's
cold and savage. It's the hatred of the powerless, turned
crooked."[31]

The story ends in a question posed by the accusing
second-person voice. Again, Milagros is inscribed in a
cinematic discourse, although this time the reference is to
Fellini. She acquires gigantic proportions in the mirror,
where the narrator is also reflected for her own contemplation.

Un temblequeo, apenas perceptible, comienza a
apoderarse de tus rodillas, pero aún así no
logras apartar los ojos del espejo donde la
Milagros se agranda, asume dimensiones colosales,
viene hacia tí, sí, viene hacia tí en busca de
una respuesta, de esa respuesta que ella urge
y que tendrás que dar, no puedes aplazarla,
Marina, mírate y mírala, Marina, ¿qué re-
sponderás? (There is a barely perceptible
shaking in your knees but you cannot take
your eyes from the mirror where Milagros takes
on enormous proportions as she moves toward
you, moves toward you in search of an answer,
an answer that she has to have, an answer
that you will have to provide. You cannot put
her off Marina; look at her, look at yourself
Marina. How will you respond?)[32]

The impossibility of the choices before Marina/Milagros
are those of "woman's place." What subject position is
there for the woman? What position is there that does not
subject her to the seemingly opposite although perhaps
complementary positions of virgin and whore? The ironic
discourse of Marina's imaginary striptease points to this
complementarity. If religious and secular discourses equally restrict women, religious terminology is as appropriate
for a debased secular dance like the striptease as it is
for the tambourine dances of the fundamentalist church.
The place offered by beauty magazines is no real alternative. Hence, the question at the end of the text, which
is addressed as much to Marina as it is to Milagros, and
to the reader: "What will you tell her?"
    The fictive narrator of this story has masculinized
herself by gazing at Milagros in her imagination, by creating for her own private viewing a kind of striptease in
which she, the narrator, identifies with the cop during the
raid. She, therefore, is not a woman at that moment, for
she "becomes" a man through identification. When Milagros
returns to the salon at the end of the story, she is ready
to "go out into the world," but what identity shall she
have? Who shall she be? This is a problem without a
solution, for there is no way to be a "woman."
    In this story, the end of innocence that marks ado-
lescence gives rise to the larger problem of identity, female
complicity, possible subject positions for women in the

script or cultural text written for them, and the impossibility of apprehending the Other without somehow subjecting that Other to our own desire, our own script.

ADULTHOOD

The title of Carmen Valle's first book of prose suggests intimacy and illegitimate access to private writings: Diarios Robados (Stolen Diaries),[33] consists of 12 diary entries, fictive artifacts that structure the reader into the narrative as a voyeur. This choice of form allows the author to position the reader into the narrative through irony: the reader is allowed to see more deeply than the fictive narrator, who is unreliable. Wayne Booth states that unreliable narrators are those who do not speak for or act in accordance with the implied author's norms.[34] This rhetorical device allows the reader to see what escapes the narrator because the narrator is culturally inscribed, through language, in a situation that blinds her. This distance between the reader and the narrator makes possible feminist critical readings of the social position known as "woman."

These texts are self-referential in their questioning of the act of writing. Making an entry means something different to each of the fictive narrators of the collection, but in each case the narrative voice is that of a subject engaged in the act of constructing for herself a position in the social order through language. The situations presented allow few choices, they foreclose desire, but not before it peeks out, if only tentatively at times. It is this manipulation of an absence, a lack, that gives each "story" its tension. The protagonists write because they are missing something, and the diary form allows them to give that something a name. Each story is a projection by the author of a possible position or place within Puerto Rican society. The collection defines several stops along a continuum, a variety of imagined social subjectivities.

As stated earlier, there is a formal split in the narrative as the narrator is addressing herself. This split points to the deeper structural split that takes place upon entry into the symbolic, into language. Language here is speaking the (fictive) subject, but as the place spoken for women in Puerto Rican society is precarious from the point of view of her desire, the narrators of these pieces work to reconstruct the positions that are reserved for them in the cultural order. But although several of the diary entries index the struggle against that culturally assigned place called "woman," they also acknowledge that the human subjects, women, are not passive victims in this process of inscription. They are accomplices, if uneasy ones, in the creation of the category "woman," a socially prescribed position to be taken up, an imaged ideal, the projection of male desire, that static image of his Other. What is imaged here in these prose pieces is women's constitution of a "self" through language in an uneven, oscillating movement, a female's inscription into the symbolic order, an inscription that is always taking place even as it is always being resisted.

In reading these fictive diary entries we catch glimpses of some ways in which women create the fictions that smooth their entry into the larger discourse of society and culture. The ways in which the place "woman" is spoken in society are supposed to become the very ways in which women learn to speak themselves. That is, women are supposed to accept the culture's mysogynism. But that is both possible and impossible; the fit is imperfect and the speaking subject of these entries continuously searches for a satisfaction, a wholeness, an authenticity that must escape her, for identity is not a given in human psychic life, but is instead an ideal, something yearned for, something that is never completely achieved. Our desires undermine our socially acceptable identities. One of the implications of this choice of narrative strategy is that it indexes the way that women, even as they seize upon writing as a way to break through social constraints, are themselves being written by culture.

In this section I will focus on the first fictive diary entry. This is a representation of the oscillating movement that the female human subject makes in the process of trying to establish for herself an identity; the narrator is constructing an internal narrative, which we read. She is trying to make for herself a place, a mirror with which she can see herself; she thereby participates in the social, the legal, and the cultural construction of woman's place. The entry is a wry comment on the tenacity of the socially prescribed position for women in Puerto Rican society and the impossibility of this place.

The first-person narrator is a woman who finds herself widowed, finally free of an abusive husband. She begins to write in her diary at the moment when her husband has been buried, stating that she is writing in order to clarify her thoughts. Prior to this entry she has had no voice for she has been in a state of emotional confusion due to having had to repress the voices of resistance within her. The clarity she seeks is the resolution of her deep ambivalence toward her husband, an ambivalence that has marked her life with him for many years. The clarity she wants will continue to escape her, but we, the readers, will have access to her verbal ambiguity as she tries to make sense of the life she has led with him until his death. We are structured in as illegitimate readers of her private story of emotional abuse.

The entry begins "Ya que pasó el entierro quiero estar sola y escribir un poco. Tengo pena, aunque a la verdad, no tanta." (Now that the funeral is over, I want to be alone and write a little. I'm sad, but to be honest, not that sad.)[35] The narrative consists of tentative expressions of relief circumscribed by statements that reveal her awareness of the social expectations about what a recently widowed woman should feel and say. In this quote, the main clause of the sentence, "tengo pena," is immediately undercut by the subordinate clause. Ambivalence shapes this entry as the woman finds herself in a moment rich with possibilities, a moment in which she can finally choose how to structure her own life now that her husband is no longer there to dictate to her.

In the first paragraph she tells of how her husband would go to cockfights and return late into the morning of the next day. On such occasions she would alternately wish for his return and for his death. Her accounts of their life together oscillate between expressions of appreciation and statements of resentment.

The symbol of his dominance is a cage of fighting cocks he kept next to the house. He had forced her to remove her hydrangeas so that he could keep an eye on the cocks. Now that he is dead, she states unequivocally, she will get rid of the fighting cocks, give them away if necessary, and replant the flowers. She thus plans to take charge of her living space, and by extension, her life. She dislikes the animals that have so held her husband's interest—fighting cocks—that in Puerto Rican culture represent an exclusively male domain of belligerent catharsis similar to that of boxing in the United States.

A series of anecdotes makes it clear to the reader
that the man, while alive, used a combination of sadism
and solicitude to keep his wife emotionally dependent on
him. Her tie to him was strong, based as it was on fear,
masochism, and self-hatred. "Y yo le creía todo, y le
tenía miedo, y lo odiaba. Y lo envidiaba porque yo no
tenía ni la mitad de las gallas que él tenía." (I believed everything he said and I feared him. I hated him.
And I envied him because I didn't have half the guts he
did.)[36]

Femininity is here defined as lack. Compared to
her husband, her not-having, her powerlessness, makes
his power normative. She recognizes her weakness compared with his strength, but she does not accept it. She
then tells of her one attempt at rebellion and his response
with sheer force:

> El era capaz de cualquier cosa, como cuando
> me prohibió sin darme ninguna razón de peso,
> que fuera aquel día a las tiendas y yo cogí
> mi cartera, me monté en el carro para irme y
> él, sacando la pistola, le disparó a las
> cuatro gomas; lo corrió por toda la finca
> hasta que no quedaron ni gomas, ni tubos, ni
> aros, sólo los ejes afilados que hacían paracer
> al carro como un lechón de metal con dos
> varas atravesadas. (He was capable of any-
> thing, like the time he forbade me to go shop-
> ping without giving me any good reason and
> I grabbed my purse, climbed into the car to
> go and he took out his gun, shot out all
> four tires and ran the car all over the farm
> till there were no tires, no inner tubes, no
> rims, only the sharpened axles that made the
> car look like a metallic pig on a spit.)[37]

He turned her car, symbol of mobility and freedom,
into a pig on a spit, an image coded for rural, domestic
celebration on holiday occasions. Lechón asado, the main
dish of the traditional Christmas meal, is associated with
the patriarchal culture of the countryside. The conflation
of the two symbols, car and pig, affirms the patriarchal.
The woman is immobilized by extension, a victim of her
husband's brute force.

But his domination is not based on force alone. It
required her participation, which he obtains by means of
his socially sanctioned behavior. This behavior represents
a number of culturally specific codes, all of which reveal
male dominance and female passivity. The dynamic of
power is based on the husband's having certain qualities
that reflect on the wife by virtue of her connection to him.

All the qualities she enumerates are possible only
because she acquiesces or because he occupies a privileged
position in society:

(1) He is generous toward those who are less fortu-
nate than he: "Con el tiempo dejé de quererlo; aunque
me seguía enorgulleciendo su generosidad al hacerle favores
a cualquier pobre sin pedir nada a cambio." (In time I
stopped loving him, although I continued to feel pride in
his generosity. He would do favors for any poor devil
who needed them without asking for anything in return.)[38]
The recipient of the man's generosity is subordinate by
virtue of his poverty, allowing him to maintain a position
of power and moral superiority. This extends to her, although it is mediated.

(2) He is generous toward her: "O su derroche de
dinero cuando para el aniversario de casados me llevaba
a una joyería de San Juan y no importaba lo que yo
escogiera, él sacaba la chequera para pagar mi capricho."
(Or his extravagance for our anniversary when he would
take me to a jewelry story in San Juan and no matter
what I would choose, he would pull out his checkbook and
pay for my whim.)[39] He keeps his wife in the role of a
flighty, capricious dependent by indulging her whims once
a year. Later in the narrative we learn that he is able
to do this because he is the sole income earner, having
prohibited her from working outside the home despite her
professional training.

(3) He is physically attractive:

Y a veces, con chaqueta y corbata, con su
bigote entrecano y las espaldas tan anchas
era el hombre más guapo en los bailes del
club, más guapo que cualquiera de los hombres
más jovenes, porque ya no era joven él ni yo
tampoco, cosa esta última que influía en mí
para no dejarlo. (And sometimes, with his
tie and jacket, his salt-and-pepper mustache,

and his broad back, he was the handsomest
man at the club's dances, handsomer even
than the younger men because he was no
longer young and neither was I, a factor
that influenced me into not leaving him.)[40]

The way the sentence unfolds reveals ambivalence. The
qualification regarding his age leads her to express concern about her own age--a factor that kept her tied to
him. His aging is represented in her discourse only by
reference to his salt-and-pepper hair, an attribute coded
as positive for men in our culture.

(4) He provides her with a middle-class lifestyle.
Here she mentions all the elements of her social class
upon which she depends. At 40, she is a woman with
nothing better to do than wait for grandchildren to enter-
tain her. Her life is one of dependence and boredom, a
life mediated by her husband's wishes.

Now he is dead and she repeats her intention to
do as she pleases. But a final twist points to her contradictory desires for freedom and bondage.

Ahora estoy libre. Voy a ser otra. Mañana
empezaré por el jardín como había planeado
. . . aunque creo que debo hablar antes con
Augusto, a lo mejor él no quiere deshacerse
de los gallos tan ligero. (Now I'm free.
I'm going to be different. I'll start on the
garden tomorrow as I'd planned . . . but I
think I should talk with Augusto first, he
probably won't want to get rid of the cocks
so quickly.)[41]

Seizing upon her son as substitute patriarch, she refuses
any possibility of freedom as she clings to her subordinate
position by putting her son in the dominant place formerly
occupied by her husband.

CONCLUSION

The three stories analyzed here point to the difficulty Puerto Rican women have occupying the place that
has been socially prescribed for them. Each text under-

mines a culturally assigned role, whether it be alienated worker, virgin, whore, or dutiful wife. However, this takes place in a complex manner, for all three stories refer to a vacillation on the part of women. The temptations of sexual desire, consumer goods, the desire to be beautiful, the desire to subject another woman to the male gaze, as well as the comforts of a middle-class life, all play a part in keeping the protagonists vacillating between what they want and what they can have in society as it is now structured. The three narratives problematize this structure and "women's place" in it differently, but in each case the reader can see that it is both possible and impossible to be a woman in Puerto Rico. Narrative strategies vary, but in each case we see a deep dissatisfaction with those cultural practices that define women in Puerto Rico. From a fairy tale for children and adults to a story that calls into question the authority of the narrative voice as well as women's complicity in the patriarchy, to a fictive diary, each narrative structures the reader into a position where s/he too must question the cultural code's inscription of women.

While there are numerous other stories that also lend themselves to productive gender analysis, it is clear from this initial reading that short-story writing by contemporary Puerto Rican women is a practice deeply marked by women's desire to break through the constraints placed on them by culture.

ACKNOWLEDGMENT

I would like to thank Brown University's Pembroke Center for Teaching and Research on Women for fellowship support that made possible part of the research for this article. All English translations are my own.

NOTES

1. Catherine Belsey, Critical Practice (London: Methuen, 1980), p. 109.
2. Ibid., p. 135.
3. Ana Lydia Vega, "De bípeda desplumada a escritora puertorriqueña con E y P machúsculas: testimonios autocensurados, La Torre del Viejo 1, 2 (julio-agosto 1984):44-48.

4. An excellent discussion of this mindset or world view appears in José Luis González, El País de Cuatro Pisos y Otros Ensayos (Río Piedras: Ediciones Huracán, 1980), pp. 45-90.

5. René Marqués, "El Puertorriqueño Dócil," in Ensayos (Barcelona: Editorial Antillana, 1972), p. 175.

6. Vega, "De bípeda desplumada," p. 45.

7. Rosario Ferré, "Pico Rico Mandorico," in La Mona que le Pisaron la Cola (Río Piedras: Ediciones Huracán, 1981), pp. 7-16.

8. Christina Rosetti, Goblin Market (Philadelphia: J. B. Lippincott, n.d.).

9. Vega, "De bípeda desplumada," p. 46.

10. Rosario Ferré, "El cuento de hadas," Sin Nombre 11,2 (1980):36-40. This author has made an important contribution to Puerto Rican culture by writing down oral narratives that, due to Puerto Rico's peculiar colonial situation, might very well have been lost to future generations. La Mona que le Pisaron la Cola is one of two collections of fairy tales by Ferré. El Medio Pollito is the other. "Pico Rico Mandorico" is one of two fairy tales she wrote herself. That is, they are not, properly speaking, oral narratives or folktales but rather tales she made up while under the influence of her readings of fairy tales.

11. Bruno Bettelheim, The Uses of Enchantment: The Meaning and Importance of Fairy Tales (New York: Vintage, 1977).

12. Ibid., p. 125.

13. Vladimir Propp, Morphology of the Folk Tale (Austin: University of Texas Press, 1968), p. 90.

14. Ferré, "Pico Rico Mandorico," p. 8.

15. Ibid.

16. Ibid.

17. Ibid., p. 9.

18. See especially, "La muñeca menor" where the guanábana fruit is the locus of a cluster of terms like "sperm," "wound,"and "smell," all of which are related to sexuality. Rosario Ferré, Papeles de Pandora (Mexico DF: Joaquín Mortiz, 1976), pp. 9-15.

19. Ferré, "Pico Rico Mandorico," p. 16.

20. Carmen Lugo Filippi, "Milagros, calle Mercurio," in Ana Lydia Vega and Carmen Lugo Filippi, Vírgenes y Mártires (Río Piedras: Editorial Antillana, 1981), pp. 27-38.

21. Lugo, "Milagros," p. 30.

22. Ibid., p. 32.
23. Ibid.
24. Ibid., p. 31.
25. Diana L. Vélez, "Power and the Text: Rebellion in Rosario Ferré's Papeles de Pandora," Journal of the Midwest Modern Language Association 17,1 (Spring 1984): 70–80.
26. Belsey, Critical Practice, pp. 108–10.
27. Lugo, "Milagros, Calle Mercurio," p. 33.
28. Ibid.
29. Ibid., p. 36.
30. Ibid., p. 37.
31. Aurora Levins Morales, ". . . And Even Fidel Can't Change That!" in This Bridge Called My Back: Writings by Radical Women of Color (Watertown, Mass.: Persephone, 1981), p. 56.
32. "Milagros," p. 38.
33. Carmen Valle, Diarios Robados (Buenos Aires: Ediciones de la Flor, 1982).
34. Wayne Booth, The Rhetoric of Fiction, 2nd ed. (Chicago: University of Chicago Press, 1983), p. 158.
35. Valle, Diarios, p. 7.
36. Ibid., p. 8.
37. Ibid.
38. Ibid., p. 9.
39. Ibid.
40. Ibid.
41. Ibid.

REFERENCES

Belsey, C. 1980. Critical Practice. London: Methuen.

Bettelheim, B. 1977. The Uses of Enchantment: The Meaning and Importance of Fairy Tales. New York: Vintage.

Booth, W. 1983. The Rhetoric of Fiction, 2nd edition. Chicago: University of Chicago Press.

Ferré, R. 1981. "Pico Rico, Mandorico." In La Mona que le Pisaron la Cola. Río Piedras: Editorial Huracán.

_____. 1980. "El cuento de hadas." Sin Nombre 11, 2: 36–40.

_____. 1976. Papeles de Pandora. Mexico, DF: Joaquín Mortiz.

Filippi, C. L. 1981. "Milagros, calle Mercurio." In A. L. Vega and C. L. Filippi, eds., Vírgenes and Mártires, pp. 27–38. Río Piedras: Editorial Antillana.

González, J. L. 1980. El País de Cuatro Pisos y Otros Ensayos. Río Piedras: Ediciones Huracán.

Marqués, R. 1972. "El Puertorriqueño Dócil." In Ensayos. Barcelona: Editorial Antillana.

Morales, A. L. 1981. ". . . And Even Fidel Can't Change That!" In This Bridge Called My Back: Writings by Radical Women of Color. Watertown, Mass.: Persephone.

Rosetti, C. N.d. Goblin Market. Philadelphia: J. B. Lippincott.

Valle, C. 1983. Diarios Robados. Buenos Aires: Ediciones de la Flor.

Vega, A. L. 1984. "De bípeda desplumada a escritora puertorriqueña con E y P machúsculas: Textimonios autocensurados." La Torre del Viejo, 1, 2:44–48.

Vélez, D. L. 1984. "Power and the Text: Rebellion in Rosario Ferré's Papeles de Pandora." Journal of the Midwest Modern Language Association 17, 1:70–80.

Vladimir, P. 1968. Morphology of Folk Tales. Austin: University of Texas Press.

Childhood and Adolescence

3

From Home to School: Puerto Rican Girls Learn to Be Students in the United States

Ena Vázquez-Nuttall, Ed.D.
Ivonne Romero-García, M.Ed.

This chapter describes the transition process Puerto Rican girls in the United States experience moving from preschool years spent in Spanish language and Puerto Rican–oriented homes to the English language and culture of the U.S. school. It focuses on the conflicts, discriminations, and discontinuities encountered by these girls as they enter school, and how these affect them as they go through different developmental stages. The impact of sexism and racism of teachers and curricular materials on their academic and social development is discussed. Ineffective and effective adaptations that the girls make to these challenges are also described.

DEVELOPMENTAL PERSPECTIVE

In the last years of preschool, conceptualized by Erikson (1959) as the stage of "initiative versus guilt," the child makes efforts to be socially active and to master new skills. During this period the child begins to identify with the parent of the same sex and to incorporate parental values. This stage plays itself out differently in a Puerto Rican middle-class family than in a U.S., middle-class one. For example, Puerto Rican mothers tend to curb a girl's initiative for fear that she might get hurt, whereas mothers in the United States tend to encourage a greater degree of initiative. Girls of both

cultures learn the female sex role expectations of their
own culture but those expectations are not the same.

The developmental tasks of the next stage, Erikson's
"industry versus inferiority," include learning the basic
skills necessary for progressing toward the adult role.
Peers become significant and children continuously compare
their accomplishments with one another. Failure to develop
these basic skills may result in feelings of inferiority.
This stage is particularly challenging for the Puerto Rican
girls, who often come to school with native language skills
but no knowledge of English or the culture of the schools
in the United States. Feelings of inferiority can easily
set in if teachers and peers are not sensitive to the special problems of a child who must learn a new language
and adapt to a new culture at the same time when she
needs to master instrumental and social skills.

In the adolescent stage the crisis of "identity versus
identity diffusion" comes to a head. A sense of ego identity is defined by Erikson (1959) as "the accrued confidence that one's ability to maintain inner sameness and
continuity (one's ego in the psychological sense) is matched
by the sameness and continuity of one's meaning for
other" (p. 89).

As Erikson states, self-esteem grows out of the con-
viction that one is taking steps toward a tangible future
and that one is developing a defined personality within a
social reality that understands and accepts one.

The inappropriate solution to this stage is "identity
diffusion." Youth suffering from this difficulty run away
in one form or another, leaving schools and other jobs,
withdrawing into bizarre and inaccessible moods. Inability
to settle into an occupational identity is one of the major
problems. To defend themselves against a sense of "identity diffusion," young people become clannish and tend to
exclude from their groups people who are of different ethnic and racial groups.

It is at this stage that serious problems can develop
for Puerto Rican girls. They have the difficult task of
defining themselves in a cultural context that is different
from their home at its best and hostile and prejudicial at
its worst. The achievement of this ego synthesis is more
challenging when one has to rebel against authority systems from two different cultures. Social and ethnic isolation are often experienced by these youngsters because they
do not form part of the majority culture. Acceptance into

groups is sometimes difficult. The generation gap between these teenagers and their parents is greater because of cultural differences.

In the remainder of this chapter we will expand in more detail on these stages and conflicts experienced by Puerto Rican girls.

CONCEPTIONS OF FEMALE ROLES
IN PUERTO RICAN CULTURE

Puerto Rican girls will identify and pattern their ways of behaving as women from their mothers, female members of their extended family, teachers, and female roles portrayed in school books and television programs. Thus, one way of predicting and understanding what kind of woman a girl will be is to find out what kind of ideal and real behaviors are shown by women from her own class group and from society at large. For Puerto Rican girls living in the United States, problems in the formation of their sex role identity are further complicated by the fact that they constitute a minority, while teachers from the majority culture will play an important role in their development. These girls will not only experience the usual discontinuities due to generational differences, but also cultural differences in the definition of what is gender-appropriate.

Many authors have tried to describe the essence of Puerto Rican womanhood (Andrade 1982; Canino and Canino 1980; Christiansen 1975a, 1975b, 1977; Comas-Díaz 1982; Mintz 1966; Minuchin et al. 1967; Torres-Matrullo 1976; Vázquez-Nuttall 1976, 1979). Descriptions of the sex roles of Puerto Rican women differ by the research methods used, age, socioeconomic class, time of the study, and whether the study was conducted in Puerto Rico or in the United States.

A series of anthropological studies conducted in Puerto Rico in the 1950s (Landy 1959; Mintz 1956; Steward 1956; Stycos 1955) have served as the foundation for later family socialization and sex role studies. These studies conducted in various parts of the island and focusing on various classes depict Puerto Rican women as supposedly being under the complete authority and control of their husbands. The husbands' authority varies by region and socioeconomic class. In some rural regions the husband's

authority is so great that the wife may be reduced almost
to the status of a child. She controls no money; is not
allowed outside the house without permission and is expected to submit to his demands without question. She
cares for the children but exercises little initiative even
in this function.

Middle- and upper-class husbands exercise less authority over their wives than do some of the men in the
lower socioeconomic class. In many of the middle-class
families the women have fewer children and work outside
the home. The husbands have relinquished the control of
the money and the children to them.

Landy (1959), in discussing the power of women,
notes a great inconsistency in the cultural expectations
and socialization patterns. He states that in a culture
where the men are supposed to be absolute rulers of their
homes, it is the women who are brought up to be stable
and responsible. Puerto Rican women hold responsibility
not only for their siblings and parents, but ultimately for
their children and families. They stay at home to impart
continuity and stability to the family group.

In the 1970s a group of family therapists including
Minuchin, Montalvo, Guerney, Rosman, and Schumer (1967)
studied low-income families in the United States using a
systems analysis perspective. The major purpose of their
study was twofold: (1) to explore the structure and dynamics of delinquent-producing, disadvantaged, and disor-
ganized families; and (2) the kinds of techniques and interventions in therapy that would work best with them.
They included 12 families, each with one delinquent child,
and 10 "equivalent" families with no delinquent children.
Of these 22 families, four were Puerto Rican.

The families that were studied in depth were administered before and after therapy a pictorial projective
technique and a specially developed behavioral questionnaire and they were seen for 30 family therapy sessions.
From this intensive contact, Minuchin and his collaborators
obtained impressions of the sex roles and family structure
of the various ethnic groups participating. They state
that the Puerto Rican woman is expected to be submissive
and loyal. She has no right to question her husband's
activities, but has authority in her home and in regard
to her children's well-being. They assert:

> The woman's self picture is one of being ex-
> ploited by the man and powerless to defend

> herself. The only alternative to this exploitation, she feels, is separation from her husband, and she wavers between the alternatives of resignation and self-assertion, the latter implying the destruction of her family. Caught in this dilemma, one of her most palpable reactions is resignation and depression. She seems to deny her real strength, actually manifested quite clearly in her practical adaptation to the new culture, her management of the new household, her relationship to her children, and her ability to press for role revision on the part of her man [p. 240].

However, researchers who concentrate on normal middle-class populations present a more optimistic view of Puerto Rican women. Christensen (1975a, 1975b, 1977), based on 10 years of empirical research, clinical work, and educating Puerto Rican college students, states that Puerto Rican women tend to adapt more readily, are more striving, and are more oriented toward achievement than are the Puerto Rican men. They learn to accomplish things through peaceful, typically educational endeavors rather than through direct exertion of power. In a similar vein, King (1974) notes that Puerto Rican women have played an important role in academic and public life and have been the mainstay of their children.

Recent empirical research by Pugh and Vázquez-Nuttall (1983), using Spence and Helmreich's (1978) conceptual schemes and measures with college subjects in the United States, corroborates the findings of Christensen, described previously. In their study, which included Black, Hispanic, and White women using the Personal Attributes Questionnaire, Puerto Rican women came in second after Black women in describing themselves as possessing masculine traits. White women described themselves as the least masculine. However, when asked to report on their "ideal woman," Puerto Rican women rated their ideal selves as the least masculine. Thus, they reported themselves as being more masculine than U.S. women but also as ideally desiring to have fewer masculine traits. These findings indicate that Puerto Rican women are willing to and do act in masculine ways, but internally do not want to lose their traditional femininity. Rosario (1982), using Spence and Helmreich's Attitudes Toward Women Scale in a sample of

45 women living in New York City, found that younger, working, and better educated women tended to be more liberal in their attitudes toward women's status than were their counterparts. In addition, the results suggest that Puerto Rican women born in the United States have a more liberated attitude than their sisters born in Puerto Rico. Thus, migration to the United States changes the Puerto Rican woman's concept of her femininity and masculinity (Vázquez-Nuttall 1979). Women who, in Puerto Rico, are expected to be subservient to men and loyal to their extended families and children become more assertive and independent when they migrate to the United States, a society that has different values and sex role expectations. How are women socialized into these gender roles on the island? Are Puerto Rican child-rearing patterns consistent with those in the United States?

CHILD-REARING PATTERNS

Although child-rearing patterns differ by socioeconomic class and region of the country, there are some patterns that seem to hold constant for all Puerto Ricans on the island (Christensen 1975a, 1975b, 1979; Landy 1959; Mintz 1966; Steward 1956; Stycos 1955). The sexes are strictly separated, with the female's role more narrowly defined than the male's. Since early childhood she is restricted in dress, conduct, freedom, language usage, and social associations. Controls on her mobility are intensified when she migrates to the United States due to the dangers that prevail in urban settings. She is also expected to be submissive--a restriction imposed since early childhood to assure that she will be a virgin when she marries and that the families' honor will be preserved.

However, Christensen (1977) points out that this narrow but clearly defined role simplifies the female's developmental tasks. He feels that the reward for following the role facilitates the development of achieving and persevering behavior in women. In contrast, the greater freedom with its emphasis on male behavior that includes sexual conquest, heavy drinking, and physical encounters, and lower requirements to perform household tasks leaves the male Puerto Rican child often ill-prepared for the educational and vocational challenges he will have to meet later in life.

Even though willingness to be aggressive is one of the basic tenets of machismo, its presence is strongly suppressed in children, especially in girls, of all classes. Landy (1959) noted that in the village he studied, children who were involved in a fight were punished, no matter whose fault the fight was. However, while aggression is severely punished in young children, attachment is nurtured. Since birth, children are rewarded for being close to their parents and other adults. Parents and extended family reinforce attention-getting and nurturance-seeking behaviors of children (Landy 1959). This close attachment to adults will later bring difficulties to the child, since most mainstream teachers in U.S. schools do not recognize this behavior but rather discourage it.

DISCONTINUITIES BETWEEN HOME AND SCHOOL

The role of the school in socialization is important for everyone. It is doubly important for children entering school in a new country. In addition to learning academic skills, new patterns of relating to adults and children have to be mastered. The Puerto Rican girl has heretofore developed primarily in the protected context of an intimate group of kin of similar culture and language. Now she associates with adults who are strangers to her, as well as with other children of her age and status but of a different culture and language.

The role that formal education will play in her life differs strikingly from the role it played for her mother. While her mother may have had little use for schooling, this woman-child needs education and schooling if she is going to develop into an economically independent female. To obtain this education she will have to surmount many obstacles and adapt herself to many inconsistencies between the way she was brought up and the way the school expects her to behave. In Table 3.1 we present a summary of many of the conflicts the Puerto Rican girl will face when she enters school in the United States.

Although Table 3.1 presents many conflicts experienced by Puerto Rican girls attending schools in the United States, because of space limitations we will discuss only the ones that seem most acute. We described earlier the anthropological work done in Puerto Rico in the 1950s (Landy 1959; Mintz 1956; Steward 1956) that pointed out

Table 3.1

Home/School Cultural and Value Conflicts

Home	School
Nurtures dependency	Values independence
Children loved and enjoyed	Teacher seen as distant or cold
Nurtures cooperation	Values competition
Authoritarian style	Democratic style
Low-income children usually do not have preschool experiences	Expects preschool experiences
Low-income families are forced to value daily survival more than the educational needs of their children	Expects parents to value education above other values
Girls do not need to be educated as much as boys	Both sexes should be educated equally
Admonishes immodesty in girls	Physical education requires changing in front of others
Promotes ignorance of sexual matters	Advocates sex education
Achievement is for family satisfaction	Achievement is for self-satisfaction
Nonsegregated age groups	Segregated age groups
Segregated sex groups	Nonsegregated sex groups
Machismo for boys	Less sexually typed male ideal
Marianismo for girls	Less sexually typed female ideal
Some low-income families do not see the connection between school-related behaviors, such as daily school attendance, and doing well in school	School assumes that families know the types of child and family behaviors that lead to good school performance

the prevalence of fostering from very early on dependency, warmth, and protection of females in the child-rearing patterns of most subcultures in Puerto Rico. This style of child rearing is the opposite of the U.S. middle-class pattern, which tends to nurture autonomy by encouraging independent, exploratory behaviors for both sexes (Maccoby and Jacklin 1974). Majority teachers who have been raised this way have a hard time understanding and valuing children whose dependency has not been discouraged. This conflict is felt more strongly by girls, who are caught between the divergent developmental demands of the two cultures. Elam (1960) describes this situation well when she states,

> The little girl who has been compliant is now expected to be active and responsive, to take initiative, to face new people and situations on her own. In the schoolroom she is expected to talk and play with boys and to socialize more freely with her peers. There are rewards in our culture for this, but when she goes home she is forbidden to go out on the street to play. At home there is no reward for enterprising deeds, but rather the awaited and expected punishment [p. 334].

As Mintz (1966) states, in Puerto Rico small children are universally loved and enjoyed. Puerto Ricans demonstrate their love redundantly through verbal and nonverbal means. In general, mothers smile openly, keep close physical proximity and eye-to-eye contact, and hug and touch their children frequently. This pattern of social interaction does not repeat itself in school. The U.S. teacher will seem cold and distant, since she keeps a different cultural "space" and is not accustomed to physical contact with strangers.

Schools in the United States foster competition among students, both by requiring classroom work to be performed individually (Prewitt Díaz 1979) and by using competition as an incentive. Puerto Rican culture, on the other hand, values cooperation (Steward 1956), and families promote help-giving and help-seeking behavior among children. Thus, the Puerto Rican girl might become unsatisfied in school when she finds that the way to complete her school work successfully is not the way to which she is accustomed and enjoys. The high importance of family and the restricted definition given to the woman's role in Puerto Rican culture needs to be clarified in order to understand its implication for schooling. Girls will be kept home from school when more important family needs emerge. Sex and physical education may be opposed by parents and uncomfortably endured by daughters. The value of educating females at all is still questioned in some families (Tumin and Feldman 1961).

CONFLICTS WITH TEACHERS
IN THE UNITED STATES

As previously stated, schools are a major socializing agent with great impact on students' achievement, behavior, and sex-role development. They are the exponent of the needs and values of a particular society and are responsible for the transference of those norms to younger generations (Guttentag and Bray 1977). Through teachers, textbooks, curriculums, and overall classroom practices, schools reinforce the ideology of male supremacy and further communicate a common sociocultural model to which students are expected to conform.

Investigators from various countries have documented the important role that teachers play in the socialization of sex roles (Brophy and Good 1970; Dempsey 1973; Meyer and Thompson 1956; Picó 1983; Serbin 1973). A review of the literature done by Guttentag and Bray (1977) indicates clear differences between behaviors exhibited by teachers in the United States toward boys and toward girls. They report that, although teachers do not seem aware of this differential treatment, an analysis of their interactions and classroom behaviors shows that they give more attention to boys than to girls, both in terms of approval and disapproval. The only exception to this pattern is the dependent girl, who tends to receive more teacher approval than the dependent male.

Differences in teacher-student interaction can decrease initiative and autonomy in girls, as well as hinder the development of confidence in their own abilities. According to Guttentag and Bray (1977), girls are called on less often than boys, are ignored more frequently, and receive more global and less specific feedback. Emphasis on friendly, agreeable behavior and lack of discipline problems, rather than good work habits and performance, seem to be the characteristics that teachers actively or passively support in girls. Guttentag and Bray also point out that this makes it harder for girls to make a realistic and accurate assessment of their performance or to develop confidence in their own abilities.

A similar trend is revealed in a study done with elementary school teachers in Puerto Rico (Picó 1983). It was found that Puerto Rican teachers interact differently with boys and girls. Boys in the sample received more attention than girls in terms of both praise and censorship. In addition, when boys were reprimanded, teachers tended to use a louder tone and nonverbal forms of discipline, while this style was seldom used with girls.

In this same study teachers were asked if they made any comments on the girls' clothing or manners. Sixty-seven percent of the teachers responded affirmatively, and when their comments were evaluated it was found that more than half of the comments were sexist or based on stereotypes that reinforced traditional feminine behaviors. Included are some of the comments more frequently used by the Puerto Rican teachers (authors' translation):

> Girls can't raise their voices. They should talk in a softer tone.
> Girls don't fight with boys.
> Girls don't run in the classroom.
> Girls must be soft, delicate, and patient.
> Girls should cover their bodies more than boys do.
> Sit down like ladies. You are a lady.
> Girls must be decent so they are respected.
> Girls must behave with delicateness so they won't lose their femininity. [p. 85]

Not only do teachers in the Puerto Rican sample show differential interaction patterns by sex, but their expectations of appropriate behaviors for girls and boys vary along traditional sex-role lines as well. Teachers expect that girls will be involved in passive activities twice as much as boys. More than 37 percent believe that girls should not play with cars, airplanes, or soldiers, and that boys should not play with dolls. Ultimately, "these attitudes contribute to the traditional sex-role

socialization of boys and girls through games and toys"
(p. 83).

As we have seen throughout this section, teachers,
both in Puerto Rico and in the United States, have a great
impact in the sex-role socialization of girls from their own
cultural group. But what about the Puerto Rican girl in
the United States who is not only a female but a member
of an ethnic minority group? Are the behaviors and expectations of teachers in the United States affected by the
Puerto Rican girl's ethnic membership? Is she treated
differently, not only for being female but also for being
Puerto Rican? Although no studies were found investigating
teacher interactions with Puerto Rican students in the
United States, two studies done with Mexican-American
students could help answer some of these questions. It
seems plausible to believe that comparable results would
have been obtained with Puerto Rican students.

An investigation done by the U.S. Commission on
Civil Rights (1973) offers important information on how
Anglo teachers treat Mexican-American and Anglo students
in the same classroom. The results of this study indicate
that Mexican-American students receive less praise, encouragement, attention, and approval than Anglo students.
Teachers spent significantly less time addressing questions
or speaking noncritically to their Mexican-American students and were less apt to accept or use the ideas they
expressed.

Wahab (1973) also demonstrated that many teachers
treat Mexican-American students in a different manner
than they treat Anglo students. It was found that they
interact most with Anglo-American boys, then Anglo-American girls, next Mexican-American boys and, lastly, with
Mexican-American girls.

From this information it is clear that Mexican-
American students are not receiving the same quality of
education and are not involved in the teaching process to
the same extent as Anglo students. Lower teacher expectations of Mexican-American students are an important
factor influencing the quality of their interactions. Evidence suggests that some teachers in the United States believe that Mexican-American students are "not a normal
bunch of kids," and probably not as capable of learning
as other children (U.S. Commission on Civil Rights 1973, 23).

We have presented data indicating the impact that
teachers have in perpetuating stereotyped roles of girls,

as well as their differential treatment of Hispanic and Anglo students. It is to this somber picture that the Puerto Rican girl is introduced when she enters school in the United States. Not only will she receive less praise, encouragement, and attention because she is a female, she will suffer doubly because she is not Anglo. As Silvia Viera (1980) expressed it, "Not only will future generations of white, Anglo women internalize their own inferiority, but they will not allow the Hispanic, working-class females to destroy the myth and discard the image of her dual inferiority: first, for being 'non-white,' and second, for being female" (p. 281).

THE ROLE OF TEXTBOOKS

Textbooks are another major way in which sex-stereotyped roles for girls are reinforced in the schools. In a book by Isabel Picó (1983), an analysis is made of basic textbooks used to teach reading and history in Puerto Rico (and in many bilingual programs in the United States). Not only were female characters significantly underrepresented in the textbooks, but when presented at all, they are portrayed in traditional roles and occupations (housewives) and always in a position inferior to the male characters. Girls were presented as mainly involved in passive activities like playing with dolls, observing the boys at play, or just waiting for them. In socially valued characteristics like courage, creativity, perseverance, and adventurousness, males were presented as surpassing females, while in weakness, passivity, dependence, and fear, girls and women greatly outnumbered males.

In the United States the severe sex and social bias and underrepresentation of minorities and women in school textbooks has been extensively documented (Women on Words and Images 1972; Weitzman and Rizzo 1974; Britton 1975). Not only do textbooks quantitatively discriminate against women by underrepresenting females, they do it qualitatively as well by stereotyping human qualities and activities along lines of sex and race (Council on Interracial Books for Children 1980).

A 1972 study of elementary school reading texts by Women on Words and Images (1972) indicated that males appear in the books in overwhelmingly larger numbers than females. In a significant number of the child-centered stories, boys are portrayed as possessing active mastery traits, while girls are presented as passive, dependent, incompetent, and are frequently humiliated or victimized.

In 1974 Weitzman and Rizzo examined the presentation of minority and majority females and males in elementary school text illustrations. They found that white males were overrepresented, while both minority and majority females were underrepresented in the illustrations. They also observed that as textbooks increased in terms of grade level, the portrayal of minority and female characters was significantly reduced. Thus, adolescent females are deprived in their textbooks of female role models with whom to identify to a greater extent than are young girls.

In a 1975 study done by Gwyneth Britton examining reading textbooks, little difference was found between 1975 editions and those published earlier. Both minority and majority females were still underrepresented, while males were not. Men had a greater variety of career roles than women, with 134 different roles for men but only 31 for women. There continued to be a predominance of sexual and cultural stereotyping, with females often appearing as goddesses or princesses and 71 percent of minority women represented in domestic roles. Similar stereotyping occurred with minority males, who were portrayed primarily in roles such as tribal chiefs.

Puerto Rican girls are not only exposed to stereotyped images of themselves in school textbooks, but also in books of fiction and fantasy. In 1972 and later updated in 1983, the Council on Interracial Books for Children conducted an analysis of children's books about Puerto Ricans and Puerto Rican themes that are available in the United States (Nieto 1983). They report that the books available are plagued with sexism, and that in the majority of cases Puerto Rican women are portrayed in subordinate and demeaning roles. An article entitled "Feminists Look at the 100 Books," which was published in the 1972 issue of Interracial Books for Children, further indicates that in those books Puerto Rican girls were seldom main characters. They were depicted performing dull activities and were almost totally devoid of personality (Prida et al. 1972). The article goes on to say, "Not only is the female role in the books more constricted than a comparable Anglo American girl's would be, but it is even more limited than the Puerto Rican female role is in actual fact. A Puerto Rican girl faced only with the prospects presented in these books might reasonably choose not to grow up at all" (p. 7).

As can be seen from this brief review, textbooks and even fiction books present a limited and stereotyped image of women, which in many cases is far from reality. In this way, the girl's normal development as an individual is affected, her future contributions to society are hindered, and inequality between men and women is perpetuated. By socializing children to integrate sexually and racially stereotyped behavioral patterns and roles, schools impede individual growth and possible preparation to confront life's problems. These ascribed roles are constrictive to females, and even more so to Puerto Rican girls in the United States. Are Puerto Rican girls able to survive these negative influences? The next section discusses some of the routes these girls take.

EFFECTIVE AND INEFFECTIVE ADAPTATIONS TO SCHOOL

As stated earlier, for many Puerto Rican girls, their first direct interaction with the culture of the United States is in the public schools. They come in with high aspirations, but, unfortunately, the reality they encounter is plagued with a set of conditions that hinder participation and academic achievement. Often, the schools they attend are overcrowded, poorly equipped, and have lower per-pupil budgets than other schools. Many do not have even one Spanish-speaking counselor to guide these girls through curricular choices consistent with the high aspirations they report when entering school (National Commission on Secondary Schooling for Hispanics 1984). Teachers and other adults expect very little of them, the limited amount of feedback they receive is discouraging, and their needs as bilingual, bicultural females are not acknowledged or addressed. It is not surprising, then, to observe the high dropout rates of Puerto Rican girls.

Statistics describing the enrollment of Puerto Rican females in the U.S. public school system indicate alarmingly low levels of educational attainment, particularly in the 14 to 17 and the 18 to 24 age groups (National Puerto Rican Forum 1980). Although the percentage of Puerto Rican children who are enrolled in elementary schools is comparable to the national average (U.S. Commission on

Civil Rights 1976), the difference grows more acute as they reach high school. By this time, they are more likely to be two or more years below grade level than their peers (National Puerto Rican Coalition 1985), and to have been tracked into weak academic programs that limit the possibilities of their pursuing a college education. According to the 1980 U.S. Census, the percentage of White and Black female high school graduates is 69 and 52 percent respectively, while for Puerto Rican females in the United States it is only 39 percent. The comparable rates for Puerto Rican males is 41 percent.

In trying to identify the variables that contribute to the high dropout rate among adolescent Puerto Rican females in the United States, several investigators have pointed to the quality of the educational experience as a crucial factor affecting their decision to remain in school or to drop out (Santiago Nazario 1981; Gutiérrez and Montalvo 1982). By tenth grade, which appears to be the "peak year for dropping out" (Gutiérrez and Montalvo 1982, 3), feelings of alienation, rejection, and an overall perception of school as a hostile environment predominate (Santiago Nazario 1981). The schools have not been able to identify the early signs of distress and are ill-prepared to meet the complex and multiple needs of the Puerto Rican adolescent.

A three-year longitudinal study of Puerto Rican youth done by Gutiérrez and Montalvo (1982) found that for Puerto Rican tenth-grade girls in the United States, dropping out was strongly correlated with pregnancy but not with delinquency. They describe the potential Puerto Rican girl dropout in the following way:

> While academically she is likely to have repeated a grade, she tends to be easily overlooked as a problematic student. She is mostly bored, unchallenged, and does not like school, where she brings aspects of the unmotivating environment usually prevailing in her family. But none of this makes her visible. Only when she becomes actively truant or already pregnant is she identified in the school as requiring assistance, at which point it might be too late [p. 4].

Not only do school factors determine the Puerto Rican girl's decision to stay out of school, the family's impact is a major determiner as well and must be examined when searching for answers to the dropout problem.

At a time in which the adolescent Puerto Rican girl is starting to experience the need to achieve independence and gain a sense of self, she is confronted at home with increased parental restrictiveness and conflict. This is especially true in families characterized by "diffuse generational and interpersonal boundaries and little tolerance for self-differentiation." Parents in these families exhibit difficulty in allowing the girls "to develop autonomous behavior and to differentiate from the family system" (Canino 1982, 29). These conditions result in conflicts around traditional sex-role values, disagreements around male-female relationships, and a strong curtailment of outside activities (Lacot 1978) that limits honest encounters with the opposite sex.

According to Preble (1968), the Puerto Rican girl at the courtship age has three choices: "She can stay 'upstairs' (in the house), she can attempt to deceive the parents regarding her activities outside, or she can marry at a young age" (p. 64).

Early pregnancy, often one of the most important contributing factors to an adolescent Puerto Rican female dropping out of school, can be a result of the limited options available to her. However, this is not the only explanation for early pregnancies. Ortiz (1982), in a study of pregnant Puerto Rican teenagers, found that they knew little about contraception before their pregnancies. Many reported great difficulties in communicating with their parents about sexual matters and showed poor understanding of normal body functioning, particularly the reproductive system. They end up pregnant at an age at which they will have to assume new roles and responsibilities, often before they are developmentally capable. Not only is the educational future of these pregnant girls in serious jeopardy, but the adolescent period of social exploration and development of autonomy is denied them.

While "an unsupportive [home] atmosphere for school achievement, infrequent discussion of school work, and older siblings [or friends] who have dropped out from school" have been found to be characteristic features common to the dropout girl's family (Gutiérrez and Montalvo 1982, 4), it has been demonstrated that school factors also impinge on the Puerto Rican girl's decision to stay in or drop out of school. Nor can we ignore a whole range of environmental and social factors--poverty, unemployment, discrimination, inadequate housing and health facilities, deteriorated neighborhoods--that influence family life and parental practices (Linares 1980), and ultimately contribute to the high drop-out rate among Puerto Rican adolescent girls in the United States. Since there are multiple and extensive sources of stress impacting upon the Puerto Rican girl (Linares 1980), the development of new interventions that address several levels in unison are needed if her opportunities for educational participation and achievement are to be enhanced.

Throughout this section emphasis has been placed on describing the sad state of Puerto Rican girls in U.S. schools, with the hope of creating an awareness of the seriousness of this problem. However, it has not been our intent to overlook the accomplishments of individual Puerto Rican girls who have been able to overcome all obstacles and move forward in acquiring an education and greater occupational mobility.

SUMMARY AND RECOMMENDATIONS

The present status of Puerto Rican girls attending schools in the United States is alarming. They do not receive adequate support and encouragement for their educational interests from either their homes or the schools. Value conflicts between both environments abound, leaving these girls caught in the middle. While some of them are able to surmount these conflicts, the majority have a hard time making it through high school, consequently missing the expanding work opportunities now available to more-educated women. What can be done to ameliorate this situation? We propose the following:

1. Teachers in the United States need to become aware, through in-service training and workshops, of the school-home conflicts and negative treatment of these girls in schools

2. Efforts to remediate the situation must start in the early school years. Learning and emotional difficulties should be diagnosed and treated early and appropriately.

3. Guidance counselors need to take a more active role in orienting these girls to the world of work early in their school careers. Models of Hispanic women who have been successful in different occupations should be presented, and girls should be encouraged to enter careers in the professions and high technology. The immense family responsibilities awaiting these girls should be emphasized.

4. Book and curriculum publishers must become aware of the absence or negative treatment given to these girls in most textbooks. Puerto Rican female role models need to be included in regular school textbooks.

5. Research on the educational achievements of Puerto Rican girls should be funded and carried on. Ineffective and effective adaptation patterns in low- and middle-class samples should be studied. New studies that are well researched and designed are badly needed in this area, as most studies are outdated, sample sizes are too small, and work is of a more anthropological nature.

REFERENCES

Acosta-Belén, E., ed. 1979. The Puerto Rican Woman. New York: Praeger.

Andrade, S. J. 1982. "Family roles of Hispanic women: Stereotypes, empirical findings, and implications for research." In R. E. Zambrana, ed., Work, Family and Health: Latina Women in Transition, pp. 95-107. New York: Hispanic Research Center.

Britton, G. E. 1975. "Sex stereotyping and career roles." Journal of Reading 17:148.

Brophy, J., and T. Good. 1970. "Teacher communication of differential expectations for children's classroom performance: Some behavioral data." Journal of Educational Psychology 61:365-74.

Canino, G. 1982. "Transactional family patterns: A preliminary exploration of Puerto Rican female adolescents." In R. E. Zambrana, ed., Work, Family, and Health: Latina Women in Transition, pp. 27-36. New York: Hispanic Research Center.

Canino, I., and G. Canino. 1980. "Impact of Stress on the Puerto Rican Family: Treatment considerations." American Journal of Psychiatry 50:535-41.

Christensen, E. W. 1975a. "Counseling Puerto Ricans: Some cultural considerations." Personal and Guidance Journal 5:412-16.

_____. 1975b. "The Puerto Rican woman: The challenge of a changing society." Character Potential 7, 2:86-89.

_____. 1977. "When counseling Puerto Ricans." American Personnel and Guidance Association 53:349-57.

Comas-Díaz, L. 1982. "Mental health needs of Puerto Rican women in the United States." In R. E. Zambrana, ed., Work, Family, and Health: Latina Women in Transition, pp. 1-11. New York: Hispanic Research Center.

Council on Interracial Books for Children. 1980. Guidelines for Selecting Bias-Free Textbooks and Storybooks. New York: Author.

Dempsey, A. 1973. "Sexual stereotyping of elementary school boys and girls by pre-service elementary school teachers." The Teacher Educator 8, 2:34-36.

Elam, S. 1960. "Acculturation and learning problems of Puerto Rican children." Teachers College Record 61: 258-64.

Erikson, E. H. 1959. "Ideology and the life cycle." Psychological Issues 1:1-173.

Gutiérrez, J. J., and B. Montalvo. 1982. "Puerto Rican youth: Dropping out and delinquency." Paper presented at the Annual Convention of the American Psychological Association, Washington, D.C. (ERIC Document Reproduction Service, No. ED 221 638).

Guttentag, M., and H. Bray. 1977. "Teachers as mediators of sex-role standards." In A. G. Sargent, ed., Beyond Sex Roles, pp. 395-411. New York: West Publishing.

King, L. M. 1974. "Puertorriqueñas in the United States: The impact of double discrimination." Civil Rights Digest 6:20–27.

Lacot, M. S. 1978. "Freedom in making personal decisions as perceived by Puerto Rican ninth-grade girls." In F. Parker and B. J. Parker, eds., Education in Puerto Rico and of Puerto Ricans in the United States: Abstracts of American Doctoral Dissertations, pp. 241–43. San Juan: Inter-American University Press.

Landy, D. 1959. Tropical Childhood. Chapel Hill: University of North Carolina Press.

Linares, I. M. 1980. "The Hispanic child: A multidimensional approach to mental health." Hispanic Research Center: Research Bulletin 3, 1:9–10.

Maccoby, E., and C. Jacklin. 1974. The Psychology of Sex Differences. Stanford, Calif.: Stanford University Press.

Meyer, W., and G. Thompson. 1956. "Sex differences in the distribution of teacher approval and disapproval among sixth grade children." Journal of Education Psychology 47:385–96.

Mintz, S. 1956. "Cañaveral: The subculture of a rural sugar plantation proletariat." In J. Steward, ed., The People of Puerto Rico, pp. 314–418. Urbana: University of Illinois Press.

_____. 1966. "Puerto Rico: An essay in the definition of a national culture." In Status of Puerto Rico: Selected Background Studies, pp. 339–435. United States-Puerto Rico Commission of the Status of Puerto Rico.

Minuchin, S., B. Montalvo, G. Guerney, B. Rosman, and F. Schumer. 1967. Families of the Slums. New York: Basic Books.

National Commission of Secondary Schooling for Hispanics. 1984. "Make Something Happen" Hispanics and Urban High School Reform, vol. 1. Washington, D.C.: The Hispanic Policy Development Project.

National Puerto Rican Coalition. 1985. Puerto Ricans in the Mid '80s: An American Challenge. Alexandria, Va.: ERIC Document Reproduction Service, No. ED 253 605.

National Puerto Rican Forum. 1980. The Next Step Toward Equality: A Comprehensive Study of Puerto Ricans in the United States Mainland. New York: ERIC Document Reproduction Service, No. ED 197 026.

Nieto, S. 1963. "Children's literature on Puerto Rican themes--Part 1: The messages of fiction." Interracial Books for Children Bulletin 14, 1-2:6-9.

Ortiz, C. G. 1982. "Teenage pregnancy: Factors affecting the decision to carry or terminate pregnancy among Puerto Rican teenagers." Unpublished doctoral dissertation, University of Massachusetts, Amherst.

Picó, I. 1983. Machismo y educación en Puerto Rico, 2nd ed. Rio Piedras: Universidad de Puerto Rico.

Preble, E. 1968. "The Puerto Rican-American teenager in New York City." In E. B. Brody, ed., Minority Groups Adolescents in the United States, pp. 48-71. Baltimore: Williams and Wilkins.

Prewitt Díaz, J. 1979. The Conflicts in In-School Cultural Behaviors of the Puerto Rican Migrant Children on the Mainland. (ERIC Document Reproduction Service, No. ED 197 035.)

Prida, D., S. Ribner, E. Davila, I. Garcia, C. Puigdollers, and A. Rivera. 1972. "Feminists look at the 100 Books." Interracial Books for Children 4, 1-2:7-10.

Pugh, C., and E. Vázquez-Nuttall. 1983. "Are all women alike? Reports of White, Hispanic and Black women." Paper presented at the Meeting of the American Personnel and Guidance Association, Washington, D.C.

Rosario, L. 1982. "The self-perception of Puerto Rican women toward their societal role." In R. E. Zambrana, ed., Work, Family, and Health: Latina Women in Transition, pp. 95-107. New York: Hispanic Research Center.

Santiago, Nazario, N. I. 1981. "Social psychological correlates of expected school drop out among mainland Puerto Rican females." Unpublished doctoral dissertation, University of Massachusetts, Amherst.

Serbin, L. A. 1973. "A comparison of teachers response to the pre-academic problem behaviors of boys and girls." Child Development 44, 4:796-804.

Spence, J. T., and R. L. Helmreich. 1978. Masculinity and Femininity: Their Psychological Dimensions, Correlates, and Antecedents. Austin: University of Texas Press.

Steward, J., ed. 1956. The People of Puerto Rico. Urbana: University of Illinois Press.

Stycos, J. M. 1955. Family and Fertility in Puerto Rico: A Study of the Lower Income Group. New York: Columbia University Press.

Torres-Matrullo, C. 1976. "Acculturation, and psychopathology among Puerto Rican women in mainland United States." American Journal of Orthopsychiatry 46:710-19.

Tumin, A., and A. Feldman. 1961. Social Class and Social Change in Puerto Rico. Princeton, N.J.: Princeton University Press.

U.S. Commission of Civil Rights. 1973. Teachers and Students: Differences in Teacher Interaction with Mexican-American and Anglo Students. (Report V: Mexican-American Education Study.) Washington, D.C.: U.S. Government Printing Office (USGPO).

_____. 1976. Puerto Ricans in the Continental United States: An Uncertain Future. Washington, D.C.: USGPO.

U.S. Department of Commerce and Bureau of the Census. 1983. 1980 Census of Population. General Social and Economic Characteristics, U.S. Summary, vol. 1. Washington, D.C.: USGPO.

Vázquez-Nuttall, E. 1976. "Coping patterns of Puerto Rican mothers heading single family households." Inter-American Journal of Psychology 12:5–13.

_____. 1979. "The support systems and coping patterns of the female Puerto Rican single parent." Journal of Non-White Concerns 7, 3:128–37.

Viera, S. 1980. "The need for an anthropological and cognitive approach to the education of Hispanic women." Proceedings of the Conference on the Education and Occupational Needs of Hispanic Women, pp. 277–89. Washington, D.C.: U.S. Department of Education and National Institute of Education.

Wahab, A. Z. 1973. "The Mexican-American child and the public school." Dissertation Abstracts International 34, 01A: 74–75.

Weitzman, L., and D. Rizzo. 1974. Biased Textbooks. Washington, D.C.: Resource Center of Sex Role in Education, National Foundation for the Improvement of Education.

Women on Words and Images. 1972. Dick and Jane as Victims: Sex Stereotypes in Children's Readers. Princeton, N.J.: Author.

4

Adolescent Pregnancy and Childbearing: Psychosocial Consequences during the Postpartum Period

Cynthia T. García Coll, Ph.D.
Maribel Escobar, B.A.
Pedro Cebollero, M.S.
Marta Valcárcel, M.D.

Pregnancy and new parenthood are considered life transitions requiring the expectant and new parent to make major psychosocial adjustments. Many investigators have viewed pregnancy as a biologically determined period of psychological stress (e.g., Benedek 1959). Traditionally, pregnancy is considered, like puberty or menopause, as a period of crisis involving not only somatic changes, but also profound psychological alterations (Bibring 1959; Bibring, Dwyer, Huntington, et al. 1961a, 1961b). However, although profound psychological changes are expected during the course of pregnancy and following the birth of a new baby, these changes are more recently conceived of as the product of normal adaptation processes, with individual variations determined by multiple internal and external factors (Osofsky and Osofsky 1983).

In this chapter we will explore the psychosocial consequences of adolescent childbearing among primiparous Puerto Rican women from an urban, low socioeconomic background in San Juan, Puerto Rico. We will start with an examination of the literature on the psychological effects of pregnancy and childbearing in general. Subsequently, we will review the literature on adolescent pregnancy and childbearing, emphasizing our current knowledge of these phenomena among Puerto Rican women. Finally, we will present the findings of a study comparing young and older adolescents and adult Puerto Rican women in psychosocial variables during pregnancy and the immediate postpartum period. It is our purpose to explore the complexity of teenage pregnancy and childbirth, including the normative aspects of a major life stage (adolescence) superimposed on a major life transition (pregnancy and delivery) and further influenced by a particular sociocultural context (traditional Puerto Rican culture).

HOW MUCH OF A CRISIS IS PREGNANCY AND CHILDBIRTH?

The crisis and critical nature of a first pregnancy and childbirth in a female's life cycle have been emphasized in the extant literature. Chertok (1969) speaks of pregnancy as a progressively developing crisis that has labor and delivery as its peak, both because of the final results of the confinement (separation of the mother and child) and because of its isolation in time as an event. Caplan (1957) also describes pregnancy as a crisis for the woman and suggests that the woman's emotional state varies at various stages during pregnancy, depending on her adjustment to the physiological and psychological changes. The woman's emotional status during the course of pregnancy also reflects her psychological development into the role of mother.

Although most early writings and even recent studies (e.g., Levy and McGee 1975) have viewed pregnancy as a crisis and an abnormal state of health that only returns to normal sometime after delivery, wide individual differences have been noted in reaction to pregnancy and delivery. For example, Chapple and Furneaux (1964) tested women twice during pregnancy, once on an introversion-extroversion scale, and again on a neuroticism scale. They found that as pregnancy progressed introverted women tend to become more neurotic, while the extroverted women become less neurotic. Pregnancy, they concluded, acts as a nonspecific stress and the response of women varies according to their personalities. Caplan (1957) also noted that in pregnancy, as in all human crises, the outcome depends not only on the long-standing personality patterns of the participants, but also on their current life situations. Thus, the outcome may be influenced by helping figures in the family and environment and services in the community, and not solely by intrinsic factors.

Following a thorough review of the studies of normative psychological adjustment as well as emotional disturbance during pregnancy, Osofsky and Osofsky (1980)
conclude that a wide variation of reactions to pregnancy
can occur. These reactions may differ for an individual
woman or a couple, but other factors, including age of
the parents, available support systems, previous psychological adjustment, and parenting experience contribute
significantly to the process. Although they conclude that
women experience profound psychological changes during
the course of pregnancy and following the birth of their
new babies, they suggest that emotional disturbances seem
to be related to maturational and psychological readiness
for the process, emotional stability and instability at the
time of pregnancy, early life experiences, the overall
social situation, and, probably, the very significant hor-
monal shifts that occur. Thus, the crisis or upheaval
nature of a first pregnancy and delivery is experienced
by some individuals but not others and is influenced by
both internal and external factors.

During the immediate postpartum period, emotional
reactions have been described ranging from "very happy
and well adjusted, to those for whom the experience pro-
duces depression and dependency" (Ball 1987, 19). Most
studies have found an incidence of 3 to 10 percent of postpartum depression (Tod 1964; Pitt 1968; Dewi-Rees and
Lutkin 1971; Dalton 1971; Cox 1978). These studies related
differences in postnatal emotional well-being to intrinsic
factors such as personality and previous childhood experiences (e.g., early separation from parents), as well as
additional stresses arising from marital tension and other
life crises that have a detrimental effect upon the adjustment process. In a recent study, Ball (1987) found a
wide range of reported feelings immediately after the baby
was born: 55 percent were gloriously happy or tired but
happy; 29 percent said they felt relieved; 7 percent said
they felt too tired to care for the infant; and 2 percent
felt disappointed (primarily because of the sex of the infant). More important, emotional well-being six weeks
after birth was related to postnatal feelings of well-being
as well as specific life stress events that had occurred
within the one year prior to the baby's birth (e.g., marital conflict or a transition at home). Mothers who reported being too tired to care for the infant, or disappointed during the postpartum period, or who had moved

or experienced marital tension during the previous year had lower emotional well-being scores six weeks after delivery. Thus, stress during pregnancy as well as negative feelings toward the infant during the immediate postpartum period might have predictive value concerning later emotional well-being.

The postnatal period does not mark only the end of the pregnancy but, more important, the beginning (or continuation) of the motherhood role. Maternal self-esteem has been implicated as a central factor related to the quality of a woman's adaptation to motherhood (Tronick and Shea, in press). As it is the case for general emotional well-being, many diverse factors affect a woman's adaptation to motherhood. Parity, birth experience, and infant medical status are all closely related to maternal self-esteem. Primiparous mothers express less confidence in their mothering abilities than do multiparous mothers (Seashore, Leifer, Barnett, and Leiderman 1973; Westbrook 1978). Following a Cesarean section delivery, mothers generally experience significantly more negative feelings toward pregnancy and motherhood than do mothers who deliver vaginally (Pederson, Zaslow, Cain, and Anderson 1980; Grossman 1980; Field and Widmayer 1980). Dramatic and intense feelings of inadequacy and/or failure are reported when an infant is born with a congenital anomaly, a chronic disease, or prematurely (Greenberg 1979; Klaus and Kennell 1976). The occurrence of even minor health complications of infants negatively affect maternal self-esteem during the initial adaptation period after delivery (Tronick and Shea, in press). Thus, variables that are directly related to the birth process and outcome influence maternal self-esteem.

Research has also demonstrated the importance of family support and acceptance in predicting positive maternal attitudes as well as high ratings of maternal involvement immediately after delivery for mothers of all ages (Cohen 1966; Barnard and Gortner 1977; Tronick and Shea, in press). Moreover, in the Tronick and Shea study, family support alone accounted for 52 percent of the variance of maternal self-esteem one month after discharge from the hospital. Thus, the family support network available to the mother during the early postpartum period affects how confident a mother feels about her ability to care for her infant.

In summary, psychological well-being during pregnancy and after delivery is determined by a variety of
factors including maternal and infant characteristics as
well as the family context. Although less extensively explored, the role of cultural and socioeconomic factors has
also been substantiated. The impact of social definitions
of pregnancy and the importance of cultural pressures for
parenthood are seen as major determinants in the psychological consequences of pregnancy and motherhood (Brody
1978; Goshen-Gottstein 1966; Hoffman and Hoffman 1973;
Pohlman 1969; Hubert 1974; Veevers 1973). Oakley (1974,
190) states, "In Western cultures today, motherhood is the
chief occupation for which females are reared." Although
women's roles are undergoing dramatic changes in the
twentieth century, this quote might reflect a prevalent and
accurate cultural perception of women in the Western
world: Adulthood for women is determined largely by
motherhood. In addition, within cultures, socioeconomic
factors also permeate attitudes toward pregnancy and
childbirth (Nelson 1983; Bello 1979). Thus, both cultural
and socioeconomic backgrounds should be considered as
influences on the psychological consequences of pregnancy
and childbirth.

ARE ADOLESCENT MOTHERS AT A HIGHER RISK?

Adulthood for women is determined largely by motherhood. If first pregnancies and deliveries are potential
sources of stress and of psychological disequilibrium, are
adolescent mothers at a higher risk for psychopathological
symptoms during the postpartum period?

Most writers assume that adolescent mothers are at
higher risk due to both internal and environmental factors. Internally, adolescent mothers are seen as coping
with two major sources of stress: the developmental tasks
of the adolescent period and the transition to motherhood
(Reedy 1983). As an adolescent, she is moving from
childhood to adulthood; as a pregnant woman, she is moving from individual to parent.

Many theorists have described various developmental
"tasks" of adolescence (Havighurst 1972; Erikson 1963;
Helms 1981; Kreipe 1983). In general adolescence as a
developmental stage is seen as a major transitional phase
that involves physical, cognitive, emotional, and social

changes of major consequences for adulthood. The major developmental task of adolescence, according to Erikson, is establishing an identity (Erikson 1968). This is the process by which the adolescent establishes a relatively stable self-concept and defines his or her uniqueness from others in the environment. Individual, social, and vocational goals are also broadly defined in this stage. Peer acceptance is crucial; however, although increasing detachment from adults and adult values is typical, teenagers also seek "models" in their environment. The establishment of a consistent self-image or a stable role identity prepares the female for the next stage--that of the young adult, where the establishment of intimate relationships becomes the major developmental task.

Other theorists have acknowledged other important processes that are dealt with during the adolescent period. One refers to the acceptance of physical maturation (e.g., pubescence) and consolidation of a body image (Kreipe 1983; Handwerker and Hodgman 1983). Indeed, the major task of early adolescence (13 to 15 years of age) is considered to be the achievement of awareness and comfort with body image.

An adolescent's body image, or the image of her body she forms in her mind, or the way in which her body appears to herself (Kolb 1975) must change as well. Frequently, the internalization of these outward changes lags far behind the changes themselves. In adolescents, this process is dependent on a number of factors: the adolescent's ideal body image, the input they receive from bodily sensations, the awareness of how parents and peers see them, and their own interpretation of these evaluations (Handwerker and Hodgman 1983).

Another major task during adolescence is the attainment of the formal operational stage of thinking that is characteristic of adult development as described by Piaget (see Ginsburg and Opper 1979). Formal operational thinking is characterized by the ability to make abstractions, to see the long-range consequences of behavior, to plan for the future, and to be able to "think about thinking." Although Piaget's theory marks the beginning of formal operations at age 11 or 12, research has shown that a significant percentage of the adult population do not display formal operational thinking (Dasen and Heron 1981). Other cognitive phenomena associated with normal adolescent development are the reemergence of egocentrism (self-centeredness), the notion that "all eyes are on them" (perception of an imaginary audience), and the application of magical thinking to themselves (personal fable) where the adolescent idealizes and thinks of herself as a special person, feeling invulnerable and immortal (Elkind 1970). Emergence from dependence upon the parents and family to self-sufficient independence is another important task of normal adolescence development (Kreipe 1983; Reedy 1983). This process is described as an emotional turmoil, whereby fluctuations between periods of dependence and independence are the norm. It encompasses changes in intellectual, sexual, and functional aspects of development, including educational and vocational choices.

A final but extremely important aspect of adolescent development is the establishment of satisfactory relationships with peers of both sexes (Reedy 1983). During early adolescence the establishment of relationships with same sex peers is crucial, since they become the major source of support, advice, and pressure for the adolescent. Late adolescence is characterized by the decreased importance of the same sex peer group and the emergence of important individual relationships, especially with one person of the opposite sex.

This brief overview of the developmental tasks of normal adolescence highlights the profound internal changes that are hallmarks of this period. How do pregnancy, delivery, and parenting affect these processes? Several possibilities can be derived from the extant literature:

1. The superimposition of pregnancy, delivery, and parenting over these processes can deter the individual from attaining these major developmental goals.
2. The adolescent's attitudes and behaviors around her sexuality, pregnancy, and childbearing will be determined by where she is in terms of these developmental processes.
3. At the least, teenage childbearing will add to the stress experienced by the adolescent that stems from the normal developmental processes she is undergoing.

Not only are these internal factors placing the adolescent at a higher risk than an adult mother, but environmental circumstances also might be important contributors. In the United States, adolescent childbearing frequently is associated with conception out of wedlock, and lower educational and financial resources. A large percentage of adolescent mothers are single, school dropouts from lower socioeconomic backgrounds (Baldwin and Cain 1980). In addition, the rejection by peers, teachers, family, and other adults because of pregnancy is experienced by pregnant adolescents because of societal expectations of childbearing within marriage and at a later age.

Recognizing both sources of stress (adolescent's development and pregnancy/childbearing), adolescent mothers can be expected to experience more stress and display more psychopathological symptoms. However, several caveats have to be made before we can accept this generalization.

1. Wide individual differences have been observed in the reaction to pregnancy and delivery by adult women (see previous section).

2. The "turmoil" aspects of adolescent development vary tremendously from culture to culture (Mead 1929).

3. Environmental variables (e.g., good family relations) serve as buffers for at-risk adolescents (Hauser and Follansbee 1984).

Thus, we can expect to observe wide individual differences in reactions to pregnancy and childbearing during the adolescent period, and that these reactions will be also greatly influenced by the immediate family and sociocultural environment.

TEENAGE PREGNANCY AND CHILDBEARING
AMONG PUERTO RICAN WOMEN

We have argued elsewhere (e.g., García Coll et al. 1982; García Coll, 1988) that traditional Puerto Rican culture is relatively positive toward teenage pregnancy and childbearing, as long as it is within a marriage.

This is based on the positive maternal attitudes reported by Puerto Rican teenage and adult mothers toward early childbearing in comparison to Anglo-Saxon teenage and adult mothers. We have also previously found a more positive outcome for infants of teenage mothers in Puerto Rico in comparison to that obtained in other populations (García Coll, Sepkoski, and Lester 1982; Lester, García Coll, and Sepkoski 1983).

Studies with Puerto Rican mothers and other Hispanic groups in the United States report similar findings. Becerra and deAnda (1984) suggest that acculturation is the key variable influencing adolescent marital status and peer networks. More important, this variable also affects attitudes, behavior, and knowledge about reproduction and contraception. Several studies indicate that the majority of adolescent pregnancies, although conceived while the Hispanic teen is single, are legitimized before the infant's birth (Smith, Weinman, and Nenney 1984; Smith, McGill, and Wait 1987). In addition, in contrast to births of Black adolescents, a greater proportion of these deliveries are reported as actually desired. One study (Smith et al. 1984) further suggested that marriage was seen as the preferred resolution primarily by adolescents who prefer to speak Spanish rather than English, again pointing out that teenage childbearing within marriage is a preferred option for more traditional Hispanics. Based on an exploratory study of pregnancy and motherhood among Mexican-American adolescents (13 to 20 years of age), Becerra and deAnda (1984) state,

> In general, women's perception of self as mother and wife is strong in the traditional Mexican-American culture. This may help explain why the self-concept of the Spanish-speaking Mexican-American respondents in the study sample often seemed to consist of the idea of being wife and mother and keeping house rather than working. This view of self was less strong among the English-speaking Mexican-American respondents [Becerra and deAnda 1984, 115].

Thus, for the more traditional Hispanic adolescent, the perceived cultural acceptance of teenage pregnancy and childbearing becomes internalized as a positive aspect of the self-concept.

METHODOLOGY

The purpose of the present study was to document the sociocultural context of teenage childbearing in a primiparous, low socioeconomic status (SES), urban population in San Juan, Puerto Rico. Demographic characteristics such as marital status, pregnancy circumstances (planned/unplanned), and prevalence of teenage pregnancy and childbearing within the family and immediate community were compared among groups of young and older adolescent and adult women. The distinction between young and older adolescent was deemed necessary, given the heterogeneous nature of adolescence as a period of development as it is described by most theorists (Erikson 1963; Kreipe 1983; Reedy 1983).

The groups were also compared in other aspects of their experience of pregnancy and delivery: how did significant others react to the news of their pregnancy, how much previous experience they have had in taking care of babies, how much stress did they experience throughout the pregnancy, and how much support are they expecting in their role as a new mother?

Subsequently, the groups were compared in measures of depressive symptomatology and maternal self-esteem during the postpartum period. Are Puerto Rican adolescents at a higher risk for postpartum depression or low maternal self-concept?

We were expecting very few group differences--that is, that adolescent mothers would show the same demographic characteristics and perceive their families and communities as positive toward teenage pregnancy and childbearing as adult mothers. However, we were expecting younger adolescents, as a group, to experience more stress and more depressive symptomatology and lower maternal self-concept. This expectation was based on the fact that even when the sociocultural context might be positive, the internal demands of early adolescence might be too much to cope with for these young women.

Finally, a more interesting set of questions related to the range of individual differences observed in postpartum psychological well-being. Wide individual differences have been observed in both reactions to the demands imposed by adolescent development and by pregnancy and delivery. A second set of analyses related sociocultural and environmental factors (e.g., marital status, planned pregnancy, previous experience in childcare, life stress, and support) to depressive symptomatology and maternal self-esteem for the various groups. It was expected that these sociocultural and environmental factors would have a stronger association to psychological well-being than maternal age per se.

SAMPLE

The sample consisted of 59 primiparous, Puerto Rican women delivering full-term healthy infants at the University Hospital, Río Piedras, Puerto Rico. The sample was divided into three groups: young adolescents ($n=20$), with a mean age of 16 years (range 14 to 17 years); older adolescents ($n=19$), with a mean age of 18 and a half years (ranging from 18 to 20 years); and adult women ($n=20$), with a mean age of 25 years, ranging from 21 to 30 years. Table 4.1 shows the demographic characteristics of these groups. The groups were similar in marital status, maternal occupation, family composition, and income source.

Table 4.1

Demographic Characteristics of the Sample

Variables	Groups			
	Young Adol. (n=20)	Older Adol. (n=19)	Adult (n=20)	p <
	#(%)	#(%)	#(%)	
Married	17(85)	15(79)	17(85)	N.S.
Married After Pregnancy	8(40)	6(32)	3(15)	N.S.
High School Graduate	6(30	17(89)	16(80)	.001
Homemakers	17(85)	15(79)	17(85)	N.S.
Nuclear Family	7(35)	9(47)	13(65)	N.S.

Maternal education was significantly lower for younger adolescents, as expected for their chronological age.

PROCEDURE

A research assistant reviewed daily the medical records of the infants born at the hospital. Recruitment criteria included maternal age, parity (primiparous), health status of the infants (healthy), and socioeconomic background. Since most of the families of adolescent mothers were from working-class backgrounds, we made an effort to recruit adult mothers of similar backgrounds (not college graduates).

After informed consent was obtained, we conducted a one and a half hour interview that consisted of the following measures:

1. Demographic Information: including questions about the mother's age, education, occupation, family composition, and so on.

2. Life Stress: To document the characteristics of the life stress during this pregnancy, a list of 37 life events was read to the mother. This was a modified version of a stress checklist derived from Cochrane and Robertson (1973), previously utilized by Crockenberg (in press) in a study with adolescent mothers and by us in a previous study with this population (García Coll, 1988) and with Caucasian adolescent mothers (García Coll, Vohr, Hoffman, and Oh 1986; García Coll, Hoffman, and Oh 1987; García Coll, Hoffman, Van Houten, and Oh 1987; Levine, García Coll, and Oh 1985). If the life event had happened during pregnancy, the mother was asked to rate, on a 6-point scale, how stressful it was. The total number of events and the total average perceived stress were derived as summary scores. In addition, the scale was divided into sub-scores, depending on the kind of life event: (1) general life event; (2) interpersonal conflict with relatives, (3) interpersonal conflict with others, (4) economic problems, (5) legal problems, and (6) health problems.

3. Social Support: The interview on child care support was an adaptation of Mattei's (1983) and Crockenberg's (1981; in press), which we used extensively in our previous research. For the child care network, the mother was asked who the persons were who would be involved in some aspect of child care (changing diapers, baby sitting, etc.), their ages, and in how many different child care activities and how frequently they would be helping out. For

each category (except for number of persons) an average score was determined. Since this interview was done during the perinatal period, it is better conceived of as a measure of the mother's perception of how supportive the environment will be to her as a mother.

4. Beck's Depression Inventory (BDI): The BDI (Beck, Ward, Mendelson, Mock, and Erbaugh 1961) is one of the most standard scales for measuring the severity of depressive symptomatology. It consists of 21 items, each containing four or five items ranked in order of severity. The patient chooses the statement closest to his/her present state.

The split-half reliability is around 0.9, and its test-retest reliability is approximately 0.75. It has consistently been found to correlate well with clinicians' ratings of severity of depression, as well as with other scales of depression. It has the advantage of being useful across a great range of severity levels and in both clinical and analogue populations, and has been used extensively in subclinical and student populations (Williams 1984).

In scoring, each item is given a score ranging from 0 to 3. The total scores can range from 0 to 63. Normative data suggest the following categories of severity level: mild, 14-20; moderate, 21-26; severe, > 26.

5. Maternal Self-Esteem Inventory (MSI): The Shea and Tronick Maternal Self-Esteem Inventory (revised 1982) was used to measure maternal self-esteem defined as a mother's feeling of self-confidence in her mothering ability. This inventory consists of 26 items to be rated on a 1 to 5 point scale that ranges from completely true to completely false. Scores on the MSI have been correlated with theoretically established criteria such as health of the infant, family support, and maternal behavior in a mother-infant interaction task (Shea and Tronick 1982; Tronick and Shea, in press). To obtain a MSI score, the responses are summed, adjusting values for negative statements. The higher the score, the higher the maternal self-esteem of the subject.

The interview was conducted in our behavioral laboratory to ensure a comfortable environment for the mother. Of those approached, five mothers refused participation. The interviews were later coded for analyses by another research assistant unaware of the respondents' group membership.

RESULTS

Sociocultural Context of Teenage Childbearing

In the United States teenage pregnancy and child-bearing occurs in a very particular context. Most teenage mothers are unmarried, come from lower socioeconomic backgrounds, and are considered ill-prepared for parenting (Baldwin and Cain 1980). What is the context experienced by primiparous, lower SES adolescent mothers in comparison to adult mothers in Puerto Rico? As shown previously (Table 4.1), most adolescent mothers (younger and older) are married. Although a larger percentage of adolescents get married after becoming pregnant, this percentage was not statistically different from adult mothers. Unlike the United States, teenage childbearing occurs within marriage in this low SES, urban Puerto Rican population.

Moreover, the difference in the rates of unplanned pregnancies observed among young (70 percent) and older adolescents (74 percent) and adults (50 percent) was not statistically significant. Again, adolescents within this population behave very similar to adult primigravidas.

Another aspect of the sociocultural context refers to how common the phenomena of teenage pregnancy and childbearing are in the immediate community. We asked our subjects, as part of our demographic questionnaire, how many relatives, friends, or neighbors of hers had become parents during the adolescent years. As shown in Table 4.2, adolescent mothers (both young and older) gave more frequent affirmative answers to these questions ($X^2 = 7.24$, $p < .05$). Thus, within their immediate community, adolescent mothers report a higher frequency of adolescent parenting among relatives, friends and/or neighbors.

Another way we measured indirectly how accepted teenage pregnancy and childbearing are within this population was by asking how positive, negative, mixed, or neutral the reactions of the baby's father, grandparents, and other relatives and friends were when the mother told them about this pregnancy. As shown in Table 4.3, no significant differences were found among the groups on the reaction of these significant others to their pregnancies. Besides, reactions by most significant others were predominantly positive for all groups.

Finally, we were interested in assessing how much previous experience these first-time mothers had in care-taking. Again, as part of our demographic questionnaire,

Table 4.2

Frequency of Responses to the Following Questions:
Do you know any (1) relatives (2) neighbors or
friends that are or were adolescent parents?

	Groups			
Responses	Young Adol.	Older Adol.	Adult	p <
Yes[a]	24	26	16	
No[a]	15	12	24	.05

[a]Table reflects number of affirmative answers to two separate

questions. One referring to relatives and the other to neighbors or

friends.

we asked if they had previous experience in taking care
of babies (e.g., siblings, other babies in the family, or
neighbors' or friends'); how many years of experience
they had and in how many different categories (e.g.,
changing diapers, baby sitting). The groups did not
differ statistically in the percentage of mothers who had
some previous experience in caretaking: 89 percent of
young adolescents, 82 percent of older adolescents, and
56 percent of adult mothers. In addition, most mothers
reported having less than two and a half years of experience: 75 percent of young adolescents, 89 percent of
older adolescents, and 90 percent of adult mothers had
some caretaking experience, but this was less than two
and a half years. Moreover, all mothers had a variety
of experience, including at least two different categories
of caretaking activities: 88 percent of young adolescents,
93 percent of older adolescents, and 80 percent of adult
mothers. Thus, based on these self-reports, these first-
time mothers have had similar amounts and types of previous caretaking experience, again a very different context than that reported by teenagers in the United States
(e.g., Baldwin and Cain 1980).

Table 4.3

Reactions of Significant Others to Pregnancy

	Groups			
	Young Adol.	Old Adol.	Adult	$\underline{p}$ <
Baby's father				
positive	17	14	19	N.S.
other[a]	3	5	1	
Baby's grandparents				
positive	13	15	15	N.S.
other[a]	7	4	4	
Other relatives				
positive	16	14	16	N.S.
other[a]	4	5	4	
Other friends				
positive	18	15	20	N.S.
other[a]	1	3	0	

[a]Includes negative, mixed and neutral reactions.

In summary, young and older adolescents are very similar in social characteristics (e.g., marital status, planned pregnancies) to adult, primigravidas of similar educational levels (not college graduates). In addition, these adolescent mothers report higher frequencies of relatives, neighbors, or friends who have experienced adolescent childbearing and similar reactions to their pregnancies by significant others. Finally, they report having the same amount and kind of previous caretaking experience as adult mothers. These findings suggest that these mothers experience a relatively positive sociocultural context toward teenage childbearing.

Life Stress and Social and Child Care Support

In a previous study (García Coll, 1988) we found that adolescent mothers reported more stressful life events than adult mothers in the United States, but not in Puerto Rico. In addition, adolescent mothers in Puerto Rico reported expecting more frequent help from their child care network than adult mothers, again suggesting a maternal perception of a less stressful and more supportive context for teenage childbearing in Puerto Rico.

How do young and older adolescents compare to adult mothers in their reports of life events and social support? Table 4.4 shows the means and standard deviations by age group on the number of life events and average perceived stress by category for each age group. No significant differences were found among the various age groups in any of the stress variables.

Table 4.5 shows the social and child care support variables for the various age groups. Differences were found between young and older adolescents in two social support variables: younger adolescents listed fewer persons as sources of support [$F(2,58)=4.4$, $p<.02$], especially adults [$F(2,56)=3.7$, $p<.03$]. No differences were found among any of the groups in any of the child care support variables: the number of persons expected to help, the different caretaking activities, or how frequently they expected help were very similar among the groups.

In summary, young and older adolescents are similar to primiparous, adult mothers of the same educational background in their reports of life stress and support. Older adolescents receive social support from more persons, especially adults, than younger adolescents, but these differences do not carry over to their expectations for child care support.

Depressive Symptomatology and Maternal Self-Esteem

One of the main goals of this study was to assess the psychological consequences during the immediate perinatal period, in addition to the sociocultural context of teenage childbearing (demographics, stress, and support). Table 4.6 shows the means and standard deviations for the Beck's Depression Inventory (BDI) and the Maternal Self-Esteem Inventory (MSI) for the different age groups.

Table 4.4

Number of Life Events and Perceived Stress

Variables	Young Adol. $\bar{X}\pm SD$	Older Adol. $\bar{X}\pm SD$	Adults $\bar{X}\pm SD$	p <
Life events:number	3.7±1.3	4.2±1.3	3.5±1.1	N.S.
:perceived stress	2.6±1.1	2.1± .8	2.4± .8	N.S.
Conflict relatives:number	1.6±1.5	1.9±1.1	1.6±1.7	N.S.
:perceived stress	1.9±1.5	2.9±1.4	2.1±1.9	N.S.
Conflicts others: number	.6± .8	.3± .5	.4± .7	N.S.
:perceived stress	1.3±1.7	.7±1.3	1.0±1.7	N.S.
Economic problems:number	1.0±1.2	1.1±1.1	1.3±1.3	N.S.
:perceived stress	1.2±1.5	1.5±1.4	1.4±1.7	N.S.
Legal problems: number	.2± .5	.2± .4	.1± .45	N.S.
:perceived stress	.6±1:6	.4±1.	.3±1.4	N.S.
Health problems: number	.9± .7	.7± .5	.8± .8	N.S.
:perceived stress	2.3±1.9	2.6±2.	1.8±1.9	N.S.
TOTAL number	8.5±5.	8.4±2.6	7.7±2.9	N.S.
:perceived stress	2.5± .8	2.5± .6	2.6± .8	N.S.

There were no significant differences among the groups in either of these variables, suggesting similarities among these groups during the postpartum period. However, seven of the 59 subjects had BDI scores in the mild depression category (between 14 and 20) and one subject had scores on the moderate category (between 21 and 26). All eight subjects were adolescents (three younger and five older). Thus, there was a significant difference in the incidence of mild and moderate depression between adolescents and older mothers ($\underline{X} =4.7$, $\underline{p}<.03$).

The scores of the maternal self-esteem inventory theoretically can range from 26 to 130. The mean scores of the three groups were reflective of relatively high maternal self-esteem.

Table 4.5

Social and Child Care Support

Variables	Groups			
	Young Adol.	Old Adol.	Adult	p <
Social support	$\bar{X}\pm SD$	$\bar{X}\pm SD$	$\bar{X}\pm SD$	
Number of people	.75±.7	1.4±.8	1.0±.6	.05
Number of adolescents	.11±.3	.16±.37	0.0±0	N.S.
Number of Adults	.70±.7	1.3±.7	1.0±6	.05
Frequency of contact[a]	3.3±2.6	4.5±1.6	4.3±2	N.S.
Intimacy[a]	2.3±1.8	2.8±1	3.0±1	N.S.
Child Care Support				
Number of people	1.9±1	2.0±1	1.8±.8	N.S.
Number of activities[a]	7.0±1.5	7.0±2	6.8±2	N.S.
Frequency of help[a]	5.0±.9	5.0±8	5.0±8	N.S.

[a]Average, taking into account number of people.

Table 4.6

Beck's Depression Inventory (BDI) and Maternal Self-Esteem Inventory (MSI)

Variables	Groups			
	Young Adol.	Old Adol.	Adult	p <
	$\bar{X}\pm SD$	$\bar{X}\pm SD$	$\bar{X}\pm SD$	
BDI	7.6±5.6	8.2±7.6	4.4±4.7	N.S.
MSI	100.6±14	102±11	105±17	N.S.

Correlates of Depressive Symptomatology
and Maternal Self-Esteem

A question that remains is: What are the correlates
of psychological well-being during the perinatal period
for young and older adolescents and adult mothers?

Demographic Variables

We expected that certain demographic variables, like
marital status and circumstances around the pregnancy
and marriage, would affect the psychological status of the
mother during the postpartum period. For these analyses,
linear regressions using dummy variables for dichotomous
variables were computed.

Marital status, planned pregnancy, marriage before
or after pregnancy, and previous experience in caretaking
were used as predictor variables, and depressive symptomatology (BDI scores) and maternal self-esteem (MSI
scores) were used as dependent variables for each age
group. For younger adolescents higher BDI scores (more
depressive symptoms) were associated with marriage after
pregnancy ($F(1,16)=4.3$, $p<.05$], accounting for 22 percent
of the variance in BDI scores. For older adolescents,
higher BDI scores were associated with unplanned pregnancies [$F(1,18)=5.5$, $p<.03$] accounting for 24 percent of
the variance. No significant correlates of BDI scores were
found for adult mothers.

No significant correlations were found between these
demographic variables and maternal self-esteem (MSI)
scores in young adolescents. For older adolescents, higher
MSI scores were associated with having more previous caretaking experience [$F(1,14)=6.3$, $p<.03$]. For adult mothers,
higher MSI scores were related to planned pregnancies
[$F(1,19)=10.4$, $p<.01$]. Thus, circumstances around the
marriage and pregnancy affect differentially the psychological well-being of young and older adolescents and
adult women during the postpartum period.

Life Stress and Social Support

Another set of analyses were conducted to assess the
associations between life stress and support variables and
psychological well-being (BDI and MSI scores) for each
age group.

For young adolescents, more depressive symptoms (higher BDI scores) were associated with higher total perceived stress ($r=.59$, $p<.01$), especially the number of stressful life events ($r=.46$, $p<.04$) and the perceived stress associated with these events ($r=.53$, $p<.02$). For older adolescents, higher BDI scores were associated with a higher number of conflicts with relatives ($r=.46$, $p<.05$). No significant correlations were found between stress and support and BDI scores for adult mothers.

Maternal self-esteem scores (MSI) were not significantly correlated with life stress or support variables for either of the adolescent groups. However, lower MSI was related to a higher number of total stressful events ($r=-.56$, $p<.01$), especially a higher number of conflicts with relatives ($r=-.47$, $p<.04$) and the perceived stress associated with health problems during pregnancy ($r=-.46$, $p<.04$) for adult mothers. Thus, life stress and social support variables are again differentially associated with psychological well-being of young and older adolescents and adult women.

Discussion

Although based on a small sample size, our findings suggest some interesting patterns on how Puerto Rican adolescent and older mothers compare on their experiences of their pregnancies and their psychological well-being during the postpartum period.

First, we found striking similarities among the groups in demographic characteristics (especially marital status). Although we chose adult mothers of similar educational backgrounds, what is significant in this population is that most of these women (even the younger adolescents whose ages range from 14 to 17 years) are experiencing the birth of their first child within a marriage. This is very different from the context of teenage childbearing in the United States among all ethnic groups, including Puerto Rican teenage mothers in the United States (Darabi, Dryfoos, and Schwartz 1986). Since marriage seems to serve the function of "legitimizing" the pregnancy and birth of the child, we can expect that societal reactions and support toward these events will be more favorable.

The maternal reports seem to suggest this is the case. Most women in this sample, regardless of their age, report mostly positive reactions to the news about being pregnant from significant others (e.g., the baby's father or grandparents, other relatives, and friends). In general, these women's perception of their pregnancy and birth of their first child was described as a positive experience. The groups, in addition, did not differ in their experienced life stress, including the specific events or the perceived stress during pregnancy. These findings replicate our previous study (García Coll, 1988) in which general attitudes about teenage pregnancy and childbearing and experienced life stress did not differ between teenage and adult mothers. Within this low SES, urban population, adolescent pregnancy does not seem to be experienced as a more stressful event than a first pregnancy during the adult years.

The groups were also quite similar in social and child care support. One difference emerged between young and older adolescents: Older adolescents receive social support from more persons, especially adults, than do younger adolescents. But these differences do not carry over to their expectations for child care support. The differences between younger and older adolescents are in agreement with the distinctions made by theorists of adolescent development between early and late adolescence (e.g., Kreipe 1983; Reedy 1983). Younger adolescents are expected to be more oriented toward same-sex peers than to adults, and this orientation might explain, in part, the differences in the number of adults listed as support by young and older adolescents. However, the groups do not differ in their perceived support in their roles as new mothers, as measured by the number of people, activities, and frequency of help they expect with their baby.

Finally, we compared the groups in psychological well-being as measured by the Beck's Depression Inventory and the Maternal Self-Esteem Inventory. In general, most of these mothers, regardless of their age, reported very few depressive symptoms and a relatively high maternal self-esteem. However, all eight mothers whose BDI scores were in the mild or moderate depression category were adolescent mothers. In fact, this represents an incidence of 21 percent in the adolescent sample, which is substantially higher than the 3 to 10 percent of postnatal depression found in other studies (Tod 1964; Pitt 1968; Dewi-Rees and Lutkin 1971; Dalton 1971; Cox 1978). Thus, we have found some evidence that mild and moderate depression during the immediate postpartum period is more prevalent among adolescent mothers, regardless of their age.

What are the correlates of psychological well-being (e.g., absence of depression or high maternal self-esteem) during the postpartum period? Aside from having a higher incidence of mild or moderate depression, we found more significant correlations between environmental variables and depressive symptoms in adolescent mothers (both young and older) than in the sample of adult mothers. Specifically, the circumstances around the pregnancy (e.g., marital status, planned or unplanned pregnancy) and experienced life stress were significantly associated with depressive symptoms for both groups of adolescents but not for adults. Thus, we found evidence that adolescent mothers who were single at conception, or had an unplanned pregnancy, or experienced certain kinds of life events during pregnancy reported more depressive symptoms during the postpartum period.

In contrast, for adult mothers, maternal self-esteem seems to be a more sensitive measure of well-being than depressive symptomatology. Although adult mothers did not differ from either group of adolescents in maternal self-esteem, similar patterns of associations between environmental variables and psychological well-being were observed, but this was defined as higher maternal self-esteem. Unplanned pregnancies and higher life stress were associated with lower maternal self-esteem, but not with depressive symptomatology in adult mothers.

These patterns of results suggest several important theoretical considerations of the impact of adolescence, pregnancy, and delivery on psychological well-being. First, the similarities between young and older adolescent mothers in this population are striking, suggesting that chronological age per se might not be a good indicator of maturation level within this developmental stage. The distinction between early and late adolescence refers mainly to a psychosocial, not physical or chronological, stage of development (Kreipe 1983). We have previously found (Levine et al. 1985) that for some aspects of mother-infant interaction, like those required in a teaching situation, chronological age is an important determinant of individual differences. For other aspects of mother-infant interaction, such as displays of pleasure or acceptance during a face-to-face interaction, ego development becomes a more important variable. Since in the present study, chronological age was not correlated with psychological well-being, nor were there differences among the adolescent groups in the associations between environmental variables and BDI or MSI, future studies should assess psychosocial or stage of ego development in addition to chronological age.

Another theoretical implication of our findings is the fact that poor psychological status was reflected for adolescent mothers as depressive symptomatology, while for adult mothers, maternal self-esteem seemed to be a more sensitive measure of psychological well-being. This might be due to the differences between the groups in developmental status in their self-esteem. Since most adolescent mothers are expected to be in the process of establishing a relatively stable self-concept, their self-esteem might be influenced or threatened by other more relevant aspects of their psychosocial development (e.g., peer relations) than by motherhood. In other words, other aspects of self-esteem might be more salient to these women than their maternal role. A general measure of self-esteem, rather than specific to the maternal role, might be more sensitive for assessing psychological well-being in adolescents. For an adult Puerto Rican woman, in contrast to an adolescent mother, their role as a mother might be a more central aspect of their self-concept. Therefore, negative environmental circumstances might be more influential and threatening to their maternal self-esteem, especially for a first-time mother.

There is one important methodological limitation of the present study that should be considered in interpreting our results. Our findings might be relevant only to primiparous, low SES, urban populations in San Juan, Puerto Rico. The demographic characteristics of various samples of Puerto Rican adolescent mothers in the United States (Darabi et al. 1986; Ventura 1985) are more similar to other minority populations in the United States than to adolescents in Puerto Rico. Therefore, extrapolation of our results to other samples should be avoided.

However, our findings suggest the importance of the immediate family and sociocultural context for the psychological well-being of the mother, a similar conclusion reached by work with other populations (e.g., Friedman and Phillips 1983). Future research should try to replicate our findings in other populations and examine whether these observations have any predictive power to psychological well-being or parenting skills beyond the postpartum period. Longitudinal studies are the only way to assess the unfolding processes of development and their impact on both maternal and infant well-being.

ACKNOWLEDGMENTS

We would like to thank Gladys Capella for the scoring and coding of the data and Maureen McElroy for word processing.

REFERENCES

Baldwin, W., and V. Cain. 1980. "The children of teen-age parents." Family Planning Perspectives 12:34-43.

Ball, J. A. 1987. Reactions to Motherhood: The Role of Postnatal Care. Cambridge: Cambridge University Press.

Barnard, K. E., and S. R. Gortner. 1977. Nursing Child Project. Division of Nursing, Bureau of Health Resources and Development, U.S. Department of Health, Education and Welfare.

Becerra, R. M., and D. deAnda. 1984. "Pregnancy and motherhood among Mexican-American adolescents." Health Soc Work 9:106-23.

Beck, A. T., C. H. Ward, M. Mendelson, J. Mock, and J. Erbaugh. 1961. "An inventory for measuring depression." Archives of General Psychiatry 4:561-71.

Bello, T. A. 1979. "The Latino Adolescent." In R. T. Mercer, ed., Perspectives in Adolescent Health Care, pp. 57-64. New York: Lippincott.

Benedek, T. 1959. "Parenthood as a developmental phase: A contribution to the libido theory." Journal of the American Psychoanalytic Association 7:389-417.

Bibring, G. L. 1959. "Some considerations of the psychological processes in pregnancy." Psychoanalytic Study of the Child 14:113-21.

Bibring, G. L., T. F. Dwyer, D. S. Huntington, and A. F. Valenstein. 1961. "A study of the psychological processes in pregnancy and the earliest mother-child relationship." Psychoanalytic Study of the Child 16:9–27.

Bibring, G. L., T. F. Dwyer, D. S. Huntington, et al. 1961. "A study of the psychological processes in pregnancy and the earliest mother-child relationship. II. Methodological considerations." Psychoanalytic Study of the Child 16:27–72.

Brody, E. B. 1978. "The meaning of the first pregnancy for working class Jamaican women." In W. B. Miller and L. F. Newman, eds., The First Child and Family Formation, pp. 92–197. Chapel Hill, N.C.: Carolina Population Center.

Caplan, G. 1957. "Psychological aspects of maternity care." American Journal of Public Health 47:25–31.

Chapple, P. A., and D. Furneaux. 1964. "Changes of Personality in Pregnancy and Labour." Proceedings of the Royal Society of Medicine 57:260–61.

Chertok, L. 1969. Motherhood and Personality. London: Tavistock Publications.

Cochrane, R., and A. Robertson. 1973. "The life events inventory: A measure of the relative severity of psychosocial stressors." Journal of Psychological Research 17:135–39.

Cohen, R. L. 1966. "Some maladaptive syndromes of pregnancy and the puerperium." Obstetrics and Gynecology 27:562–70.

Cox, J. 1978. "Some socio-cultural determinants of psychiatric morbidity associated with childbearing." In M. Sandler, ed., Mental Illness in Pregnancy and the Puerperium, pp. 91–98. Oxford: Oxford University Press.

Crockenberg, S. B. 1981. "Infant irritability, mother responsiveness, and social support influences on the security of infant–mother attachment." Child Development 52:856–65.

_____. In press. "Support for adolescent mothers during the postnatal period: Theory and research." In C. F. Z. Boukydis, ed., Research on Support for Parents and Infants in the Postnatal Period. Norwood, N.J.: Ablex.

Dalton, K. 1971. "Prospective study into puerperal depression." British Journal of Psychiatry 118:689–92.

Darabi, F., J. Dryfoos, and D. Schwartz. 1986. "Hispanic Adolescent Fertility." Hispanic Journal of Behavioral Science 8:157–59.

Dasen, P., and A. Heron. "Cross–cultural tests of Piaget's theory." In H. C. Triandis and A. Heron, eds., Handbook of Cross–Cultural Psychology, vol. 4, Developmental Psychology, pp. 295–341. Boston: Allyn and Bacon.

Dewi–Rees, W., and S. G. Lutkin. 1971. "Parental depression before and after childbirth." Journal of the Royal College of General Practitioners 21:26–31.

Elkind, D. 1970. Children and Adolescents. New York: Oxford University Press.

Erikson, E. H. 1963. Childhood and Society. New York: Norton.

_____. 1968. Identity: Youth and Crisis. New York: Norton.

Field, T., and S. Widmayer. 1980. "Eight–month follow-up of infants delivered by Caesarean section." Paper presented at the International Conference on Infant Studies, New Haven, Conn.

Friedman, S. B., and S. Phillips. 1983. "Psychosocial risk to mother and child as a consequence of adolescent pregnancy." In E. R. McAnarney, ed., Premature Adolescent Pregnancy and Parenthood, pp. 269–77. New York: Grune and Stratton.

García Coll, C. T. 1988. "The consequences of teenage childbearing in traditional Puerto Rican culture." In K. Nugent, B. M. Lester, and T. B Brazelton, eds., Cultural Context of Infancy. Norwood, N.J.: Ablex.

García Coll, C. T., J. Hoffman, and W. Oh. 1987. "The social ecology and early parenting of caucasian adolescent mothers." Child Development 58:955-63.

García Coll, C. T., J. Hoffman, L. J. Van Houten, and W. Oh. 1987. "The social context of teenage child-bearing: Effects on the infant's care-giving environment." Journal of Youth and Adolescence 16:345-60.

García Coll, C. T., C. Sepkoski, and B. M. Lester. 1982. "Effects of teenage childbearing on neonatal and infant behavior in Puerto Rico." Infant Behavior and Development 5:227-36.

García Coll, C. T., B. R. Vohr, J. Hoffman, and W. Oh. 1986. "Maternal and environmental factors affecting developmental outcome of infants of adolescent mothers." Journal of Developmental and Behavioral Pediatrics 7:230-36.

Ginsburg, H., and S. Opper. 1979. Piaget's Theory of Intellectual Development, 2nd ed. Englewood Cliffs, N.J.: Prentice-Hall.

Goshen-Gottstein, E. 1966. Marriage and First Pregnancy: Cultural Influences and Attitudes of Israeli Women. London: Tavistock.

Greenberg, D. M. 1979. "Parental reactions to an infant with a birth defect: A study of five families." Paper presented at the biennial meeting of the Society for Research in Child Development, San Francisco, Calif.

Grossman, F. K. 1980. "Psychological sequelae of Caesarean delivery." Paper presented at International Conference on Infant Studies, New Haven, Conn.

Handwerker, L. B., and C. H. Hodgman. 1983. "Approach to adolescents by the perinatal staff." In E. R. McAnarney, ed., Premature Adolescent Pregnancy and Parenthood, pp. 311-27. New York: Grune and Stratton.

Hauser, S. T., and D. J. Follansbee. 1984. "Developing identity: Ego growth and change during adolescence." In H. E. Fitzgerald, B. M. Lester, and M. W. Yogman, eds., Theory and Research in Behavioral Pediatrics, vol. 2, pp. 207-62. New York: Plenum.

Havighurst, R. J. 1972. Developmental Tasks and Education. New York: Longmans.

Helms, C. 1981. "What is a normal adolescent?" Maternal Child Nursing 6:405-6.

Hoffman, L. W., and M. L. Hoffman. 1973. "The Value of Children to Parents." In J. T. Fawcett, ed., Psychological Perspectives on Population, pp. 19-76. New York: Basic Books.

Hubert, J. 1974. "Belief and Reality: Social Factors in Pregnancy and Childbirth." In M. P. Richards, ed., The Integration of a Child into a Social World, pp. 37-51. London: Cambridge University Press.

Klaus, M. H., and J. H. Kennell. 1976. Maternal-Infant Bonding. St. Louis: C. V. Mosby.

Kolb, L. C. 1975. "Disturbances of the body image." In S. Arieti, ed., American Handbook of Psychiatry, vol. 4, pp. 539-47. New York: Basic Books.

Kreipe, R. E. 1983. "Prevention of adolescent pregnancy: A development approach." In E. R. McAnarney, ed., Premature Adolescent Pregnancy and Parenthood, pp. 37-59. New York: Grune and Stratton.

Lester, B. M., C. T. García Coll, and C. Sepkoski. 1983. "A cross-cultural study of teenage pregnancy and neonatal behavior." In T. Field and A. Sostek, eds., Infants Born at Risk: Physiological, Perceptual and Cognitive Processes, pp. 147-69. New York: Grune and Stratton.

Levine, L., C. T. García Coll, and W. Oh. 1985. "Determinants of mother-infant interaction in adolescent mothers." Pediatrics 75:23-29.

Levy, J. M., and R. K. McGee. 1975. "Childbirth as crisis: A test of Janis's theory of communication and stress resolution." Journal of Personality and Social Psychology 31:171-79.

Mattei, M. L. 1983. "Autonomy and social support network in a Puerto Rican community." Unpublished doctoral dissertation, University of Massachusetts, Amherst.

Mead, M. 1929. Coming of Age in Samoa: A Psychological Study of Primitive Youth for Western Civilization. New York: Morrow Quill Paperbacks.

Nelson, M. K. 1983. "Working-class women, middle-class women and models of childbirth." Social Problems 36: 284-97.

Oakley, A. 1974. Woman's Work. New York: Pantheon.

Osofsky, H. J., and J. D. Osofsky. 1980. "Normal adaptation to pregnancy and new parenthood." In P. M. Taylor, ed., Parent-Infant Relationships. New York: Grune and Stratton.

_____. 1983. "Adolescent adaptation to pregnancy and parenthood." In E. R. McAnarney, ed., Premature Adolescent Pregnancy and Parenthood, pp. 195-206. New York: Grune and Stratton.

Pederson, F., M. Zaslow, R. Cain, and B. Anderson. 1980. "Caesarean childbirth: The importance of a family perspective." Paper presented at the International Conference on Infant Studies, New Haven, Conn.

Pitt, B. 1968. "'Atypical' depression following childbirth." British Journal of Psychiatry 114:1325-35.

Pohlman, E. W. 1969. The Psychology of Birth Planning. Cambridge, Mass.: Schenkman.

Reedy, N. J. 1983. "Birth Alternatives for Adolescents." In E. R. McAnarney, ed., Premature Adolescent Pregnancy and Parenthood, pp. 329-50. New York: Grune and Stratton.

114 / García Coll et al.

Seashore, M. H., A. D. Leifer, C. R. Barnett, and P. H. Leiderman. 1973. "The effects of denial of early mother–infant interaction on maternal self–confidence." Journal of Personality and Social Psychology 26:369–78.

Shea, E., and E. Z. Tronick. 1982. "Maternal self-esteem as affected by infant health and family support." Paper presented at the American Psychological Association, Washington, D.C.

Smith, P. B., M. Weinman, and S. W. Nenney. 1984. "Desired pregnancy during adolescence." Psychological Reports 54:227–31.

Smith, P. B., L. McGill, and R. B. Wait. 1987. "Hispanic adolescent conception and contraception profiles: A comparison." Journal of Adolescent Health Care 8: 352–55.

Tod, E. D. M. 1964. "Puerperal depression: A prospective epidemiology study." Lancet 2:1264.

Tronick, E. Z., and E. Shea. 1988. "The maternal self–report inventory: A research and clinical instrument of assessing maternal self–esteem." In H. E. Fitzgerald, B. M. Lester, and M. W. Yogman, eds., Theory and Research in Behavioral Pediatrics, vol. 4. New York: Plenum.

Veevers, J. E. 1973. "Voluntary Childless Wives: An Exploratory Study." Sociology and Social Research 57:356–66.

Ventura, S. J. 1985. "Birth of Hispanic parentage, 1982." Monthly Vital Statistics Report, National Center for Health Statistics 34, 4 Supp. DHHS Pub. No. (PHS) 85–1120. Public Health Service, Hyattsville, Md.

Westbrook, M. T. 1978. "The effect of the order of birth on women's experience of childbearing." Journal of Marriage and the Family 165–72.

Williams, J. M. G. 1984. The Psychological Treatment of Depression. New York: Free Press.

Adulthood and Growing Old

5

Developmental Issues during Adulthood: Redefining Notions of Self, Care, and Responsibility among a Group of Professional Puerto Rican Women

María T. Margarida Juliá, Psy.D.

INTRODUCTION

The growing body of literature on women's development that incorporates a feminist orientation addresses the issue of development as not simply about differentiation and movement from fusion to autonomy, but about integration and movement from dependent connections to more complex and articulated relations (Miller 1976; Gilligan 1982a,b; Surrey 1985). The growing number of feminist theorists have posited that a primary developmental task for women as they achieve a greater degree of differentiation during adulthood involves a movement toward bringing the attitude of care toward the self (Surrey 1985; Kaplan 1984; Jordan 1984). The paradox in women's development during adulthood seems to involve the dilemma of how to stay connected while growing more differentiated within their connections with others.

Recently, women theorists have also stressed the importance of understanding the context in which women develop (Miller 1976). Without understanding context, it is impossible to understand development. However, virtually no empirical or theoretical studies done address women's developmental processes within various cultural contexts. Studies on Puerto Rican women have tended to focus only on how structural, sociocultural, and economic factors determine women's lives and roles. In doing so, they underemphasize women's experiences of growth and change and fail to acknowledge them as active meaning makers of

115

their experience and reality. Recognizing the importance of context in individual development, the study on which this chapter is based focuses on the interface between sociocultural and familial contexts and the individual development during adulthood for a group of middle-class, professional Puerto Rican women.

Female Adult Development:
Dimensions to Be Explored

The developmental framework chosen to examine the above-mentioned interface is based on the structural developmental theories of Kegan (1982) and Gilligan (1982a). Their work forms part of a growing body of constructivist theory based on the fundamental assumption that each person is an active agent in perceiving and making meaning out of their experience in the world. They both follow a Piagetian tradition in their delineation of an invariant sequence of stages, which I will refer to as developmental positions. These stages involve a succession of qualitative differentiation and reintegration of what gets defined as "self" and "other" resulting in an increasingly more complex social perspective.

This study particularly focuses on two fundamental changes outlined by these theorists: (1) developmental changes in a person's definition and construction of the self-other relationship (Kegan 1982), and (2) developmental changes in women's orientation of care and responsibility (Gilligan 1982a).

Kegan depicts the third of his five stages of ego development as the "Interpersonal" position, in which the self is defined by the expectation of those interpersonal relationships in which the person is embedded. At this developmental position, the self derives its meaning from its interpersonal roles and contexts: that is, from other's needs, wishes, expectations, and values. People at this position tend to think about the self within the context of a relationship rather than to conceptualize a self that is differentiated from interpersonal situations. Focus of authority is the interpersonal other. As the person transitions to an "Institutional" position (Stage 4), there is a growing differentiation from a sense of self that defines itself in its own terms and can now coordinate and reflect upon his/her relationships with others, making them the object of his/her attention. At the "Institutional" position, the self now has its own internal standards for evaluation, values, goals, and attitudes that are internally chosen rather than derived from external standards and expectations.

The second developmental dimension to be explored involves women's changes in the orientation of care and responsibility as outlined by Gilligan. Gilligan's research on women's moral development has led her to suggest that women balance and equalize responsibility to themselves within the orientation of care for the needs of others through a developmental progression.

Gilligan's framework for differentiating the stages of women's moral development includes a sequence of three levels and two transitions, each transition representing a critical reinterpretation of the moral conflict between responsibility and selfishness. Alvarez's (1985) research has suggested that there is a strong correspondence between Kegan's transition from an "Interpersonal" definition of self to an "Institutional" position and Gilligan's second and third levels.

At the second level the orientation of care and responsibility centers on the ability to be sensitive and responsive to others' feelings and needs. The needs of the self at this level are taken to be synonymous with the needs of others. The transition to level three begins as the woman starts to ask whether it is selfish or responsible to include her own needs within the compass of her care and concern. This question, Gilligan argued, leads her to reexamine the concept of responsibility, juxtaposing the outward concern about what other people think with a new inner judgment. Thus, in this transition the woman strives to encompass the needs of both self and other.

At the third level there is an expanded conception of the obligation to care, which now encompasses both care of self and others and directs the self to balance and resolve the multiple and at times competing responsibilities. Care for the self is no longer construed as incompatible with care for others, but rather as essential for true care for others. Gilligan has used the metaphor of "women's voice" to refer to women's inclusion of themselves in the experience of care and has suggested, "There must be a sense of equality to foster a sense of voice. If the only options for women as they attempt to integrate responsibility to self are hurt and isolation, voice can be silenced or submerged, resulting in continued subordination to the needs of others" (Gilligan 1982b).

A crucial element that facilitates growth within relationships is the ability and responsiveness of the other to the changing and evolving needs of the person involved. The processes of differentiation and integration require a reciprocal process or context in which to evolve and develop (Surrey 1985). Society's affirmation or lack of it holds a deep power over the establishment of individual identity, differentiation, and equalizing of care in women (Hancock 1981).

Puerto Rican Women within the Historical
and Sociocultural Context

A second major exploration of this study involves examining the role of women's relational and sociocultural context on the developmental changes mentioned above. In order to do so, we need to describe the social experience of Puerto Rican women within the historical context of a colonial and patriarchal society (Zambrana 1982; Zavala-Martínez 1981; Andrade 1982).

The psychological consequences of colonialism documented by Fanon (1963), Memmi (1967), and others (Zavala-Martínez 1981; Urdang 1979) describe the process of internalization of oppressive ideologies and stereotypes created about the colonized person, which in effect perpetuates the oppressive system. These ideologies and myths are in turn mediated by social institutions and through larger cultural beliefs and behaviors that have an impact on men's and women's development and personal choices (Pantoja 1980). The ideological myths most frequently cited involve: (1) the orientation toward the supremacy of male authority, and (2) the value of selflessness and sacrificial stance in which women are encouraged to place others' needs above their own as a way of deriving personal fulfillment and satisfaction. This ideology is personified in the role of mother and is embedded in the process of socialization that rewards her passivity, self-sacrifice, and abnegation as daughter, wife, and mother (Bernal and Alvarez 1983; Seda Bonilla 1958).

Furthermore, little is known about the role that the orientation toward "familism" plays within Puerto Rican society in perpetuating women's continued subordination to the needs of others at the expense of the development of her separate goals and strivings. This family orientation is based on the predominant value toward economic, emotional, and social support and protection among kinship relationships with the reciprocal obligations and loyalties that it entails, even when family members have established their separate families (Vales 1977).

Although this orientation was the mechanism for survival in rural and urban settings as the Spaniards colonized the island, it has persisted with a transformation in its role and function according to the needs of the different social classes. Vales has stated, "in the middle urban class family, 'familism' tends to take the form of an emotional dependence which sustains the sense of reciprocal family obligations and responsibilities" (Vales 1977, 3). This family orientation is sustained largely through the ideology of the "theory of sacrifice" in which a good woman is defined by her self abnegation and by placing the family and community needs before her own. Women's selflessness and "sacrifice" is crucial in order to assure the continuity of care, responsibility, and reciprocity of family obligations and ties among generations as parents grow older (Nieves Falcón 1972; Bernal and Alvarez 1983). In this way, ideological beliefs interface with the structure of family relationships in ways that reinforce women's continued dependency and subordination.

The last three decades have brought considerable social and economic changes that have touched on fundamental structures and processes, altering traditions, norms, and values within Puerto Rican society. However, many scholars have argued that in spite of increased participation of women in education and in the work force, the traditional orientation toward sharp sex-role segregation and women's continued subordinate and dependent roles within their relationships with men have minimally changed, since these are embedded within cultural beliefs, ideologies, and other institutional practices that remain untouched by the nature of these changes (Pantoja 1980; Ramírez 1974). Thus, although recent changes in family structure and women's roles suggest that there is a movement toward egalitarian expectations with regard to women's role in marital relationships, there are still many instances where modern or egalitarian arrangements exist alongside more traditional patterns of behavior (Muñoz-Vázquez 1979). In other instances, studies have shown that women's ability to control their personal growth is still a distant reality (Alonso 1979).

Areas of Study and Exploration

Recognizing the structural and sociocultural factors impinging on women's growth while acknowledging them as active meaning makers to their experience and reality, the present study was designed to explore the following areas: First, I speculated that there would be a similar distribution of women's changing definition of self and the corresponding orientation toward care and responsibility as outlined by Kegan and Gilligan in a group of middle-class, professional Puerto Rican women. Second, I speculated that there would be ideological beliefs and practices within society and family relationships that had direct bearing on the developmental changes being explored. However, our working hypothesis was that women at different developmental positions would perceive and negotiate those sociocultural and familial expectations in different ways. Third, given the prevalent cultural emphasis on continuity of family attachments in Puerto Rican society, it was speculated that the family's recognition and/or lack of support of the developmental changes being explored would be extremely influential in how these developmental shifts were negotiated and experienced by the women. For example, the strong orientation toward the morality of self-sacrifice and placing others' needs above one's own might render particularly difficult the transition depicted by Gilligan in which women achieve a balance between their responsibility toward others in a way that included the self. It is the contention of this researcher that this is perhaps the most cultural developmental transition for the Puerto Rican woman as a way of evolving from relationships that foster continued subordination and oppression. Societal pressures reinforcing the morality of self-sacrifice as the ultimate definition of goodness are strong binding forces that might tend to silence the woman's emerging inner voice.

METHOD

Sample

Subjects were 20 middle-class women who had been raised in Puerto Rico and who continued to live there.

Subjects ranged in age from 30 to 40 years. Among the single women, who included three divorced women without children, the mean age was 34 years, and 36 years was the mean age among married women. The following variables were held constant: The women had spent their childhood and adolescence in Puerto Rico and had not lived outside of Puerto Rico more than five years, they held a minimum of a B.A. degree, and they presently held a job. The level of education for the single and married women in this sample ranged from a B.A. to a Ph.D., with a mean of 18 years of education for the whole group (e.g., the equivalent of a Master's degree). Their professions covered a wide range of fields such as business, art, administration, law, and different health and mental health professionals. In order to begin to get some idea about the role of motherhood in Puerto Rican women's development, the sample was divided between women who had children (10 subjects), and those who did not (10 subjects).

Subjects were recruited through professional networks of the investigator. Friends, acquaintances, and colleagues were asked to identify persons with whom they were acquainted and who met the selection criteria stated in the previous section. Several subjects themselves referred other acquaintances for the study. The interviews required approximately two hours. They were audiotaped with verbatim transcripts made for the purpose of analysis.

Design

This study sought to give a voice to the phenomenological experience of Puerto Rican women with respect to the developmental and relational context in these changes. Selltiz, Wrightsman, and Cook (1976) have argued that studies that seek to capture uncharted phenomena in areas of inquiry where little is known are best suited to qualitative and descriptive research designs. Furthermore, Baltes and Schaie (1973) have suggested that a qualitative approach to inquiry into developmental processes is best suited since it can encompass the individual as well as his/her context as the unit of analysis, as opposed to taking the individual as the only unit of analysis with set categories to be tested and confirmed. Thus, a qualitative exploratory design was chosen as best suited for this study in order to attend to the different aspects of

the phenomena studied in an area where little is known.
The advantage of a qualitative design involves its ability
to capture, clarify, and describe phenomena with the purpose of formulating emergent hypotheses and areas for
more precise investigation. Currently in the discovery
phases, developmental research on Puerto Rican women requires a fluid approach for generating hypotheses and
capturing uncharted phenomena. Although the obvious
limitations of qualitative research like this involve the
generalizability of its findings and the inherent difficulties minimizing bias and reliability, a quantitative research model would not have yielded the richness of phenomenological data sought. Since our purpose was not to
confirm or test hypotheses of casual relationships between·
variables, but rather was to uncover and discover new
categories and ways of understanding women's experience
of their changing self-definition, a qualitative design was
best suited to meet these goals.

This qualitative study employed an extensive semi-
structured interview that consisted of four parts: (1) a self-
description interview (Gilligan 1979, 1982a), (2) an interview designed by this researcher that examined women's
experience of the role of their relational and sociocultural
context in the process of change, (3) demographic information, and (4) family questionnaire or genogram. These
instruments were utilized to gather data about women's
internal experience and perceptions about themselves and
their developmental changes, and the role of the different
relational contexts (e.g., family, friends, community, work
group) and sociocultural context in their process of change.
Probes were specifically designed to elicit spontaneous information about those relational and sociocultural contexts,
expectations, and/or norms that they perceived facilitated
or impeded their growth. The way in which women negotiated these changes within these contexts was also explored.

Analysis of Interviews

We separated the sections of the interview that were
designed to yield specific scores based on the theoretical
and empirical work of Kegan and Gilligan as well as
Alvarez's (1985) elaboration of the themes that evolved
from women in her study at the different developmental

positions. These sections were scored by two independent coders as well as by the researcher. Inter-rater reliability for content themes and developmental position according to Kegan and Gilligan's levels was done for one-half of the interviews by comparing the developmental level scores assigned by the raters and the researcher. Gilligan's levels were able to be differentiated with 100 percent inter-rater reliability, and Kegan's levels with a 70 percent reliability. Frequency counts were made of the recurrent themes that evolved both spontaneously or in response to predetermined probes. These were used to determine developmental themes as well as recurrent sociocultural assumptions, norms, and beliefs reported implicitly or explicitly by the women. These will be elaborated in the following section.

RESULTS

Developmental Differences

The findings of this study suggest that there were developmental differences among women's definition of self and the corresponding orientation toward care and responsibility as outlined by Kegan (1982) and Gilligan (1982a). Themes of care and responsibility were woven spontaneously by all the women into the fabric of their description of their sense of themselves and of their relationships with others. This finding was consistent across development positions. Five of the 20 women (25 percent) were found to define themselves and their changes according to others' needs, wishes, and expectations. An example of a typical response was: "I am someone who tends to feel according to how my environment feels . . . it is important for me to have good relations with everybody . . . by gettng to know how other people feel, I get to know how I feel as well" (34-year-old married woman). Another five women (25 percent) were found to be in transition from an "Interpersonal" definition of self, toward an "Institutional" sense of self in which women described themselves as more differentiated from others' expectations and needs than before. For example,

It is very important for me to be able to make my own decisions . . . to develop my

own criteria without external influence from
my family . . . of course this does not mean
I will not consider their points of view, but
at least I need to feel that I make my own
decisions, and not just do what they [family]
expect or want me to do" [35-year-old single
woman].

Ten of the 20 women (50 percent) described themselves as having consolidated a clear and internal sense
of who they were. These women seemed to fit into what
Kegan has described as the "Institutional" position, that
is, they defined themselves as having their own internal
standards for evaluation, values, goals, and attitudes
that were internally chosen rather than derived from
others. An example of how women at this developmental
position described themselves was the following:

I am aware of how my beliefs are shocking to
people around me, of how they challenge their
preconceived ideas of what a woman should be
like. But it is essential for me to live by my
own sense of who I am and what I believe in
and deal with the consequences of my choices
and actions [38-year-old single woman].

When asked to describe their responsibilities to themselves
and to others, these women expressed a need to care for
themselves and their needs that they saw as indispensable
for true care for others.

Sociocultural Themes

A second major exploration of this study involves
examining the role of women's relational and sociocultural
context on the developmental changes being negotiated.
Women in the sample addressed consistently several implicit and explicit sociocultural assumptions as they talked
about themselves and their processes of change. These
had direct bearing on women's sense of themselves and of
their relationships with family (both nuclear and biological), community, and society. These themes emerged in
the interviews independently of developmental position and
marital status, but were experienced and dealt with dif-

ferently by the women in the sample according to developmental position. This will be further elaborated on in a later section. These themes were the following:

(1) <u>Self-fulfillment strictly through caretaking roles.</u> Fifteen out of 20 women (75 percent) commented on the implicit social assumption that the only source of self-fulfillment and actualization for women was through her role as a caretaker of others. They perceived society, and in some cases family, as implicitly or explicitly not recognizing their professional or academic pursuits and competence as sources of personal satisfaction and fulfillment. These pursuits were encouraged and valued as safeguards for personal and financial protection rather than as ways for a woman to establish a self-authoring identity as an adult in her own right. "In this society you are taught that the only choices for a woman are to be fulfilled as a housewife and mother. No one teaches you that being a single woman does not mean that you cannot realize yourself as an adult, and that you can choose something else for yourself" (35-year-old divorced woman).

(2) <u>Placing others' needs above one's own.</u> The second predominant implicit social assumption mentioned by women involved an orientation toward placing other's needs above one's own. Some characteristic ways of describing this involved the value of selfless giving; and placing group or collective needs, primarily those of family, above one's own. Eighteen out of the 20 women (90 percent) made implicit or explicit reference to this theme. "I am always solving other's problems. I feel that I take on too much sometimes, I take on the burden of everyone else's problems and end up with no time for my own things. However, if I stopped doing it I would feel very selfish, like I wasn't being myself" (38-year-old single woman).

(3) <u>Continuity of close family relationships, loyalties, and responsibilities.</u> This third sociocultural theme that was implicitly or explicitly addressed by most women involved the emphasis on continuity of close attachments and affiliation among women and their families (nuclear or original) throughout life. Eighteen out of 20 women articulated the social assumption of sustaining close family relationships, loyalties, responsibilities, and obligations, independently of age and marital status. As expected, this theme was related to the orientation of "familism" cited in the literature of Puerto Rican women and family.

Most women made reference as well to the expectation by society and/or family that women's caretaking role within families required them to place family needs and interests unconditionally above their own. The following quote illustrates one of the ways women made reference to this theme.:

> I am very different from what my family expects of a woman. They expect a woman to limit her life to her husband and children and have her life revolve around them being a provider of services within the household. Any participation in any activity outside the home or after work hours are big sources of conflict and arguments. Besides, they believe that a mother is responsible for her children all her life and I believe that my responsibility is only until a certain age [40-year-old married woman].

(4) Women were implicitly encouraged to remain in dependent relationships. This theme was addressed by 12 of 20 women (60 percent). It involved the cultural sanction that made it acceptable for women to remain in relationships of emotional and functional dependency on their family of origin, husbands, or lovers. These women mentioned the way in which some families and men reinforced and sustained women in subservient, submissive, and dependent relationships as caretakers within their families in exchange for the protection, security, and support they provided. An example of this theme is reflected in the following quote:

> I feel the way I have been raised and the way my family is has made me very dependent on them for support, approval, and making decisions. I know I have imposed on myself many responsibilities toward them . . . no one forces me to do so, but I feel there is a way in which they do expect me to be this way [33-year-old single woman].

It is important to clarify that the sociocultural themes described in this study, which emerged from the interviews of the women, attempted to capture the general

cultural tendencies and orientations that are merely
still frames of a constantly evolving and changing sociocultural reality. The choice of highlighting these specific
themes, social assumptions, and expectations was a prag-
matic one for the purposes of this research, since they
had direct bearing on the developmental issues explored
in this study. They should not be understood as stereo-
typical and rigid images of culture, which is truly a
dynamic and changing phenomenon.

Relationship between Sociocultural and
Relational Contexts and Women's
Developmental Position

An important working hypothesis of this study involves the notion that women at different developmental
positions would perceive and negotiate their changes with
respect to sociocultural and relational contexts in different
ways. In this section the sociocultural themes described
above will be discussed as they were experienced and
dealt with by the women at the three developmental positions found in this study.

(a) For the women who defined themselves according
to others' needs, wishes, and expectations (Interpersonal
position), these sociocultural expectations represented the
very essence of how they understood and gave meaning
and coherence to their sense of themselves. Although they
found value and gratification from their professional roles,
their sense of self-worth was ultimately tied to their ability to be unconditionally sensitive and responsive to
others' needs, wishes, and expectations. For instance,
all the women in this group, single or married, prided
themselves on their ability to unconditionally place their
family needs above their own needs for personal and professional development. Visions of maturity for women at
this developmental position revolved around a compelling
need to place the needs of family and friends above their
own, and avoiding difference or conflicts with their families, preserving their loyalty to the values, expectations,
and responsibilities toward their nuclear and biological
families.

In their interviews, these women defined responsibility to themselves as synonymous with their wish to care
for and be responsible to others' needs, particularly their

families'. For the married women, this involved remaining
loyal, first to their nuclear family needs and expectations,
and second to their families of origin. For the single
women, this involved remaining loyal to the needs of their
family of origin above their own. Whenever there was conflict between the pursuit of professional or work-related
responsibilities and family responsibilities, they experienced any need or wish that took them away from family
responsibilities as selfish or bad and therefore discarded
it.

Although most women in this developmental position
saw themselves as independent decision makers within the
domestic sphere, one woman reflected on how she felt her
husband implicitly reinforced her dependency on him for
decision making:

> I find myself being very dependent on my
> husband for making all the decisions. I feel
> he limits my wish to grow in other areas.
> For example, I can't participate in profes-
> sional activities after work hours or go out
> with friends because he demands that I dedi-
> cate my time to the children and to him. I
> usually comply, but I guess I am really
> afraid of bringing conflict or friction to my
> relationship with my family. This is some-
> thing that I want to change, not be so afraid
> of creating friction and making more decisions
> on my own. However, I am not willing to
> sacrifice my marriage for my profession or
> anything else [35-year-old married woman].

Women at this developmental position felt compelled to avoid
conflicts within their family and sustain the interpersonal
concordance. The pursuit of personal needs that were
separate from family needs represented a threat to the
connections and responsibilities toward the family and
thus were discarded. Therefore, she continued to place
the need for interpersonal concordance above her wish to
attend to needs and goals that were separate from those
of the family.

(b) Women at the transition between "Interpersonal"
to an "Institutional" position reflected critically on the
social assumptions described earlier and prided themselves
on their ability to "realize" themselves, not only through

their roles as caretakers within their families, but also by setting personal and professional goals and fulfilling them. The meaning most of these women attached to being "actualized" and "fulfilled" encompassed not only their traditional roles as caretakers, but also other parts of the self, such as meeting their individual goals and expectations outside the traditional domestic sphere. These women incorporated work identity as an important source of self-definition and of an emerging self-authoring identity.

In contrast to the women at the "Interpersonal" position, these women were able to negotiate differences of values and opinions within their nuclear and extended families, although these remained for the most part similar to those of their families. The following quote reflects this change.

> My mother believed that it was the woman's role to serve her husband at all times, and that she was the one responsible for meeting all the family needs. She saw it as her duty to sacrifice herself for everything or anybody at her own expense. I don't see it like that. In my family we all share the responsibilities and the sacrifice for each other. I do have a responsibility to sacrifice some things or activities for my family, but not always [40-year-old married woman].

Although these women were more able to differentiate their values and expectations from those of their families, their personal needs continued to be defined as synonymous with their wish to care for and attend to the needs of others. Women described their great efforts at juggling these multiple responsibilities and trying to fulfill everyone's needs at once. They describe their conflicts in responsibility to self and to others as involving competing loyalties and responsibilities within different relationships with friends, family, and work--for instance, between wanting to help a friend in need and sustaining responsibilities toward their professional roles, or between spending time with their parents and their nuclear family.

(c) Women at the "Institutional" position consistently described themselves as having their own internal standards for evaluation, goals, and expectations. They critically examined the ways in which societal and sometimes familial expectations (particularly those of their husbands or lovers) did not allow women to pursue personal or professional growth. They commented on how these expectations structured an artificial dilemma for women in terms of having to choose between responsibilities to their families and wishes for personal and professional development. The following is an example.

> One of the most important struggles that women have today is that of being recognized as individuals who have a right and a capability to develop ourselves in areas other than as mothers or wives, such as professionally, politically, and personally. I feel men in particular place barriers and limits that go against our own wish to develop ourselves as individuals. We need to educate our husbands, our children, and our men to realize that by developing ourselves in other ways, we are not going to stop being less feminine, or stop being good mothers, wives, or daughters. But rather, that like men we are also searching for a balance [35-year-old married woman].

These women were reexamining the concept of selfless giving and placing others' needs above their own. They juxtaposed the outward concern and value of what was expected or what other people thought with a new inner judgment that scrutinized the logic of self-sacrifice.

> I am beginning to question my tendency to always be available when other people need me. That may seem like a virtue but for me it is now a defect. Goodness is one thing and "servility" is another. It used to be important for me to be available to meet others' needs at all costs. I think there is a fine line between being unconditionally available for others and being accessible for their needs. It is possible for the first one to stem out of a need for recognition, a need to be loved and accepted. Now I believe people should be responsible for their life, therefore I have to look at this tendency to always be avail-

able for others, since it may lead to dependency [30-year-old single woman].

All of the women at this developmental position described
the need to care for themselves as a precondition for the
true care for others. They now questioned the sincerity
and meaningfulness of their motivations. Most of the
women mentioned that caring for others out of guilt or
fear of losing acceptance or attachments was not honest or
truthful to their sense of themselves. Rather, they saw it
as a weakness that they sought to understand and transcend. Most of the women expressed a strong sense of being disloyal to themselves when they had difficulty saying
"no" to others and later regretted it. For example,

> I accept myself more, accept the limits of
> what I can and cannot give or do for others.
> I no longer feel guilty or afraid to say "no"
> to other people if I don't feel I can help
> them at some point. Other people have also a
> responsibility to take care of themselves. As
> a result of this change, I feel much more at
> peace with myself, more self-assured. More
> accepting of who I am and what my limits
> and strengths are [34-year-old single woman].

Furthermore, women at this developmental position
recognized the inescapability of conflict and accepted responsibility for the difficult choices they made as they
balanced the multiple needs and wishes of the self with
the wish to be responsible to their families. They consistently described a willingness to engage in open, honest
dialogue--even conflict, if necessary--with their families
and husbands as a way of negotiating the various needs,
values, and expectations for themselves and for their families.

Family Relationships and Developmental Change

The role of the family in supporting the acceptance
and inclusion of the woman's individual needs and feelings
in the equation of care seemed crucial as they attempted to
resolve the moral and emotional dilemma of care for self
versus placing others' needs above their own. This was

particularly true for women who were transitioning from a definition of self based on others' needs, wishes, and expectations to a more self-authoring identity. For these women, meeting their needs and being responsive to the needs of their family was experienced as incompatible and seen as an either/or choice that created, much emotional instability and had to be avoided at all cost.

The two women at this transition who described their families as directly or indirectly making it more difficult for them to attend to their separate needs had no consistent way of being able to reconcile these seemingly contradictory needs for themselves and their wish to care for others.

Women who had achieved more self-authoring identities and held more internal definitions of themselves (Institutional position) commented on the ways in which their families provided an important context that paradoxically could both facilitate and impede their attempts to integrate and balance their responsibility to themselves and to their families. As a result, they saw themselves as consistently seeking to change the nature of their relationships and renegotiate their responsibilities toward their families so as to make room for the mutual respect of their personal choices and the pursuit of personal needs that were separate and different from those of others.

Half of the women in this group described their families as making room for the exercise of their self-authoring identities, personal choices, and pursuit of needs that were separate from the families' own. The two single women reported have set limits and boundaries around their responsibilities for their caretaking roles within their families. They also felt they had succeeded in getting respect for their opinions and personal decisions, even when these went against their family's belief systems and expectations. The three married women in this group reported having negotiated equal participation around household chores and child care responsibilities with their spouses.

In contrast to these women, the other half of the women at this developmental position continued to struggle with their husbands and their family of origin to make room for the differences of opinions, respect for personal choices, as well as the wish to integrate their own needs into their wish to remain connected and responsible to their families. The married women described the major sources of struggle with their husbands and families of origin as involving their wish to share the caretaking responsibilities equally within their families and finding time to pursue their individual interests, needs, and goals outside the domestic sphere.

The single women's attempts to negotiate their relationships and responsibilities toward their families involved setting limits around the responsibilities for the well-being, happiness, companionship, and assistance expected by their families of origin. The following is a quote from a 38-year-old single woman:

> Before, I used to get them [parents] to respect my personal decisions and lifestyle through extensive and draining confrontations. Now, I deal with them through distance. It has been a long and painful process because it has involved changing all those expectations and messages of guilt that mothers instill in their daughters, of how their happiness depends on what you do or fail to do.

For this woman as well as for the other women, setting limits and engaging in conflict as they sought to transform the nature of their relationships and responsibilities toward their families meant facing the possibility of disruptions and loss of connections and attachments. This left them feeling very isolated and vulnerable to self-doubt. In such instances, all the women sought support, validation, and reciprocation for their changing needs and goals from their relational contexts outside the family for support. Thus, they identified nondomestic factors, such as participation in educational, professional settings, involvement in political and ideological movements, as well as friendships as contexts facilitating change.

DISCUSSION

Sociocultural and Relational Context: Implications for Women's Development

Feminist theorists have argued that differentiation and integration of women's needs for separateness and connectedness require a reciprocal context, one that can support and affirm both the need for separateness and for

connectedness. In contrast, a context that would value
one need at the expense of the other would be seen as inhibiting rather than facilitating the developmental process.
In that light, it is possible to suggest that the predominant social orientation that fostered the morality of self-
sacrifice and placing others' needs above their own militated against the integration of women's separate needs.
Society and family, according to these women's perceptions,
recognized women's yearning for connectedness but did not
recognize their needs for separateness and self-determination. Defining their needs as synonymous with the needs
of others, and placing others' needs above their own would
be consistent with the expectations of their social context.
It is possible that this may be a significant reason why
women experience no need to differentiate from this valued
way of knowing themselves and being in their relationships
with others. In fact, this was a finding for the five
women who were at the "Interpersonal" position.

The developmental dilemma for women of how to stay
connected to their families while differentiating from them
was intensified further by the cultural emphasis on the
continuity of family attachments, loyalties, and responsibilities. The data showed how these social assumptions
structured an external layer of conditions that highlighted
women's experience of the either/or, rather than integrated
constructions of the dilemma as women tried to reconcile
their wish to integrate their separate goals and expectation for themselves with their wish to care for their families.

Therefore, it was not surprising that the process of
differentiation and integration was facilitated in families
who recognized and supported the developmental changes
taking place and made most difficult for women whose families did not. For some women, the absence of relational
and social contexts that affirmed and recognized their
separate needs as valid still tended to "silence" their
emerging voices, leaving them with an extreme fear of
loss of attachments and crippling self-doubt. This was
particularly true for women who experienced themselves as
disembedding from relationships of extreme emotional dependency on their families or spouses. The fear of hurt
and loss of needed family supports was seen as the possible outcome of including their personal needs in the equation of care. Some of these women described themselves as
unable to reconcile this dilemma and felt trapped or stuck,

unable to change unless prompted by changes in the family system, or through psychological help.

The data also highlighted the value of continuity of family relationships. The married women in particular experienced less stress and isolation in relation to their multiple roles and responsibilities than what is reported by mainstream North American women in similar involvements.

In general, the findings suggested that the sociocultural expectations, assumptions, and roles described by the women in this study (e.g., the primacy of "familism," self-sacrifice, and placing others' needs above one's own) contribute to the ways in which women are reinforced to remain in positions of subordination to the needs of others at the expense of their development as self-authoring individuals who can determine and control their personal choices.

Transcending the Limits of the Colonial Context

Although it seemed clear that certain cultural elements foster dependency and limit women's development as self-authoring and integrated individuals, the findings of this study show that these limitations co-exist with other elements that allow growth and development to occur. This argument is supported by the finding that 50 percent of the women in the sample described themselves as more self-determining and self-defining than before, better able to articulate and balance the multiple needs and expectations for themselves within their relationships with others. This finding suggests that the sociocultural context, like developmental phenomena, is not static but rather is dynamic and, as such, it contains elements that militate both for and against development of more self-defining and integrated relation individuals. For instance, support and encouragement for women to attain educational and professional achievements and self-sufficiency coexisted in many instances with expectations for their continued subordination to the needs and expectations of their families and/or spouses. As these women recognized that conflict was often an inherent part of the process of transforming the nature of their relationships with others, they challenged the assumptions and expectations that limited their growth. They assumed responsibility for the risk of losing connec-

tions with others and for choices that fell short of their
desire to fulfill all the various wishes for themselves and
for others. The following quote from a 31-year-old single
woman illustrates this point.

> I guess that part of being true and honest to
> oneself involves accepting that being who you
> are and standing by what you believe in and
> need may have as a consequence losing people
> you want to have by your side. But you come
> to a point where you have to decide whether
> you are going to stop being yourself in order
> to please others, and avoid losing their love
> or being true to what you feel you need.

In instances when women challenged their families'
expectations and rejected their values, it seemed that the
emphasis on continuity of family connections implied that
families in fact did not ostracize or reject women who
sought to reintegrate their needs for connection and attachments with their families while becoming more differentiated. This constant reworking and renegotiation of
their differences with their families seemed, in turn, to
promote changes in the relationships among family members.

Concluding Remarks and Areas for Further Study

An area of special concern that evolved from the
findings of this study involves questions concerning the
long-term implications of women's embeddedness in relationships that can foster extreme dependency in terms of
later psychological adjustment. Although some of the
women in this study had been able to transcend this dependency, their enduring inner struggles with self-doubt
and the intense experience of vulnerability leave questions
about possible future difficulties in coping with other life
changes or events. How women resolve their long-standing
histories of dependency on their families and/or spouses is
an area that deserves future longitudinal exploration and
research.

Furthermore, it is crucial to explore how differences
within Puerto Rican society provide different contexts
structuring and shaping developmental processes and goals--
for example, exploring the differential impact of social

class, level of education, and other family characteristics or dynamics and their role in shaping developmental phenomena.

In conclusion it seems that within the social context portrayed by women in this study there are elements that militate for and against the exercise of self-determination and the integration of a more differentiated and integrated relational self in women. Women's embeddedness within a social matrix of family relationships and responsibilities was presented as a source of both strain and strength in women's lives, in the exercise of self-determination, and the pursuit of integration of their needs for separateness and affiliation.

The finding that half of the women in the sample were committed to continue to make room for their need to be recognized as self-authoring individuals with separate needs and goals for personal growth outside the context of their families, even when this involved open conflict, was a hopeful sign for the gradual individual and collective evolution toward a more differentiated and integrated community and society.

REFERENCES

Alonso, I. 1979. "Conjugal role relationship and social networks among 30 Puerto Rican families." Unpublished dissertation, Harvard University, Cambridge, Mass.

Alvarez, M. 1985. "The construing of friendship in adulthood: A structural developmental approach." Unpublished doctoral dissertation, Massachusetts School of Professional Psychology, Dedham, Mass.

Andrade, S. 1982. "Family roles of Hispanic women: Stereotypes, empirical findings and implications for research." In R. E. Zambrana, ed., Latina Women in Transition. New York: Fordham University Press.

Baltes, P., and K. Schaie. 1973. "Life-span developmental research: Retrospects and prospects." In P. Baltes and K. Schaie, eds., Lifespan Developmental Psychology. New York: Academic Press.

Bernal, G., and A. Alvarez. 1983. "Culture and class in the study of families." In J. Hansen, ed., Cultural Perspective in Family Therapy. London: Aspen Publications.

Fanon, F. 1963. The Wretched of the Earth. New York: Grove.

Gilligan, C. 1977. "Women's conceptions of self and morality." Harvard Educational Review 47:481–517.

_____. 1979. "Woman's place in man's life cycle." Harvard Educational Review 49:431–46.

_____. 1982a. In a Different Voice: Psychological Theory and Women's Development. Cambridge: Harvard University Press.

_____. 1982b. Lecture at seminar Female Adolescent Development, Harvard University, Graduate School of Education, Cambridge, Mass.

Hancock, E. 1981. "Women's development in adult life." Unpublished doctoral dissertation, Harvard University, Graduate School of Education, Cambridge, Mass.

Jordan, J. 1984. "Women and empathy." Work in Progress. Wellesley, Mass.: Stone Center Working Paper Series.

Kaplan, A. 1984. "The self in relation: Implications for depression in women." Work in Progress. Wellesley, Mass.: Stone Center Working Paper Series.

Kegan, R. 1982. The Evolving Self: Problems and Process in Human Development. Cambridge: Harvard University Press.

López Garriga, M. 1980. "Estrategias de Auto-Afirmación en Mujeres Puertorriqueñas." In E. Acosta-Belén, ed., La Mujer en la Sociedad Puertorriqueña. Río Piedras: Edición Huracán.

Memmi, A. 1967. The Colonizer and the Colonized. Boston: Beacon.

Miller, J. B. 1984. "Development of women's sense of self." Work in Progress. Wellesley, Mass.: Stone Center Working Paper Series.

———. 1976. Towards a New Psychology of Women. Boston: Beacon.

Muñoz-Hernández, M. 1972. "Hacia un análisis de la clase media en Puerto Rico." In R. Ramírez, B. Levine, and C. Ortiz, eds., Problemas de Desigualdad Social en Puerto Rico. Río Piedras: Edición Librería Internacional.

Muñoz Vazquez, M. 1979. "The effects of role expectations of the marital status of urban Puerto Rican women." In E. Acosta-Belén, ed., The Puerto Rican Woman. New York: Praeger.

Nieves Falcón, L. 1972. Diagnóstico de Puerto Rico. Río Piedras: Editorial Edil.

Pantoja, A. 1980. "Oppression and the Hispanic woman with specific attention to the conditions of Puerto Rican women." Unpublished paper presented at a conference of the Hispanic Student Organization of the University of Connecticut, School of Social Work.

Ramírez, R. 1974. "Cultura de liberación y liberación de cultura." In Centro de Estudios Puertorriqueños: Taller de Cultura. New York: City University of New York.

Seda Bonilla, E. 1973. Social Change and Personality in a Puerto Rican Agrarian Reform Community. New York: Northwestern University Press.

———. 1958. The Normative Pattern of Puerto Rican Family in Various Situational Contexts. New York: Columbia University Press.

Sellytiz, C., L. Wrightsman, and C. Cook. 1976. Research Methods in Social Relations, 3rd edition. New York: Holt, Rinehart and Winston.

Surrey, J. 1985. "The self in relation: A theory of women's development." Work in Progress. Wellesley, Mass.: Stone Center Working Papers Series.

Urdang, S. 1979. Fighting Two Colonialisms: Women in Guinea-Bissau. New York: Monthly Review Press.

Vale, P. 1977. "Appreciación socio-histórica de la familia Puertorriqueña." Unpublished paper presented to the Institute of the Family, Río Piedras, Puerto Rico.

Zambrana, R. 1982. "Conclusions and policy implications." In R. E. Zambrana, ed., Latina Women in Transition. New York: Fordham University Press.

Zavala-Martínez, I. 1981. "Mental health and the Puerto Rican in the United States: A critical literature review and comprehensive bibliography." Unpublished preliminary comprehensive examination project, Department of Psychology, University of Massachusetts, Amherst, Mass.

6

An Exploratory Study of the Expression of Female Sexuality: The Experience of Two Groups of Puerto Rican Women from Different Social Backgrounds

María del Carmen Santos-Ortiz, M.A.
Marya Muñoz Vázquez, Ph.D.

INTRODUCTION

Objectives of Study

The objectives of this research were to understand some of the dimensions of the expression of adult female sexuality such as: (a) several forms of ideological[1] control to which female sexuality is subjected in marriage among a group of Puerto Rican women, and (b) how their social class affects the sexual expression of these women and distinguishes their experiences of inequality and oppression.

We cannot affirm that the constant biological sex drive of men and women has found freedom of expression in the different societies and historical eras. On the contrary, it would be inappropriate to try to understand sexuality without analyzing the historical–social variants that determine it (Cerroni 1976). As examples, we may speculate as to what factors might have led men during the feudal era to be able to own any woman he desired, deriving pleasure from owning her without her consent; or wonder how it came about for certain primitive societies to consider it natural to have relations with several persons; or, on the contrary, for the early Church to advocate sexual abstinence as the only path to salvation; and in Victorian and capitalist societies for a woman to remain a virgin until her marriage. We can also speculate how it happened that man practiced polygamy before and after marriage, or how some societies reduced or diminished a great number of women to dedicate themselves to the sexual trade in order to give pleasure to men. These examples lead us to conclude that the constant biological sex drive of humans, and particularly of women, is controlled, or its forms of expression determined, by the type of society in which it is found (Brochele mimeo; Engels 1977; Tannahill 1980; Wine 1985).

Historical Analysis of Forms of Sexual Domination

In capitalist societies the forms of sexual repression[2] and ideological control proliferate and multiply continuously. Even in marriage, which appears to be a private and free domain, men and women can only reproduce the respective roles that they are assigned in this type of society: a dominant and dominated relationship, in the last instance reducing sex to its reproductive function. These roles are reflected in passive, aggressive, potent, and frigid behaviors, among others (Brochele mimeo; Jaggar and McBride 1985).

In 1945 Wilhelm Reich had already written about the relationship between the repression of sexual expression and neuroticism. Repression via morality, he stated, increases the sexual drive or makes it antisocial. This, in turn, evokes more moral inhibitions and creates particular forms of self-protection in persons via guilt and defense mechanisms. This circle is broken if persons, through analysis (psychotherapy), renew contact with their sexual needs, thereby helping neurotic traits to disappear. Reich criticizes Freud in the sense that the problem cannot be resolved by merely replacing the mechanism of sexual repression with the renunciation of the instinct; it requires the possibility of sexual pleasure corresponding to each age or stage of development of the person. This means, for example, that we can only leave behind infantile or pathogenic desires in adulthood if the path for genital sexual pleasure is open and it can be experienced. Promoting the renunciation of sexual instincts or any other forms of sexual domination can only satisfy and be acceptable to the dominant classes (Reich 1945). The reason for this will be explained later.

Reich adds two other crucial notions to understanding repression and its effects; he agrees with Freud that the content of the unconscious is full of antisocial and cruel impulses, but sustains that they are formed by living in capitalism and repression:

> Every social order creates those character forms which it needs for its preservation. In class society, the ruling class secures its position with the aid of education and the institution of the family, by making its ideology the ruling ideology of all members of society. It is not merely a matter of imposing ideologies, attitudes and concepts. Rather it is a matter of deep-reaching processes in each new generation; of the formation of a psychic structure which corresponds to the existing social order in all strata of the population [in Burghardt 1982, 68].

The second idea, which Reich rescues from a statement made by Freud, states that the unconscious, aside from containing ideologies imposed by the dominant class, contains demands that arise from biological requirements and basic human instincts. Examples are the sexual needs of the adolescent or the needs of the person who is trapped in an unhappy marriage. In other words, when natural urges cannot be satisfied in the contemporary social situation, they are expressed in the unconscious, thereby creating an antagonistic relationship between the urges and desires of the individuals (sexual and others) and social demands. Thus, Reich emphasizes the notion that the unconscious acquires a subversive quality, which is what must be explored by those who wish to question the control that the dominant classes exercise over sexuality (Burghardt 1982).

Throughout history the forms of sexual domination have undergone multiple changes, adding to and altering the ways in which control is manifested in society and in everyday relations. These changes are the product of the ways in which economic and social conditions are transformed through class struggles and technological development. Foucault (1980) analyzes the changes in the mechanisms and forms of control of sexuality from the seventeenth century on. During this century the power of the Church, primarily exercised from the confessional, predominates. The priest or listener acquires a power that regulates and generates mechanisms to dominate any new or different "weakness of the flesh" that is brought into the confessional. In his analysis, Foucault alerts us to the power of the listener and to the fact that talking about sexuality does not necessarily lessen the control of the talker. In some instances it might augment it.

A concrete example of the way in which sexual control was exercised through the confessional during this era is described by Zaretsky in his work, "Female Sexuality and the Catholic Confessional" (1980). The woman in the confessional was talking to the priest about her precarious health, in part due to the many children she had borne, which included the possibility of death upon another birth. Nonetheless, the demands for sexual intercourse by her husband continued as they always had. In the dialogue between this woman and the priest, Zaretsky points out how control was exerted. The only solution posed by the priest consisted of having the woman convince her husband that total abstinence between them was absolutely necessary.

Furthermore, Foucault maintains that since the end of the sixteenth century, the things that were said about sex did not undergo a process of restriction (repression-defenses, censorships, denials). On the contrary they were subjected to a mechanism of increasing incitement (a transformation into discourse, a generation of knowledge, etc.) that cannot be reduced to repression.

In the eighteenth century one of the most valuable social mechanisms of exercising power was to present population growth as an economic and political problem: population as a source of wealth, as manpower or labor power; population as the balance between its own growth and the resources available. In the center of this economic and political problem is sexuality: It was necessary to analyze the rate of growth, the ages of marriage, the illegitimate children, precociousness and the frequency of sexual relations, the number of unmarried persons, the impact of the use of contraceptives, and so on. It was essential for the state to know what was happening with the sexuality of each one of its citizens.

According to Foucault, the situation was similar in the case of children's sexuality. Despite the fact that its existence was denied, a mere glance at the practices, for example, in educational establishments showed that what was being done (separation by sexes, etc.) was based on the assumption that sexuality existed, and that it was precocious, active, and present. The pedagogic institutions started to multiply the forms of discussing this subject--between educators, administrators, parents; through medicine as "nervous disorders"; psychiatry and the organization of criminal justice. Parents were warned about watching their children and the dangers of masturbation. Sexual irregularities were linked to mental illness; from childhood to old age the norm was defined, all possible deviations were described, and pedagogic and medical treatments were organized to control them. The socialization process of children became one of the mechanisms of sexual control used to eliminate the sexual expression of children and adolescents.

Sexuality between husband and wife was rife with rules and regulations; this was the era of prohibition. Among the most serious sins or conduct subject to sanctions in court were the following: adultery, incest, sodomy, "mutual caressing," homosexuality, marriage without parental consent, and bestiality.

What was pursued with this? Foucault states:

> For was this transformation of sex into discourse not governed by the endeavor to expel from reality the forms of sexuality that were not amenable to the strict economy of reproduction: to say no to unproductive activities, to banish casual pleasures, to reduce or exclude practices whose object was not procreation? [1978, 360]

In other words, Foucault is proposing that such mechanisms are generated and aimed at controlling reproduction.

We are aware of Freud's great influence by the end of the nineteenth and through the twentieth century with respect to the idea of sexuality. Most psychiatrists, psychologists, and others thought that sexuality had been restored to its proper place but were unable to see how effective Freud was in giving the study of sexuality and its control a new impetus. Examples are the labeling of some women as hysterical and the psychiatrization of "deviate" pleasures. In other words, although Freud opened the way to the study of sexuality and its repression, a thorough analysis reveals that through his theory, he reproduced the ideologies that control and repress female sexuality.

It is necessary to study the control of sexuality and its proliferation vis-à-vis the struggle that counteracts this power with its subversion. In this sense, Jackson (1983, 1984) submits an important analysis showing how the ideology of sexual freedom, promoted through the science of sexology (taking as an example the work of Havelock Ellis 1913, 1918), was really a reaction to the growing independence of some groups of women during the end of the nineteenth century. What seems to be progressive in Ellis' work in presenting the natural right of women to sexual pleasure within marriage was a form of undermining the growing affective and emotional ties developed between women of the middle class in the United States at that time. This is done by rearguing the marital status as legitimate for sexual expression.

Analyzing Ellis' arguments, Jackson reveals how his entire group of ideas are addressed to maintaining control over female sexuality within the limits imposed by the inequality of the sexes. Ellis states that power and sex are inseparable. He argues in favor of the natural aggressiveness of masculine sexuality, the unconscious inclination of women to agree to relations that go against their will, and that women need to feel pain to experience sexual pleasure, even though they claim they do not. What Ellis' ideas about sexual freedom try to achieve is greater access to the sexuality of women by men, be it through rape, harassment, or their "consent." Ellis also argues that masturbation by women can lead to avoiding sexual relations in marriage, and he states other ideas that clearly tend to control women's sexuality in the direction of yielding to aggression, power, and matrimony.

González Duro (1977) asserts that in postindustrial societies the liberation of sexuality is more theoretical than real. He adds that the requirements of contemporary living get more and more complicated (e.g., less control for the majority of people over work processes, including rising rates of unemployment, double day work for women, increasing rush and stress, breakdown of community ties, increasing violence, etc.). Furthermore, these alienating conditions make it very hard for a person to act spontaneously insofar as sexuality is concerned (as well as other aspects of life), despite the large amount of erotic stimulus that surrounds us. This author delves into the analysis of the forms of the so-called "sexual liberation," such as pornography, the "playboy" phenomenon, and erotic advertising as forms of sexual control and maintaining inequality between the sexes.

This entire concern with sexuality is caused by one basic preoccupation. In Foucault's words, "to ensure population, to reproduce labor capacity, to perpetuate the form of social relations: in short to constitute a sexuality that is economically useful and politically conservative" (1978, 37).

Dominant social classes have always been interested in controlling human reproduction so that the labor force availability (potential work capacity of workers) conforms to the requirements of the dominant form of production. The relative overpopulation resulting from this situation allows the dominant classes to exert control over the workers and maintain at least certain minimum rates of profit. Due to the type of industry, machinery, and equipment developed, modern capitalism presupposes the need for families with fewer children and more skills. Therefore, as a general rule, it is not convenient for dominant social classes to have a high birth rate within advanced capitalist societies. At the same time, there are still a large number of persons (work force) who need jobs. This factor allows them to control the salaries of the workers and to weaken labor movements, pitting the unemployed against the employed. From the dominant classes' perspective, a high birth rate presupposes overpopulation, which can tax the state's ability to meet its needs, creating multiple "social problems" and a potential for political organization that is contrary to the dominant classes' interests. Furthermore, the needs of the dominant classes to increase or reduce the persons potentially available for employment are also met through the control that they exercise over the migratory processes (N. García, personal communication, October 17, 1987).

Besides, limiting women's work to the domestic field is indirectly tied to the production of commodities (all things that are produced and are sold to obtain profit), through the function they fulfill of replacing the energy of the workers (work force) by cooking, ironing, and so on, so that men can effectively exercise their day-to-day functions. Women also fulfill a primary function in the reproduction of the future labor power. Women perform these chores without getting paid for them, which allows the dominant social classes to obtain higher profit rates by paying lower salaries, since the reproduction of the work force is cheaper because of women's unpaid labor (Larguía and Domoulin 1976).[3]

The power held over human reproduction, exerted through the control of female sexuality and the subjugation of women to domestic work, is linked and intertwined through diverse ideological practices. A single example will suffice: Man's jealousy exerts control over female sexuality and over the space women can occupy--the home.

Puerto Rican Society and Hypothesis

An analysis of the forms of controlling the sexuality of Puerto Rican women would reveal the ideologies and mechanisms described in the previous paragraphs (Nieves-Falcón 1972; Seda Bonilla 1976; Wolf 1972). The Church has played an overwhelming role by imposing its rules and punishments on the sexuality that does not conform to the function of procreation (Ramírez de Arellano 1983; Mock 1986). In addition, psychology, psychiatry, and medicine, as well as the science of sexology have played important roles in the limits and ideas imposed on sexuality (see for example Calderón 1984).

Moreover, the proliferation of erotic stimuli is obvious, be it through television, magazines, movies, or other media. The message of pseudoliberation is manifested in this stimuli. Some of the forms of controlling the population and the methods used have been more dramatic in Puerto Rico than in other countries. Two examples are: (1) the first experiments with contraceptive pills were performed on poor Puerto Rican women starting in 1956, and its subsequent mass use was carried out without considering what has subsequently been learned. Studies have shown its damaging effects on health, for example, its relationship with thrombo-embolic disease, and an increase in the probability of acquiring cancer (Epstein 1979). (2) The second example of methods of population control in our country is the policy of massive sterilization of women in childbearing years, which made Puerto Rico a country with one of the highest rates of sterilized women in the world. The rate is 48.8 percent for married women and women living consensually, and 32.5 percent for the female population between 15 and 49 years of age

(Dávila 1986). This subject has been researched by Ramírez de Arellano (1983), Stycos (1954), Vázquez Calzada (1973), and Vázquez Calzada and Morales del Valle (1982).

To counteract this power, feminists in Puerto Rico, as well as in other countries, have soundly called attention to the notion that sex is political. This struggle has been undertaken recently in Puerto Rico through the analysis of day-to-day resistance (Silva Bonilla 1982; Muñoz Vazquez and Silva Bonilla 1985), and the work advanced by feminist groups on issues such as reproductive health, domestic violence, sexual harassment, massive sterilization, and other issues.

There is no single, valid, universal strategy available to the dominant social classes that can aim to control all sexual manifestations. The central idea of reducing sex to reproduction does not include the different objectives employed in sexual policies that concern the two sexes, the different age groups, and social classes. More has been written on this subject concerning the two sexes, which is one of the reasons why we aim our study at understanding the relationship between social classes and the control of sexuality (Muñoz Vázquez 1983).

From this wide variety of relationships of power and sexual repression, psychology through research can contribute to the understanding of several concrete forms of ideologic control in the everyday practices of persons. It can also study the sexual attitudes as they reflect this control and analyze aspects of the unconscious that can reveal challenges and resistance to the dominant ideology and repression. This can be achieved by analyzing what persons state about their experiences and what these statements imply. The purpose is not to point out "deviations," but to evidence the ideologic and repressive forms of control.

To analyze the statements or discourse of the individuals is analogous to understanding how they construct their ideas and attitudes signified in this discourse. The organization of the statement is presented as institutionalized behavior that is limited by a social and economic system (Silva et al. 1984).

In addition to the analysis of the discourse, psychological research in this field can also contribute, through the use of quantitative methods, by suggesting differences with respect to the experiences of groups within various social positions, pursuant to gender, class, age, and others.

For the proposed study, two working hypotheses were formulated:

(a) The central idea of reducing sex to reproduction[4] and to forcing female inequality will be present in women's statements of their sexual experience, as will also be their resistance to this ideological control.

(b) The aim to control working-class women's sexuality is more serious, powerful, and oppressive than for women in administrative or managerial positions. This hypothesis is based on the general assumption that the aim of the social dominant classes—to control working-class women's sexuality—is one part of the domination directed at that class and the work force it presupposes, more so than at women of their own class or women in management or administrative positions.

METHODOLOGY

Subjects

In order to generate data on the subject of ideological control of sexuality and social class, 20 married adult women were interviewed. It was thought that their civil status allowed greater legitimacy for talking about the subject at hand, in addition to the fact 52.4 percent of all Puerto Rican women are legally married (1980 census). They were between 23 and 40 years of age, from two social backgrounds: working class (employees in textile factories) and managers (in management, administrative positions, or owners of small businesses). Participants were selected based on their accessibility. Gaining access to a representative sample that would also include housewives implied greater costs than what was economically feasible for the investigators at the time.

Procedure

To obtain the information, an interview was designed with over 100 open questions involving demographic data, views of their marriage, work, education, themselves, men, and areas related to the expression of sexuality.

The following are examples of some questions included in the interview:

When did you experience your first sexual intercourse?
With whom? What were your feelings at the time?
How frequently would you like to have sexual intercourse?
Have you ever pretended that you achieved orgasm? What
    were the reasons?
What is your opinion on sexual relations between women?
How would you describe the Puerto Rican male?

To guarantee greater ease, no tape recorder was used and the information was written in the questionnaire designed. The average duration of the interview was two and one-half hours.

Working-class women were contacted at their work place in a textile factory through a person known to the researchers who knew the owner of the factory. Managerial women were contacted through other professional or administrative people known to the investigators.

Both groups were approached as to their willingness to participate in this study. After an appointment was made, they were interviewed at their work place or at their home, at their convenience. Most of the interviews were carried out by the investigators. Three were performed by three trained undergraduate students.

The information obtained through the interviews was analyzed using two approaches. This method would help us in the discussion of the ways ideology is manifested by social class: the overt expression of and resistances to the dominant ideology, including unconscious resistance.

We began by analyzing the explicit content of women's answers to the interview. Their answers were placed into categories, according to response. For example, women who expressed that they suffered no inhibitions in their sexual relations were placed in one category, women who mentioned inhibitions in anal sex were placed in another, and so forth. A computation by class of the frequencies, percentages, and averages (when possible, for example, frequency of sexual relations per month) of their explicit answers was carried out. The percentages were analyzed using a Fischer's Exact Test to obtain possible statistically significant differences between groups.

A second approach to the data gathered was carried out based on the assumptions presented in this work about unconscious processes and social order. Specifically, we used this approach to try to identify the possible resistances to such control imposed on women's sexuality. Some examples are: (a) the contradictions stated by women at various times in the interviews; or (b) subtle expressions that would convey frustrations, demands, or unfulfilled desires; and (c) sexual fantasies, sickness, or emotional symptomatology that has been discussed in the literature as resistance to oppressive living conditions (Silva Bonilla 1982).

RESULTS AND DISCUSSION

The results were organized for discussion in the following areas: (a) overt expressions or conscious expressions that reflect the dominant ideology, which aims to control female sexuality; (b) expressions that reflect women's conscious resistance to the control exerted by the dominant ideology to their sexuality; and (c) women's unconscious resistances to the control of sexuality.

Overt Expression of the Dominant Ideology

In general terms, we found that the sexual expression of interviewed women was subject to the parameters imposed by the dominant ideology: sex is for reproduction, woman's sexual behavior should be passive, and the imposition of virginity before marriage. In most instances which illustrate ideological subjugation and repression in their sexual practices as expressed by the women, the experience of working women is defined as one of greater oppression than the experience of professional women.

Sex for Reproduction. The ideology of sex for reproduction is suggested in the views held by the majority of the women as expressed in their rejection of lesbianism, oral and anal sex, and masturbatory practices as accepted sexual expressions. All these practices exclude reproduction.

A strong disapproval of sexual relations between women was expressed by a majority of managers (60%) and 90 percent of the working women. Their way of thinking was that these types of sexual relations are denigrating or unjustified; they pointed out that "that's what men are for." Nonetheless, 40 percent of the managers and 10 percent of the workers said that they respected the decision of lesbian women to be so. Lesbianism has historically been one of the most sanctioned sexual practices, as it is directly in contradiction to reducing sex to a reproductive function and therefore greatly limits the control of the dominant social classes over reproduction.

The areas which appear to be of greatest inhibition when having intercourse are anal and oral sex, as seen in Table 6.1, where 60 percent of all women had inhibitions as to both practices.

Table 6.1

Percentage Distribution of the Inhibition and/or Taboos Indicated by Interviewed Workers and Managers

Inhibition or Taboo	Workers No.	%	Managers No.	%	Total No.	%
None	1	10	3	30	4	20
Anal sex	2	20	4	40	6	30
Oral sex	2	20	0	--	2	10
Anal sex and oral sex	3	30	1	10	4	20
Talk about sexuality	2	20	0	--	2	10
Very conscious of body	0	--	1	10	1	5
Take initiative in sexual act	0	--	1	10	1	5
TOTAL	10	100	10	100	20	100

The reasons stated for rejecting these sexual practices were the following: physical discomfort, feelings of repugnance and disgust, and anal intercourse was linked to latent homosexual tendencies in men and the possibility of acquiring a disease. One of the working-class women expressed the following with respect to oral sex: "I have never suffered that and I hope I don't have to do it. Women with a penis in their mouths, that's awful! I find that brings about diseases. If I do it someday, I'll do it with one of those" (she explained, pointing to a condom).

Related to the same theme, some of the managers expressed the following: "It disgusts me; just to think of it makes me want to vomit. I think of bacterias"; "I don't like to do it, it displeases me, I avoid it, but yes, he can do it."

This instance of their behavior reflects the limits imposed on sexuality, reminding us that during the last two centuries medicine and public health have combined the subjects of cleanliness and asepsis with the fear of sexually transmitted diseases, intermingling reality with the control of sexual conduct (Foucault 1978).

Another aspect related to the ideology of sexuality for reproduction was reflected in their views on masturbation, particularly among women workers; 100 percent of working-class women compared to 40 percent of the managers at the moment of the interview expressed that they did not engage in masturbation ($p < .05$). Furthermore, 70 percent of the workers and 10 percent of the managers indicated that they had never masturbated ($p < .05$). This reflects a marked difference by social sector with regard to this practice. Some of these women associated masturbation only with men. In relation to this, some workers expressed the following: "Ugh, that's filthy. Only sick women do that." "Regularly, that's done by men." "I don't think that's important to women." "If you have a man, that's what he's for." "To me, none, for men it's important because they get excited rapidly. Women don't." On the subject of masturbation, a manager stated the following: "It's ugly in women. It's common among men. It's a routine in their daily life. That's part of man's formation. They get excited when they see a woman in jeans and they go to the bathroom."

The ideology implied in this statement reflects a belief in a greater sexual urge in men and less control of sexual impulses than women and a justification of women's inequality. Also reflected in the comment of "sick women" is the relationship forced by the Church and psychiatry between disease or sickness and the performance of masturbation (Foucault 1980). Furthermore, in workers, masturbation is linked mainly to the absence of a husband. This finding corresponds to Jackson's (1983) analysis on the control imposed upon women's masturbatory practices. According to what they expressed, none of the workers presently masturbated, alleging principally, "what's the use if you have a husband?" Quite the contrary, 60 percent of the managers indicated that they masturbated, either as part of sexual intercourse or as another alternative to satisfy their sexual desires ($p < .05$).

We do not believe that differences in their present masturbation practices are due to a difference between these two groups of women in the monthly frequency of sexual intercourse. The average obtained for the managerial group was 8.7 sexual intercourses per month (it fluctuated between 2 and 16 times per month); in workers the average was 10.2 sexual intercourses per month (it fluctuated between 2 and 30 times per month). Nonetheless, an interesting finding is the wide dispersion reported by the women on the frequency of sexual intercourse (see Table 6.2).

Passive Sexual Behavior and Virginity

The control exercised to enforce feminine sexual passivity was reflected in other statements made by the participants about various aspects of their sexual practices. This ideology is dramatically manifested by the fact that 84 percent of all women in both groups expressed that the husband is the person who takes the initiative to have sexual intercourse.

Related to the imposed sexual passivity of women is the high percentage (60 percent of workers and 50 percent of the managers) who expressed that they pretended to have an orgasm. The reasons pointed out for pretending were wanting to quickly terminate the sexual intercourse, and so that the husband could feel pleased and satisfied. Rubin (1976) states that when the latter occurs, sexual intercourse becomes not an act of one's own pleasure or shared pleasure but rather a form of pleasing a man, a duty, or resignation. However, on the contrary, in the first instance it can be a way of resisting to prolong a relation that they wish to terminate and cannot express so directly.

Another piece of evidence that suggests the lack of women's spontaneity in their sexual expression and that the workers confront a more oppressive situation is the

Table 6.2

Percentage Distribution of Monthly Frequency of
Sexual Relations Informed by Workers and Managers

Frequency	Workers No.	%	Managers No.	%	Total No.	%
2	2	20	1	10	3	15
3	0	0	1	10	1	5
4	2	20	1	10	3	15
6	0	0	2	20	2	10
7	1	10	0	0	1	5
8	1	10	1	10	2	10
10	1	10	0	0	1	5
12	0	0	1	10	1	5
15	1	10	2	20	1	5
16	0	0	1	10	1	5
20	1	10	0	10	1	5
30	1	10	0	0	1	5
TOTAL	10	100	10	100	10	200

following: 80 percent of the women workers, compared to
10 percent of the managers, expressed that men need to
have more sexual intercourse mainly because it is "inherent to men," while women need more quality ($p < .05$).
This could reflect, as stated previously, an ideology of
men's greater sex drive, but also that workers have less
control over the physical and emotional quality that they
wish to have in their sexual relations. Additionally, the
inhibition of verbal expression was greater for the working-
class sector, although it was not significant ($p < .07$).
When asked with whom they talked about their sexual experiences, 90 percent of the women managers responded
with friends and husbands. Half (50 percent) of the
women workers indicated that they conversed with friends;

the other half (50 percent) said with no one. An interesting fact is that none of the women from the working class stated that they conversed about sexual matters with their husbands. Women from the working sectors usually expressed that they were kept ignorant of sexual matters while growing up, which helps to explain how control is imposed with more force upon them.

Also, the fact that working-class women confronted, in general, a more oppressive experience than women managers with regard to their relationship with their husbands partially explains their greater enforced passivity. Men from the working class are themselves subjected to greater violence than men from the management sectors, and such violence is turned, in many instances, toward women. Forty percent of the workers mentioned dissatisfaction with their husbands because of their fights; 20 percent said they had problems because of their husband's drunkenness. One said her husband kept a constant watch over her, almost to the point of being his prisoner. Altogether, working-class women described experiences that were harsher and more overtly violent than those expressed by the women who were managers.

Regarding women's claim to having sex without having children, which became part of the birth control movement at the turn of the century, almost all of the women interviewed stated they use a contraceptive method. However, birth control technology developed in a class-controlled context has not offered women the adequate social resources to explore its implications fully. Most of the women interviewed have adopted the method preferred by the state to control the birth rate: 50 percent of the workers and 40 percent of the managers are sterilized. The most frequently used contraceptive method is the pill: 20 percent of the workers and 10 percent of the managers use it. Only 10 percent of the managers and none of the workers indicated using prophylactics, and 10 percent of the managers and none of the workers indicated using the rhythm method. Most of the women interviewed said they were pleased with the contraceptive methods chosen. They raised no objections to the fact that the responsibility for birth control fell almost entirely upon them, or to the use of a drastic and irreversible method such as sterilization.

Other sexual practices described by interviewed women reflected the predominance of the ideology that

women should remain virgins until they marry, a conduct
basically controlled by instilling guilt and maintaining
women ignorant. Most of the women interviewed (70 percent) stated that their first coitus was at the time they
married. Moreover, only 30 percent of the workers and
60 percent of the managers expressed enjoying it. The
rest experienced negative or mixed feelings. The women,
during this experience, identified feelings of guilt, shame,
ignorance, and mixed emotions, partly satisfactory and
unsatisfactory.

Overt Expression of Resistance to the Control of Sexuality

In addition, intertwined with expressions that reflect ideological control and instances of oppression from
their husbands, these women individually, particularly a
group of them from each class, expressed ways in which
they gained control over some aspects of their sexuality.
For example, the majority of them reported enjoying sexual intercourse. All of them expressed reaching orgasm.
The opinion of 80 percent of these women was that reaching orgasm during sexual intercourse is important. More
than half of the managers (80 percent) expressed themselves in favor of oral sex (versus 30 percent of the
workers, $p < .05$). Some stated, "It's real nice, it's part
of sexual intercourse, it's normal." A group of them, as
stated before, demonstrated respect for lesbian relations.
Furthermore, these women expressed themselves openly during the interview, discussing the theme with relative ease.
At the same time, the demands made by these women of
their husbands became evident: that they be less selfish,
womanizing, and more warm, giving, considerate, affectionate, tender, caring, and loving in the sexual relations and for them to "take more time" to display these
characteristics (although they did not always express
their desires directly to their husbands). These expressions and others previously described, if compared to demands made by feminists in the past decades, move us to
conclude that the recovery of sexuality, reflected in these
women's expressions, represents years of social struggle
for female revindication (Jackson 1983).

Unconscious Resistance to the
Control of Sexuality

As previously stated, women's expression of the relationship between unsatisfactory conditions that they experience within their marriages, exploitation and oppression
at work, and their sexual experiences, due to ideological
concealments and repression, are expressed in subtle and
unconscious actions. These form part of the resistance
offered by these women to confront the conditions of oppression in which they live (Reich 1945; Burghardt 1982;
Silva 1984). In the following paragraphs we will discuss
certain actions and situations described in the interviews
that we additionally interpret as part of the complex
range of resistances.

Several expressions made by these women implied
some level of awareness of the existing links between the
various aspects of their material living conditions. An
example of this is the phrase stated about having difficulty in reaching an orgasm when one is "very angry,
hostile, and tense," or "if he rushes through it." More
than half of the women interviewed stated that they preferred foreplay and a feeling of togetherness to penetra-
tion, thus exposing through these manifestations their sexual and affectionate needs. One of them stated that she
took no sexual initiative because of marital difficulties,
expressing it in the following way: "If I were allowed,
I would say that lately I don't like it, and I remember
the problems and that influences a lot. A person that is
fighting all day with you and then comes to look for you
as if you were a doll . . . I tell him."

The protests expressed by these women, which are
directed toward men, were also evoked when we questioned them about views of Puerto Rican men. Seventy
percent of the managers and 80 percent of the workers
described them with negative characteristics: "macho,"
egocentric, womanizer, and others. Moreover, 70 percent
of the managers and 30 percent of workers stated that
Puerto Rican men know very little about female sexuality.

Other findings, which can be linked to unconscious
forms of protest, are the contents of their sexual fantasies.
In total, 85 percent of the women interviewed expressed
that they fantasized and 41.2 percent of those fantasies
were about sexual relations with other men. In some of

them it is possible that dissatisfaction, due to oppressive conditions in the marriage and sexual control, moved them to try, although only in their thoughts, to find a more satisfying experience while breaking away from the most rigid schemes imposed by the dominant ideology. Furthermore, some forms of resistance are also in complex ways intertwined with the dominant ideology. For example, we found that in one woman's fantasy, sex and violence were linked.

Jackson (1983, 1984), as stated previously, explains that control of male sexuality is primarily obtained through linkages between aggressiveness, violence, and sexuality. This is achieved by implanting ideas such as that men should be sexually aggressive and women should resist, otherwise men would lose interest. In Puerto Rico, there exists the idea that promulgates that a man who does not mistreat his wife does not love her.

Emotional and physical symptomatology has been described in current literature as a sign of resistance offered unconsciously to oppressive living conditions (Silva Bonilla 1982). A surprisingly large majority of women interviewed, and particularly women workers, expressed that they have at times manifested some types of illness or concerns about their health. The information offered by them regarding their concerns is compiled in Table 6.3.

Table 6.3

Percentage Distribution of Conditions Related to Illness Informed by Workers and Managers

Conditions	Workers	Managers	Total
Headaches	80	40	60 (p=.08)
Depression	90	50	70 (p=.07)
Anxiety	50	60	55 (NSD)
Nervousness	90	10	50 (p<.05)

When we asked them if the health conditions mentioned affected their sexual lives, 70 percent of both groups answered in the affirmative. They said pain, physical discomfort, and avoiding sexual intercourse are some of the consequences of these conditions.

In conclusion, we think that the information presented illustrates various concrete forms in which ideological control is exerted on adult Puerto Rican women's daily sexual practices. Furthermore, the content of these women's conscious and unconscious resistance to this control is suggested. We have also presented evidence that supports our hypothesis: The different material conditions imposed upon the working class define the experience of working-class women's sexual expression as that of greater oppression, being more subjected to control mechanisms imposed through the dominant ideology on women's sexuality than on women managers.

Trying to understand the relationship that exists between socioeconomic conditions, the oppression of women, and the control of female sexuality is one of the steps to understanding our position in society and contributing to its transformation.

This work represents an initial step in trying to understand the complexity of adult women's sexual experiences in Puerto Rico. Further investigative work can be geared to: (1) unraveling more precisely the interplay between the ideology of sex for procreation and the oppressive conditions that women confront in their marriages; (2) the socialization processes used by different social classes during earlier stages of development (e.g., childhood and adolescence) to instill the dominant ideology; and (3) the experiences of other adult women (e.g., single, divorced, or elderly) of various social backgrounds.

NOTES

1. An articulated system of representations (opinions, ideas, myths) and practices that make domination and resistance to domination possible, according to where it comes from: the dominant classes or the classes being dominated (Althusser 1984).

2. Repression in this context refers to the mechanism based on violence (including censure, negative sanctions, exclusions, selection, etc.) that lend support to social domination (Althusser 1984).

162 / Santos-Ortiz and Muñoz Vazquez

3. Another important aspect of this analysis that requires further study is the function women serve by rendering sexual services to the men, such as in the prostituted relationship. We refer to a relationship with prostitutes as a "prostituted" relationship in order to emphasize the participation of the male as well as the female in this situation.

4. Several reasons why the dominant classes continue to practice such an ideology could be to enforce less frequency of the sexual relations, less pleasure, more conformity, less questioning, and so forth.

REFERENCES

Althusser, L. 1984. Ideología y Aparatos Ideológicos del Estado. Buenos Aires: Ediciones Nueva Visión.

Brochelle, C. Mimeograph. Apuntes sobre la sexualidad, el amor, la belleza y el matrimonio en el orden burgués.

Burghardt, S. 1982. The Other Side of Organizing. Cambridge, Mass.: Schenkman.

Calderón, M. C. 1984. "La mujer en la psicoterapia: Un estudio exploratorio sobre la teoría y la práctica de un grupo de psicoterapistas en Puerto Rico." Tesis de Maestría inédita. Departmento de Psicología, Universidad de Puerto Rico: Río Piedras, P.R.

Cerroni, M. C. 1976. La Relación Hombre Mujer en la Sociedad Burguesa. Madrid: Abad Editores.

Dávila, A. L. 1986. Experiencias con otros contraceptivos entre mujeres esterilizadas. Versión preliminar, manuscrito inédito.

Ellis, H. 1913. Studies in the Psychology of Sex. Vol. 1-6. Philadelphia: F. A. Davis.

_____. 1918. The Erotic Rights of Women. London: British Society for the Study of Sex Psychology (Publication #5).

Engels, F. 1977. El Origen de la Familia de la Propiedad Privada y del Estado. Madrid: Editorial Fundamentos.

Epstein, S. 1979. The Politics of Cancer. New York: Anchor Books.

Foucault, M. 1980. The History of Sexuality. New York: Vintage.

Gonzáles Duro, E. 1977. Represión Sexual y Dominación. Madrid: Abad Editores.

Jackson, M. 1983. "Sexual liberation or social control?" Women's Studies International Forum 6, 1:1-17.

_____. 1984. "Sexology and the social construction of male sexuality (Havelock Ellis)." In L. Conbeney et al., eds., The Sexuality Papers: Male Sexuality and the Social Control of Women. London: Hutchinson.

Jaggar, A. M., and W. L. McBride. 1985. "Reproduction as Male Ideology." Women Studies International Forum 8, 3:185-96.

Larguía, I., and J. Domoulin. 1976. Hacia una ciencia de la liberación de la mujer. Barcelona: Editorial Anagrama.

Mock-Montes, G. 1986. Conceptos básicos de la sexualidad humana. San Juan, P.R.

Muñoz Vázquez, M. 1983. "Psicología de la mujer: resumen crítico y alternativas." Manuscrito inédito.

Muñoz Vázquez, M., and R. Silva Bonilla. 1985. "El hostigamiento sexual: sus manifestaciones y características en la sociedad en los centros de empleo y los centros de estudio." Disponible en el Centro de Investigaciones Sociales, Universidad de Puerto Rico, Río Piedras, P.R.

Nieves-Falcón, L. 1972. Diagnóstico de Puerto Rico. Río Piedras: Editorial Edil.

Ramírez de Arellano, A. B., and C. Seipp. 1983. Colonialism, Catholicism and Contraception: A history of birth control in Puerto Rico. University of North Carolina Press.

Reich, W. 1945. The Sexual Revolution. New York: Simon and Schuster.

Rubin, L. B. 1976. Worlds of Pain. New York: Basic Books.

Seda Bonilla, E. 1976. Cultural Character Types: The Puerto Rican Personae. Universidad de Puerto Rico, Colegio de Ciencias Sociales.

Silva Bonilla, R. 1982. "Amas de casa en la fuerza de trabajo asalariado en Puerto Rico: un estudio del lenguage como mediación ideológica en la reificación de la consciencia femenina." Tesis doctoral inédita: The Union for Experimenting Colleges and Universities, Mid-West Division.

Silva Bonilla, R., I. Alegría, A. Colón, and N. Torres. 1984. "El análisis del contenido de la práctica discursiva, sus alcances para la investigación y la práctica profesional en el campo de la psicología." Manuscrito inédito, Proyecto CERES, Centro de Investigaciones Sociales, Universidad de Puerto Rico, Río Piedras, P.R.

Stycos, J. M. 1954. "Female sterilization in Puerto Rico." Eugenics Quarterly 1, 2 (June).

Tannahill, R. 1980. Sex in History. New York: Stein and Day.

U.S. Department of Commerce, Bureau of the Census. 1982. 1980 Census of Population, vol. 1, Puerto Rico.

Vázquez Calzada, J. L. 1973. "La esterilización femenina en Puerto Rico." Revista de Ciencias Sociales, Universidad de Puerto Rico 17, 3.

Vázquez Calzada, J. L., and Z. Morales Del Valle. 1982. "Female sterilization in Puerto Rico and its demo-

graphic effectiveness." Puerto Rico Health Sciences
Journal 1, 2.

Wine, J. D. 1985. "Women's sexuality." International
Journal of Women's Studies 8, 1:58–63.

Wolf, K. L. 1972. "Growing up and its price in three
Puerto Rican subcultures." In E. Fernández, ed.,
Portrait of a Society. Río Piedras: University of
Puerto Rico.

Zaretsky, E. 1980. "Female sexuality and the Catholic
confessional." Signs: Journal of Women in Culture
and Society 6, 1:176–84.

7

Puerto Rican Women's Cross-Cultural Transitions: Developmental and Clinical Implications

Lillian Comas-Díaz, Ph.D.

INTRODUCTION

Puertorriqueñas' Role in Their Culture

The Puerto Rican woman plays a central role in her culture. Within the native Taíno society, females enjoyed the power characteristic of the matriarchal system (Steiner 1974). With the advent of a Spanish and African presence on the island, the Borincanas intermarried, initiating the mixed ethnic heritage of the Puerto Rican population (Comas-Díaz 1982). Later on, as newly emerged Puertorriqueñas, the females fought side by side with their male counterparts during political struggles. Currently, they actively shape their country's national character. To illustrate, Puerto Rico has a higher percentage of women lawyers, professors, doctors, politicians, and spiritual healers than any other Latin American country (Steiner 1974). However, women's position is far from being ideal. Acosta-Belén and Sjostrom (1979) state that although the involvement and participation of Puerto Rican women in education and the professions exceed that of other Latin American women, Puertorriqueñas still lack the necessary support from the cultural and socioeconomic structures to better utilize the educational opportunities available to them in fostering their development as equal members of society.

Once they migrate to the continental United States, Puertorriqueñas continue to play a paramount role in the

166

development of their community. For instance, Sanchez-Korrol (1980) asserts that the Puerto Rican woman in New York has emerged as a vibrant woman, helping to support her family, both emotionally and financially. However, this is not an easy transition. Puerto Rican women in the United States confront new cultural expectations from the U.S. society. First, they become a minority group, struggling with ethnocultural as well as socioeconomic conflicts. Furthermore, Puertorriqueñas face multiple types of discrimination, which are based on ethnicity, gender, socioeconomic class, and race. Thus, migration and the resulting membership in an ethnic minority group with sociocultural difficulties have created conflicts for Puerto Rican women.

This chapter discusses Puerto Rican women's cross-cultural transitions and their developmental and clinical implications. It also presents the model explaining the cross-cultural transition. These models are examined within the unique context of Puerto Rican migration. Moreover, the psychological aspects of cross-cultural transition, including the relationship between the transition and developmental stages, are discussed. Special emphasis is given to the psychological aspects of the cross-cultural transition and its effects on Puerto Rican women's identity. The chapter also examines the particular stressors that Puertorriqueñas face while coping with migration and acculturation. These stressors, translated into feelings of powerlessness, low self-esteem, and depression, appear to partly explain the high incidence of psychopathology found among some Puerto Rican women. Furthermore, the chapter presents clinical case material and treatment interventions addressing these issues.

The Puerto Rican Migration to
the Continental United States

The migration of Puerto Ricans to the United States is a complex phenomenon. Puerto Ricans tend to migrate for a variety of reasons ranging from economic, political, social, educational, health-related, and other personal factors, to the quest for adventure. The Puerto Rican migration dates back to the nineteenth century. The main motivation for migrating at that time was political. After 1917, when Puerto Ricans received U.S. citizenship, the

impetus for migrating was mainly an economic one. Due to
the political relationship between Puerto Rico and the
United States, a forced migration has developed. The high
unemployment and underemployment prevalent on the island
have led the Puerto Rican government to advertise migration as a flexible means of earning a living. The Puerto
Rican Department of Labor has worked closely with U.S.
farm and capital owners on this endeavor. Those who cannot find jobs in Puerto Rico are forced to migrate. As a
result, most of those migrating have limited education,
skills, and resources. Accordingly, the migration has
been a massive one (around 2 million), placing one-third
of the Puerto Rican population outside their country (U.S.
Commission on Civil Rights 1976).

In addition to economic reasons, Puerto Ricans also
migrate in search of better education and health services,
and as a means of coping with personal and family problems. For example, it is socially acceptable for Puerto
Ricans to send their children to live with relatives residing on the mainland when they are exhibiting behavioral
problems. Thus, regardless of reasons for migrating,
Puerto Rican women's gender roles tend to be affected.
Likewise, among the general population, cultural transitions and the subsequent cultural adaptation affect women's
gender roles. O'Reilly (1985) states that, for women, the
cultural transition is a transforming process. She argues
that most (im)migrant men desire to return to the old country and the old ways because they had status in their
homelands merely because of their male gender. On the
contrary, low-income women prefer to stay in the United
States, even though they have to struggle with the doble
jornada (double day, i.e., performing both the household
tasks and working outside the home to meet their families'
economic needs). They prefer to stay, albeit paying a
high price, because they achieve more autonomy--something
hard to obtain in their countries of origin. Likewise,
Puertorriqueñas who migrate to the mainland tend to be
actively engaged in the cultural change process of their
society due to the availability of opportunities and the
existence of more egalitarian sex roles. Puerto Rican
males tend to feel more comfortable within their traditional
sex roles and, therefore, are less invested in the transculturation process (Comas-Díaz 1988). This situation can
generate marital as well as family problems, placing the
female in a vulnerable position for the development of emotional problems.

In discussing the Puerto Rican migration to the United States, Gomez (1982) has presented a series of categories describing the various Puerto Rican patterns of migration. They are as follows:

1. Islanders. Puerto Ricans who have permanent residence in Puerto Rico. Occasionally they "migrate" to the United States for business or entertainment, to seek specialized education or health services, or to visit relatives.

2. Newcomers. Puerto Ricans who have been forced or have chosen to migrate to the continental United States for prolonged periods. They migrate primarily for socioeconomic, educational, and/or emotional reasons.

3. Merry-go-rounders. Puerto Ricans who commute back and forth between the island and the mainland through a migratory revolving door.

4. Continental Puerto Ricans. Puerto Ricans born in the continental United States or those who during their infancy or childhood settled on the mainland with their parents or extended family. They have been labeled New York Ricans (from New York), Chicago Ricans (from Chicago), Boston Ricans (from Boston), and so on.

5. Unsettled Ricans. Puerto Ricans with pervasive anomie, whereby nomadism is prevalent because they feel uncomfortable in either Puerto Rico or on the mainland.

Gomez also mentioned several other types not included in the typology. These include educated Puerto Ricans who tend to engage in social change, Puerto Ricans without a sense of ethnic identity, and Puerto Ricans who are political dissidents. Clearly, these particular patterns of migration have different developmental and clinical implications.

The type and process of migration experienced by Puerto Ricans differs from that of other ethnic groups who (im)migrated to the United States. Continuous, two-way migration provides a means of communication between Puerto Ricans on the island and Puerto Ricans in the continental United States. This is partially related to the dream of return that almost all Puerto Ricans foster when they are residing on the mainland. In fact, a significant portion of Puerto Ricans in their homeland have previously lived on the mainland. In addition to experiencing culture

shock on the mainland, Puerto Ricans also undergo adjustment difficulties when they return to the island. Pacheco
and his associates (1979) found that migrants returning to
Puerto Rico experienced difficulties with their self-esteem
and self-concept, with relationships with significant others,
and in their transactions with others, plus an alteration
in their perception of their environment. The prevalence
of migration and reverse migration among Puerto Ricans is
so high that a common joke states that there are more
Puerto Ricans in the air at any one time than on earth
(Steiner 1974). Thus, two-way migration adds to the complexity of the Puerto Rican cross-cultural transition.

PSYCHOLOGICAL ASPECTS OF
CROSS-CULTURAL TRANSITIONS

Migration involves much more than the physical move.
It is a transitional experience that affects the individual's
behaviors, feelings, and values, as well as cognitions. It
is also a pervasive condition that influences the whole
family system, even generations after the move (Sluzki
1979). Therefore, it is of crucial importance to understand the different facets and dynamics characteristic of
the cross-cultural transition process.

Cross-cultural translocation generally involves a sequence of stages. Adler's (1975) developmental sequence
of culture shock explains the transitional experience. This
model suggests the specific psychological, cultural, and
social dynamics that emerge during culture shock. The
model also implies that a successful cross-cultural transition should result in the movement of personality and identity to a new consciousness of values, attitudes, and
understandings. The five stages of this model are:

1. Contact. The migrant is still functionally integrated
   with his/her own culture.
2. Disintegration. Differences become increasingly notice-
   able. Alienation, depression, and withdrawal give
   rise to disintegration of personality and confusion
   over individual identity.
3. Reintegration. The second culture is rejected through
   anger and rebellion, thus asserting one's self and
   increasing self-esteem. This stage may be the point
   of choice, that is, returning home or moving closer to
   a resolution of difficulties.

4. <u>Autonomy</u>. The individual is able to culturally negotiate the different situations. This stage is characterized by the development of appropriate coping
skills in the second culture.
5. <u>Independence</u>. This stage is marked by attitudes,
emotions, and behaviors that are independent, but not
devoid of cultural influence. Thus, social, psychological, and cultural differences are accepted and
enjoyed.

This model is applicable to Puerto Rican women when
sociopolitical and cultural factors are considered. For instance, in a clinical study of Puerto Rican women, Comas-
Díaz (1984, 1985) found that they were expressing feelings
characteristic of the disintegration stage, where the growing awareness of being different leads to loss of self-
esteem, confusion, withdrawal, and depression. The author argues that, although the women had an average stay
of five years in the continental United States, such feelings seemed to result from constant migration between the
island and the mainland. Additionally, the resultant
membership in an ethnic minority group adds to the depressive feelings experienced by migrant Puerto Ricans.
Many Puerto Ricans become sensitive about U.S.-Puerto Rican
political relations after the experience of becoming ethnic
minorities. Some of them experience feelings characteristic
of the reintegration stage, whether they are on the island
or on the mainland.

Puerto Ricans in the stages of autonomy and even
independence are found among the continental Puerto Ricans
or among those migrants who have successfully dealt with
their transcultural translocation. Conversely, most migrant
Puerto Ricans who are merry-go-rounders tend to exhibit
behaviors characteristic of Adler's reintegration stage.

Psychological Mechanism of
Cross-Cultural Transitions

According to Piers and Piers (1982), most of the migrants share a common sociopsychological denominator: the
experience of uprootedness. These authors contend that
uprootedness frequently leads to a regressive state in
which separation from the original country is experienced
as a well-deserved rejection. Among Puerto Ricans, the

feeling of uprootedness is aggravated by the constant two-way migration and the diverse patterns of migration outlined by Gómez (1982). As a means of illustration, the pain of uprooting and the eventual loss of identity have been described as factors in the emotional problems prevalent among Puerto Ricans (Fitzpatrick 1971).

Piers and Piers further describe the dynamics characteristic of adult migrants. They are as follows:

1. <u>Splitting</u>. Migrants under stress tend to regress to a stage where trust and mistrust are not yet fused. This results in migrants not being able to assess their homeland realistically, and thus, "splitting" the image of their homeland. Therefore, countries of origin are alternately remembered as "all good" or "all bad." The splitting is extended to the host country, as well.

Splitting assumes complex dimensions for migrant Puerto Ricans. The colonial relationship between Puerto Rico and the United States frames the stage for further splitting. Believers in political independence for the island may tend to see Puerto Rico as "all good," and the United States as "all bad," while supporters of statehood may tend to perceive the United States as "all good" and Puerto Rico as "all bad." Furthermore, the current Puerto Rican political situation is becoming a polarized one. Moreover, for the Puertorriqueña, splitting is complicated due to the different and at times opposing sex roles available in both societies. To illustrate, the mainstream U.S. society reinforces individualism, assertiveness, and independence among women, while more traditional Puerto Rican society tends to reinforce a priority for the collective, nonassertive, or indirect communication of feelings and interdependence among females.

2. <u>Self-rejection and self-deprecation</u>. Migrants are also unable to see themselves as they really are. Their perceived rejection from home (in the form of the need to migrate) results in self-rejection. Furthermore, they identify with the aggressor. For Puerto Ricans, this mechanism is supported by their membership in an ethnic minority group after they migrate to the mainland. Subsequently, they experience discrimination from the majority group, with the concomitant prejudice and stereotyping. Similarly, while discussing the identity crisis of another U.S. ethnic minority group--Blacks--Erickson (1968) notes how the condition of belonging to an oppressed and exploited minority group influences the process of identity

formation, resulting in feelings of inferiority and self-hatred as well as negative identity.

3. Rebuilding the old homeland. Migrants want to restore what they lost, thus creating "a little Italy, Chinatown," or El Barrio, as well as reviving old ethnic elements such as costumes, menus, clothing, and so forth. The new ethnic diaspora is quite different from the original one. For example, the Puerto Rican barrio reflects the historical era when Puerto Ricans migrated, but due to the migration and reverse migration, the barrio constantly gets infused by the current culture from the island.

4. Passing or pseudoassimilation. Migrants tend to fluctuate between an intense desire to "belong," and a revulsion against such a desire. Thus, conflict ensues. "Passing" means that you betray your own parents, and thereby, you betray a vital part of yourself. A dilemma between the old and new ethnic identities develops. Although some individuals are more adept than others at combining aspects of both cultures, most of them cannot escape a period of distorted views of the self, the new environment, and the old one. The unique situation of Puerto Ricans further complicates this aspect of the transition. As U.S. citizens, they already "belong" to the United States, even before migrating. Hence, although not aliens or foreigners, in reality they belong to a different culture with different language and values. Pseudoassimilation, then, becomes an exercise in futility, given that they already belong to a society that perceives them as different and inferior. The Puerto Rican feels doubly rejected by the colonial power (a parental figure) and internalizes this rejection. This dynamic results in what Fanon (1965) has described as the psychopathology of the colonized.

Adler's (1975) developmental model is complemented by Piers and Piers' (1982) discussion of the psychological dynamics present during the cross-cultural transition. For example, the psychological mechanism of splitting may occur during the contact stage, in which the United States can be perceived as "all good" and Puerto Rico as "all bad" or vice versa. Moreover, living in the barrio could be perceived as an example of the psychological mechanism of rebuilding the old homeland. During the stage of disintegration, the psychological dynamics of self-rejection and self-deprecation can emerge among some individuals. As indicated previously, many Puerto Rican women express feelings characteristic of the disintegration stage, in which confusion, loss of self-esteem, and depression prevail. Others, however, may resort to the psychological dynamic of passing, or pseudoassimilation. In general, the psychological mechanisms tend to be present during the Adlerian stages of contact, disintegration, and reintegration. The stages of autonomy and independence represent a movement toward and a sense of resolution of the cross-cultural transition, and thus the psychological mechanisms are no longer required to function as coping devices.

Understanding the models of cross-cultural transition provides a framework to the series of feelings, behaviors, and cognitions that accompany the transitional experience. The developmental models of cross-cultural transition suggest that most migrants eventually manage to reconcile their previous cultural existence with their new ones and achieve a new identity. However, with Puerto Ricans, this process may be complicated by the variables of membership in an ethnic minority group and their unique migration patterns. Thus, partly due to their constant two-way migration and to the experience of being considered inferior by the mainstream society, many Puerto Ricans carry a sense of uprootedness. In other words, many Puerto Ricans do not feel a sense of belonging to the continental United States, but, as Pacheco and his associates (1979) found, once they return to the island, they continue to carry their sense of uprootedness. Hence, the reconciliation of different cultural repertoires seems highly improbable.

Factors Affecting Cross-Cultural Transitions

In analyzing the cross-cultural transition of any group, two types of factors need to be examined: extrinsic and intrinsic variables. The extrinsic variables include the type of migration, socioeconomic class, and the attitude of the host group toward the migrant group. The type of migration, whether forced or voluntary, affects the subsequent adjustment. With Puerto Ricans, this is not a clear-cut demarcation. As indicated earlier, most Puerto Ricans have been socialized into viewing migration as an acceptable way of coping with a wide range of issues, from financial problems to personal conflicts. Within this context, it is also important to examine the socioeconomic class as well as the educational level of the migrant. These factors greatly affect the adjustment and functioning

in the host society. Although a significant number of
Puerto Ricans who migrate belong to the lower socioeconomic class, some do have resources, and their motivation
for migration can range from seeking "better opportunities,"
to "cooling off," or just getting a change in scenery. Regardless of their motivation for migration, most Puerto
Rican migrants receive negative treatment from the majority
group members, who perceive them as culturally, sociopo-
litically, and racially different from them. This socio-
ecological variable suggests that the discrimination is a
result of the majority group members' stereotyping of
Puerto Ricans as inferior due to their lack of political
power.

The cross-cultural translocation is also guided by
intrinsic factors. To illustrate, Piers and Piers (1982)
emphasize that the cultural transition affects individuals
variously, according to their developmental stage. For
example, they note that children who immigrate experience
behavioral difficulties at home and at school. In school,
newcomer children often exhibit problems such as disregard
for regulations, ignorance of the mainstream customs, participation in classroom activities (over-participation—too
loud, or under-participation—inactive, or not articulate enough) and many others. Piers and Piers conclude
that the development of children who experience cross-
cultural translocation is bound to suffer due to the distorted perception of reality that accompanies the adjustment
to transition. The developmental stage in which individuals migrate has a definitive impact upon their reaction
and adjustment to the cross-cultural translocation.

Using Erickson's (1950) theory as a framework, we
can further examine this issue. For example, migration
will have limited impact on individuals who are in the
developmental states of basic trust versus basic mistrust,
autonomy versus shame and doubt, and initiative versus
guilt. These stages cover the oral-sensory, muscular-anal,
and locomotor-genital developmental phases, where the individual is usually surrounded by family members and/or
significant others, and the contact with the outside world
is often limited. However, the individual can be indirectly affected via cultural transition's impact on his/her
family.

Individuals whose transition occurs during their industry versus inferiority stage (latency) tend to be more
directly affected. During this stage they are working on

the developmental task of "entering into life." Thus, cross-cultural transition during this stage can affect their sense of mastery over the world. Dealing with two different cultures, one at home and a different one at school, could potentially create confusion, leading to emotional disturbances. The process of adaptation becomes complex with the dual adaptation to different, and at times conflicting, cultural contexts.

Likewise, an individual's translocation during the identity versus role confusion stage could have profound effects. This stage comprises puberty and adolescence, and its main developmental task is to integrate the accrued various kinds of experiences into the ego identity. As Erickson points out, the danger of this stage is role confusion. Cultural translocation can result in role confusion, thus adding more pressure and complexity to an already complicated task. This is the stage in which adolescents overidentify with the "group," at times, to the point of apparent complete loss of identity. During translocations, the "group" changes (from Puerto Rican to Anglo, Black American, or other), affecting adolescents' ethnic identity, and thus the formation of their general identity.

Puerto Rican adolescents migrating during this period face a myriad of different problems: linguistic, cultural differences, and adjustment. In particular, for the Puertorriqueña who "travels" with a cultural baggage of traditional sex roles, dealing with differing sexual mores prevalent in the U.S. mainstream society during the emergence of the sexuality could generate further complications in achieving these developmental tasks.

The Ericksonian stage of intimacy versus isolation covers the years of young adulthood. Individuals are emerging from their identity search and are eager to fuse their identity with others. According to Erickson, prejudices develop during this stage in which struggle for identity sharply differentiates between the familiar and the foreign. Puerto Ricans migrating during this stage may face ethnic and racial prejudice for the first time. This could negatively affect self-esteem, resulting in ethnic self-degradation. In addition, the migratory experience during this stage could originate the development of prejudice against other groups.

Erickson's work emphasizes more child developments and less adult developments. However, following his model, when cultural translocation occurs during adulthood and maturity, the impact of cross-cultural translocation tends to be not as profound as when the transition occurs during earlier stages, since these stages occur when the individual's sense of identity is more defined. To illustrate, the generativity versus stagnation stage that covers adulthood proposes as its main developmental tasks to teach and guide the next generation; while the ego integrity versus despair stage, which covers maturity, is more concerned with the achievement of emotional integration by participating in followership as well as by accepting the responsibility of leadership. The dynamics present during these latter developmental stages allow for a better adjustment during translocation. This is due to the existence of a more mature and integrated ego, which enables individuals to better face cross-cultural transition with a more developed sense of identity.

When individuals are exposed to cultural translocation several times and during different developmental stages, the effects tend to be additive. In the case of many Puerto Ricans who adopt a circular migration pattern, this means that a person will have to make diverse developmental adjustments according to each stage and to the total sum of translocations experienced. For example, a Puertorriqueña moving to the United States at age 12, returning to the island at age 15, and then moving back to the United States at age 21 would have to accommodate all of these diverse migrations, each of which had a different (depending on the developmental stage) additive and accumulative effect on her. A case example illustrating this issue will be presented in a later section.

Cross-Cultural Transitions and Mental Illness

Somers (1964) reports a relationship between migration, acculturation, and mental illness. On the mainland, Puerto Rican women are exposed to multiple stressful situations. They face culture shock, disintegration of family values, discrimination, and the pressures of acculturation. These stresses are usually translated into feelings of powerlessness, low self-esteem, and depression. Empirical evidence points out a high incidence of psychopathology among Puerto Rican women in the United States. For example, Torres-Matrullo (1976) found an incidence of nervousness, psychosomatic complaints, and depression among this population. Casté and his associates (1978) found a higher incidence of suicidal thoughts among Puerto Rican women as compared with Anglo, Black, and Puerto Rican males. In a similar vein, Baskin et al. (1981) found that Hispanic women in New York (most of whom were Puertorriqueñas) had a higher rate of depression than Anglo and/or Black women. Furthermore, Canino (1982) suggests that the incongruity between the Hispanic transitional sex roles and U.S. societal expectations may be a contributing factor to the development of psychopathology among women.

An area that has been minimally addressed in the literature is alcoholism among Puerto Rican women. In an article describing the treatment of alcoholic Puerto Rican females, Comas-Díaz (1986) states that this population must cope with specific stresses that may lead to drinking. Such stressors include alcoholic significant others, cultural values discouraging direct expression of assertiveness and aggressiveness, a subordinated role in their society, the single household, plus the pressure of migration and acculturation. This creates special problems, given that the higher incidence of alcoholic significant others increases their social vulnerability due to their participation in groups that are permissive about heavy drinking. Additionally, Puerto Rican women have stronger cultural and family protection against admitting being alcoholics. In sum, the incidence of alcoholism and other substance abuse among Puertorriqueñas who migrate needs to be further examined.

The studies asserting a high incidence of mental illness among continental Puerto Ricans have been questioned. For instance, Rendon (1974) indicates that migrant Puerto Ricans, in coping with the stress of acculturation, may suffer from a dissociative phenomenon, which may be misdiagnosed as schizophrenia. Although it is critical to understand the sociocultural context of Puertorriqueñas' migration and subsequent adjustment, the reality remains that many women develop symptoms at various degrees of psychopathology.

Given the high incidence of emotional problems among Puerto Rican women residing on the mainland, a question is posed: Why do some Puerto Rican women develop psychopathology while others are able to mobilize resources and adapt to stressful conditions? This is a very complex question. However, Garrison (1978) attempted to examine it by analyzing social networks and support systems of

Puertorriqueñas. She studied functional and dysfunctional migrant Puerto Rican women in reference to their support systems. Her findings indicate that seven patterns of social support with associated family and emotional status emerge. These support system patterns range on a continuum from a network of many relationships, which reflect the ideals of the culture found primarily among women who are symptom free, through four other variations found predominantly among the functional but disturbed women. Dysfunctional women exhibit two culturally deviant forms. More specifically, the patterns are as follows:

Functional Women
1. Network of many relationships of both an intimate and nonintimate nature.
2. Network of kin and friends with focus on several good friends.
3. Sectarian with emphasis on church friends.
4. Grouping with non-kin group.
5. Cultic with major relationships with spiritualists/ mediums.

Dysfunctional Women
1. One friend only.
2. No support system.

These patterns present a helpful framework for assessing resilience and vulnerability, in addition to offering a tool for psychotherapeutic interventions with migrant Puertorriqueñas.

Cross-Cultural Transition and Identity

The cross-cultural transition often impacts upon the individual's identity, generating conflict in this area. For many Puerto Ricans, their attribution of ethnic identity acquires added dimensions in that it is a chronic and pervasive issue. Bird (1982) argues that due to the effects of the Puerto Rican colonial situation, Puerto Ricans both on the island and the mainland suffer from identity diffusion in their collective self-concept. As an example, he further explains that Puerto Ricans ask, "Are we Americans?" "Are we Puerto Ricans?" or "Are we both, but predominantly one or the other?"

This identity diffusion is exacerbated when Puerto Ricans migrate to the United States. Cultural translocation tends to move individuals along the developmental pathway at a faster rate than other external factors. When individuals migrate and confront adjustment to a cross-cultural environment, part of their adjustment is struggling with their ethnocultural identities. For example, Erickson (1959) states that individuals in crisis experience a heightened awareness of their identities undergoing a "transitory excessive identity consciousness." Forced psychosocial definition may then lead to identity diffusion. Furthermore, during acculturation, ethnic minority group members may face changes in their self-images and identity crises. As indicated earlier, Adler's (1975) developmental model postulates that the cross-cultural transition creates an identity crisis leading to an awareness, reevaluation, and transformation of the individual's sense of self. Moreover, Simmons and his colleagues (1981) found that changes in self-image lead to psychological disturbances, lowered self-esteem, and depressive effects.

Identity diffusion has significant repercussions. A relationship between a conflictional ethnic identity and psychological stress has been suggested. To illustrate, Ruiz and his associates (1977) state that individuals in the midst of changing cultural values, and those lacking strong ethnic identities, tend to experience more psychological stress than do individuals with strong ethnic identities. From a more psychopathological perspective, Akhtar (1984) describes the syndrome of identity diffusion as consisting of six clinical features: (1) contradictory character traits, (2) temporal discontinuity in the self, (3) lack of authenticity, (4) feelings of emptiness, (5) gender dysphoria, and (6) inordinate ethnic and moral relativism. Regarding this last clinical feature, Akhtar argues that individuals with identity diffusion display a peculiar pallor of ethnicity, and that identity acquires a falsely liberal attitude when it is devoid of an ethnic anchor. He concludes by saying that the degree to which identity diffusion is manifested varies greatly.

The effects of cross-cultural transition on the Puerto Rican woman are multifaceted. She carries complex identities--ethnic, gender, and racial. These multiple identities are potentially conflictive. Gender roles tend to be affected by cultural transitions and subsequent cultural adaptation. Espín (1986) asserts that Hispanic (im)migrant women face the resolution of feelings of loss, the developments of decision-making skills, ego strength, and the ability to tolerate ambiguities, including sex-role ambiguities. Similarly, Puertorriqueñas struggle with culturally imposed modes of behavior while attempting to develop alternative ones. As women, they struggle with gender discrimination and oppression; and as Puerto Ricans, they cope with their ethnic identity crises. Traditional sex roles are undergoing a transformation among migrant Puerto Ricans. The machismo/marianismo sexual code behaviors are not reinforced by the new dominant culture, which, in fact, is pervaded by the impact of the Women's Liberation Movement. For example, Torres-Matrullo (1980) found significant relationships between the level of acculturation, level of education, and family and sex-role attitudes among mainland Puerto Rican women. She found that transitional concepts of Puerto Rican womanhood and manhood appear to be changing toward a more egalitarian model due to increased education and exposure to the dominant society. However, her findings suggest that other basic family values, such as sacredness of motherhood and the preeminent role of children, appear to remain relatively unchanged, despite increased acculturation and education. This apparent cultural conflict is characteristic of transculturation. Transculturation is the conflict of opposing cultural values and the emergence of a distinct new culture, resembling in some ways the old and in other ways the new (de Granda 1968). Consequently, it can be argued that mainland Puertorriqueñas are actively engaged in the transculturation process of the Puerto Rican diaspora due to the availability of opportunities and the existence of more egalitarian sex roles. On the contrary, Puerto Rican men tend to feel more comfortable within their traditional sex roles and, therefore, less involved in the transculturation process.

Sex roles among Puerto Rican women in the United States can be complicated (and confused) by the expectations imposed by the two different cultural contexts in which they live. The North American culture tends to apply masculine criteria to the evaluation of women, ascribing the greatest value to those who distinguish themselves occupationally or professionally. However, this tendency is contradicted frequently enough to send mixed messages to the female. As an example, Senour (1977) asserts that the Chicana is far surer of her role within the traditional

Mexican-American culture than she is in the mainstream, where her role is ambivalent. Apparently, this sureness of roles that her native culture provides has not stopped Chicanas, or Puerto Rican women in the midst of cultural transition, from exploring the behavioral alternatives available to them. This experimentation can lead to conflict within the nuclear unit as well as within the extended family.

Puertorriqueñas experience a conflict in their multiple identities, that is, Puerto Rican versus female. In this case, some Puertorriqueñas may choose their identities as Puerto Ricans over their gender by defending the traditional sex codes, and thus perpetuating machismo/marianismo percepts as a way of insulating the egos of their male relatives from the socioeconomic humiliations they suffer. As a means of illustration, Steiner (1974) cites Puerto Rican women who defend machismo as an understandable response to deprivation in the economic, social, and political spheres. He asserts that men take their frustrations out on women because they cannot have impact elsewhere.

Another aspect of identity that gets affected when the Puerto Rican woman migrates to the United States is her racial one. Puerto Ricans have been called the "rainbow people," denoting their wide variations of color, ranging from Black to White within Puerto Rican families. Thus, racism in Puerto Rico is covert and does not have implications for genetic inferiority. Nevertheless, it does have implications for attractiveness (the whiter the person, the more attractive he/she is considered). Additionally, in Puerto Rico, color is a social issue and not a racial one (Longres 1974). As a subjective judgment, this means that if the person belongs to a high socioeconomic class, they will be considered "White," or at least non-Black, regardless of actual racial features. In other words, the higher the socioeconomic class, the "whiter" is the person.

Racial differences are expressed according to gradations of color and traits. For example: mulato is the equivalent of mulatto; jabao is light-skinned, but with features that indicate Black ancestry--equivalent to Black "yellow"; grifo is with Caucasian features but has frizzled/ kinky hair; trigueño is olive-skinned; and negro or prieto is Black.

When the non-White Puertorriqueña migrates to the mainland, she confronts an openly racist society and thus faces an identity crisis of multiple proportions. Jorge

(1979) describes the experience of the Black Puerto Rican woman in the United States. She posits that this triple minority status engenders shame and feelings of inferiority, which are reinforced by the Puerto Rican community and the dominant society at large. She further states that if the Black Puertorriqueña develops intimacy with Black Americans, she is forced to assimilate into this group, and thus give up her identity as a Puerto Rican. Finally, Jorge states that the most difficult task for this group is integrating the three components--Black, Puerto Rican, and female--into a whole identity.

The difficulty in integrating identity is not an exclusive problem of Black Puerto Rican women. Many non-White Puertorriqueñas (trigueñas, jabas, mulatas, and grifas) also experience related difficulties. For example, trigueñas, who are considered non-Black (and thus acceptable and attractive) in Puerto Rico, are instead considered non-White (and thus, inferior and unattractive) on the mainland. Furthermore, Longres (1974) views racism as one of the most psychologically damaging experiences for Puerto Ricans, since it undermines autonomy and the initiative that they bring with them to succeed, resulting in self-doubt and feelings of inadequacy. As an example, it has been reported that non-White Puerto Ricans have higher psychiatric inpatient admission rates than White Puerto Ricans (Malzberg 1965). This situation demands an adjustment in self-concept, forcing a negative valence on self-esteem.

CLINICAL INTERVENTIONS

Clinical Assessment

In working with Puerto Rican women in the continental United States, the clinician needs to add several elements to the assessment procedure. First, the migration pattern should be explored and monitored. For example, if the client is a merry-go-rounder, special provisions should be made. Therapeutic confrontation could be used to attempt to change this behavior; however, appropriate referrals before the actual move should be made in order to ensure the continuity of care.

Another area that requires special assessment is the Puertorriqueña's developmental stage because this construct affects the perception as well as the understanding of reality. The Puertorriqueña's migration stage also requires specific assessment. Women dealing with the disintegration stage exhibit behaviors and experience psychological dynamics very differently from those women dealing with the reintegration stage. Similarly, clinical interventions could be tailored to address the specific stages of cross-cultural transition. Furthermore, the Puertorriqueña's support systems can bear prognostic and therapeutic qualities. For instance, women with only one friend or no support system are more likely to be dysfunctional than women with networks of kin and friends. In a similar vein, those women with deficient support systems could benefit more from an all-female group psychotherapy modality.

The next step in the clinical evaluation is to perform an ethnocultural assessment. Jacobsen (in press) developed the ethnocultural assessment as a simple, practical, and clinically relevant framework to be used with ethnoculturally translocated clients. This assessment involves the exploration of the ethnocultural determinants of identity in a psychotherapeutic or diagnostic setting. It consists of four stages:

First stage. Obtaining information, knowledge, and awareness of the client's ethnocultural identity or the identity aspects pertaining to the individual's ethnicity and culture.
Second stage. Focusing on the circumstances leading to the client's ethnocultural translocation.
Third stage. Exploring the client's intellectual and emotional perception of the evolution and development of the family's ethnocultural identity.
Fourth stage. Considering the evolution of the therapist's ethnocultural background to determine specific areas of real or potential overlap with that of the client.

Conducting an ethnocultural assessment with Puerto Rican women is of the utmost importance, given the degree of ethnocultural identity diffusion prevalent among this population.

Therapeutic Work

Completion of the ethnocultural assessment provides the framework for therapeutic work. Elsewhere, Comas-Díaz and Jacobsen (1987) introduced a model of the impact of cultural dislocation on the therapeutic process, which is highly relevant for working with migrant Puerto Rican women. They note that culturally translocated individuals often attribute ethnocultural qualities to their therapists. Ethnocultural identification is based on the assumption that the clients who have experienced cultural dislocation may presume and they attribute to their therapists certain ethnocultural characteristics that may or may not be accurate as a therapeutic modality. Ethnocultural identification can help the client manage cultural values, negotiate transitional experiences, and cope with the identity readjustment in a new cultural environment.

Should the assessment confirm the Puertorriqueña's identity diffusion, the therapist actively fosters the client's identification with her ethnocultural identification origin. In using the ethnocultural identification, the therapist engages in three major therapeutic functions (Comas-Díaz and Jacobsen 1987):

1. Reflection. Whereby the therapist "mirrors" the ethnocultural parts of the client's diffused identity.
2. Education. Whereby the therapist guides the client through a reformation of ethnocultural identity.
3. Mediation. Whereby the therapist helps the client integrate her ethnocultural self into a consolidated sense of self.

Reflection acknowledges the pervasive influence of ethnicity and culture on the client's life. It conveys that the therapist understands the circumstances of biculturalism. Education provides a guide in the reconstruction of the client's ethnocultural identity. In using directive approaches, the therapist helps the client examine inconsistencies among aspects of her old ethnic background, as well as those among her transcultural values and those of the new culture. Mediation attempts to integrate the ethnocultural identity with the personal identity.

Ethnocultural identification follows a developmental framework, similar to Adler's (1975) model of the individual's adjustment to cross-cultural translocation. As a therapeutic tool, it can assist clients in progressing through the five stages of Adler's model.

Following are case examples illustrating clinical intervention with Puerto Rican women struggling with transculturation pressures.

Case Vignettes

Laura is an 18-year-old Puerto Rican female living with her mother and three siblings—two brothers, ages 15 and 9, and a 12-year-old sister. She is in her senior year in high school. The family migrated to the mainland two years ago because Laura's 15-year-old brother was exhibiting behavioral problems at school. The mother, who is divorced, thought that moving closer to her children's father would help to discipline her son, "teaching him respect."

The family had a history of migration to the continental United States when Laura was 10 years old, but they returned to the island after one and a half years. Soon after, her parents separated and eventually obtained a divorce. Laura adjusted well to the divorce, being a model daughter back in Puerto Rico, earning high grades and making plans to attend college.

Upon arrival, Laura expressed resentment against her mother for leaving Puerto Rico. She verbalized that she did not like the United States and that she wanted to return home. In fact, she was expressing the psychological mechanism of splitting (Puerto Rico is all good while the United States is all bad). Moreover, she manifested discontent due to what she called "a language problem." This linguistic problem is consistent with Laosa's (1975) findings showing that Puerto Rican children tend to maintain the Spanish language more than Mexican-American and Cuban children. Laura particularly complained of school problems. Relevant to this issue is Mejia's (1983) discussion of Mexican-American children's development, where he argues that this group enters school with a particular social identity. Teachers, in turn, have a conception of a system identity for the child that incorporates personal, institutional, and societal descriptions. School assumptions and expectations tend not to be congruent with the Mexican-American children's expectations. A similar process may occur with Puerto Rican students. Likewise, Laura seemed to be caught between these conflictive expectations.

Laura began to exhibit behavioral problems. She started to get home late, to relinquish her household obligations, and to refuse to conform to her "duties as the oldest daughter." Her mother felt powerless and sought Laura's father's help, who was not available due to his "new family responsibilities."

The client's first contact with the mental health establishment was a referral from an emergency room to an outpatient substance abuse clinic. At the emergency room she was treated for an overdose of pills and alcohol. Further assessment revealed that she had a drinking problem, and she was referred to an alcohol rehabilitation program.

During the initial stages of assessment, the client revealed that she began drinking soon after her abortion the year before. Laura, a trigueña Puerto Rican, developed a romantic relationship with a Black American classmate. Her family opposed such a relationship, but Laura ended up seeing her boyfriend against their wishes. Her father, a Black Puerto Rican, was prejudiced against Black Americans, and thus very adamant against this relationship. This relationship was, in part, a reaction to the discrimination that she was experiencing from the mainstream society. As Piers and Piers (1982) and Erickson (1968) pointed out, Laura's process of identity formation was affected by her cross-cultural transitions. The conflicted process resulted in feelings of inferiority, self-deprecation, and self-hatred as well as negative identity. She embraced the Black American as a means of denying the Puerto Rican identity. (I am Black and I will have a Black child.)

After becoming pregnant, Laura was pressured by her family to have an abortion. Her drinking behavior began soon after her abortion. She stated she was very angry at her father and that the only way she could "release her anger was by drinking." Her father, a recovered alcoholic, was very strict about his children's behavior. However, Laura blamed her parents' divorce on her father's previous drinking problem.

The client's treatment consisted of group psychotherapy and individual sessions. She entered a female alcoholics treatment group. In this modality, Laura was one of two adolescents who was "adopted" by the other (elder) group members. This "adoption" facilitated the process of "future past" described by Comas-Díaz (1986) in the treatment of Puerto Rican female alcoholics. Within this format, older women represent the "future past" of the younger ones in terms of what is going to happen to them if they continue abusing alcohol. Older women are encouraged to communicate to the younger ones their experiences as alcoholics. Given the similarities in the Puerto

Rican women's backgrounds, this technique attempts to
change younger women's "future past," or the past that
they would have several years from now. Thus, older
women share their experiences with the younger women as
a means of preventing them from repeating their histories.
This treatment modality helped Laura to focus on her
drinking problem.

The group therapy also helped Laura reintegrate her
ethnic identity as a Puertorriqueña. The women in the
group validated her sociocultural reality but, at the same
time, confronted her with her destructive behaviors (suicide attempt, alcohol abuse).

An ethnocultural assessment was performed during individual psychotherapy sessions. It revealed that all of
Laura's relatives were Puerto Rican except a paternal
great grandfather, who was Dominican. As previously indicated, the client had experienced three cross-cultural
translocations at ages 10, 11, and 18. Of all of these
translocations, Laura experienced the most difficulties with
her last cultural transition.

Laura's perception of her family's migrations was
different from the mother's expressed motives. She resented
her family's merry-go-rounder migration pattern. She saw
their recent move as a means for her mother to get closer
to her father. Laura felt that she could not communicate
these feelings to her mother. The last stage of ethnocultural assessment revealed that both Laura and the therapist shared the same ethnicity and the experience of multiple cross-cultural translocations during different developmental stages.

Individual psychotherapy sessions focused on improving Laura's functioning. First, therapy helped her mourn
the loss of her baby. Indeed, she was experiencing a
delayed grief reaction to her abortion. After the completion of the mourning process, Laura's identity confusion
and diffusion were examined, helping her to increase her
self-esteem. This process helped Laura's developmental
stage of integrating her sense of self into a more consolidated identity. Within this context, the impact of her
multiple transitions was discussed, creating a higher
awareness.

An active stance in psychotherapy was taken, aimed
at improving the client's interpersonal relationship style.
Partly due to her recent move, her support system was nil.
A behavioral schedule of activities was conducted, designed

to improve Laura's communication style with her mother. This therapeutic modality was aimed at examining and identifying communication failures in order to teach Laura to communicate more effectively. Role-playing was effectively used to improve communication.

Laura's mother was invited to attend "couples" therapy with her. This strategy helped their communication style and provided the mother with some parenting skills. This was an important area for Laura, who was very concerned about the effects of her parents' divorce on her mother's emotional state. As the oldest daughter, Laura attained a parental child role after the divorce, in addition to her normal developmental tasks of adolescence. She was unable to withstand the multiple pressures that she was experiencing.

At the end of one year in treatment, Laura was free of alcohol, had increased her self-esteem, was no longer suicidal, and had improved her communication with her mother. She also felt that she had "a few friends whom she could rely on."

Laura's development of substance abuse problems is consistent with Rivera Romero and Bernal y del Río's analysis (1983). These authors assert that Puerto Rican children and adolescents who migrate to the mainland develop an eternal ambivalence about their identity, resulting in difficulties in their sociocultural and emotional adaptation. Such identity crises make these youngsters vulnerable to delinquency and/or drug addiction.

Laura's choice of romantic partner was directly related to her developmental stage at the time of her last translocation. Her peer group had suddenly changed from Puerto Rican to Black (the American inner-city school that she was attending was primarily Black). The cumulative effects of Laura's migrations (two during her infancy versus inferiority, and another during her identity versus role confusion stage) contributed to her confused sense of identity. As a trigueña Puertorriqueña, Laura encountered a different racial classification. Back in Puerto Rico she was a non-Black Puerto Rican, while on the mainland she was a non-White Puerto Rican. She began to develop a negative identity and to utilize the psychological mechanism of passing, or pseudoassimilation (in her case, with the Black American culture). Moreover, she experienced added pressure and had to negotiate differing (and at times conflictive) expectations.

Laura's choice of a romantic partner was both a way of identifying with and rebelling against her father. The rejection represented by her parents' divorce and her father's remarriage impacted upon the emergence of her sexuality and, consequently, on her act of becoming pregnant. During her identity versus role confusion stage, becoming pregnant became a means of achieving an instant identity—that of a mother. Within the Puerto Rican culture, motherhood is accorded a high status (Christensen 1975). Major changes, such as her parents' divorce, the cross-cultural transitions, her frustrated attempt at becoming a mother, and the natural process of development, all contributed to Laura's emotional problems and alcohol abuse. In this case, treatment helped Laura to recuperate from these crises and to restore her previous high level of functioning.

The following case illustrates a Puertorriqueña's cross-cultural translocation difficulties within a different developmental stage.

Sara is a 48-year-old Puerto Rican woman. She is separated from her husband and has two children from her first marriage, a female of 22 years and a male of 21. In addition, she has a seven-year-old child from her second marriage. Her oldest daughter is married and lives in a nearby state, while Sara lives with her other two children. The client has an employment record of working as a clerk in a department store.

Sara was referred to a community health center after attending a family session during her son's hospitalization for. alcohol detoxification. During the meeting, Sara became agitated and "nervous," stating that she also needed help. Her chief complaints—"I can't take this any longer," and "I have to quit my job"—were accompanied by appetite and sleep disturbances in addition to crying spells. An initial psychiatric evaluation revealed that her condition was a reactive one, and she was referred for individual psychotherapy.

Sara was seen by a female Puerto Rican clinician. During the first interview she told her therapist, "We understand each other—we come from the same place." Later, when she began to make comments such as "All of my problems come from my living outside of Puerto Rico," or "My children are being corrupted here," the therapist decided to perform a detailed ethnocultural assessment.

Results of the assessment revealed that all of Sara's relatives were Puerto Ricans. However, Sara had a British surname due to her second marriage to a West Indian. For financial reasons, Sara migrated to the mainland after her first divorce, at age 38. She stated that her best friend "convinced her to have a change in scenery." Thus, migrating for Sara was associated with her divorce, and as such she perceived it as a failure in her role as a woman. Sara, who had never been employed before, began to receive governmental financial aid and attended several vocational programs. She obtained a job as a clerk and eventually met and married her second husband. This marriage was very controversial within her family because her husband was a Black West Indian. The client, who was herself a <u>jabá</u> Puerto Rican, began to socialize and identify with Black West Indians. While discussing this marriage and subsequent legal separation, Sara expressed a lot of anger and violence toward her husband, admitting that she used to engage in physical fights with him.

During the last stage of the ethnocultural assessment, the clinician's own ethnocultural background is examined for potential overlap with the client's. In this case, the overlapping areas identified are that both are Puerto Rican women raised in small towns, both bear mixed racial characteristics, and both have experienced cross-cultural transition.

During the initial stages of therapy, Sara discussed her feelings about migration and its effects on her and her oldest children. As a newcomer Puerto Rican, she stated that adjusting to the move created problems for her children. Sara also expressed difficulties at what she called "finding out who she really was." As a <u>jabá</u> Puerto Rican, Sara was very angry at "being treated like a Black by Americans as well as some Puerto Ricans." She mentioned that marrying her second husband offered her another ethnic group to identify with and belong to. However, this behavior alienated her from the Puerto Rican community. Given her marital separation, Sara withdrew from her West Indian friends, feeling alone and without a group of reference or support.

In order to treat her presenting symptoms, the clinician taught Sara relaxation techniques that offered her relief from her present complaints. The treatment also aimed at helping restore the level of functioning she had attained before the crisis. After alleviation of her symptoms,

Sara began to identify with her clinician. Statements such as, "You resemble my cousin. I could swear that we are related," allowed the clinician to act as a guide in the reformation of Sara's ethnocultural identity.

During this stage in treatment Sara was able to disclose that she was sleeping with her ex-husband, even though she had received divorce papers from him. This conflictive situation engendered more anger in Sara, who confessed to harboring homicidal intentions toward him. A therapeutic contract was made. Sara was able to control her homicidal impulses and, thus, stay out of the hospital during her divorce proceedings. The clinician used culturally relevant assertiveness training to teach her to express her feelings in a more adaptive manner. During this period, Sara was able to return to work.

In returning to work, themes of Sara's multiple identities merged--mother, woman, Puerto Rican, and non-White. The clinician took a directive stance in helping her integrate these multiple identities. Treatment was the forum for guiding Sara in redefining her identity as a Puerto Rican woman residing in the United States. Cultural inconsistencies and mixed societal messages were examined. In addition, the cultural behavior alternatives available to her and their likely consequences were explored.

At this stage in treatment, Sara revealed that although she was not a practicing espiritista (medium, person who can communicate with spirits) like her mother, she had facultades espirituales (spiritual faculties). This revelation was examined within the ethnocultural context and was assessed as Sara's process of identification with the healing functions of her clinician. Furthermore, the therapist framed the healer identity as a means of cultural self-awareness. Within this context, Maduro (1983) suggests that Hispanics' identification with folk illness and folk healing is a means of reintegration into the Hispanic/ Latino culture.

Treatment was terminated when Sara decided to migrate to another state. Some of her relatives had already moved there and she stated that she wanted to be supportive of her relatives, in addition to obtaining support from them.

In this case example, ethnocultural identification was utilized as an auxiliary to behavior therapy. This clinical vignette illustrates how the diffused identity can be pervasive in a Puertorriqueña's mental health presentation. Sara's rationale for migrating was a response to a perceived failure in her role as a woman. As a "forced" translocation, Sara's reaction to culture shock was difficult. Her translocation occurred during a period of Sara's early adulthood when she was trying to settle down in preparation for entering her mid-life transition. Levinson's (1978) model of adult development, although based primarily on male development, can also be applied to women. Within this model, Sara's migration at age 38 coincided with her developmental tasks of corresponding to the second adult life structure. The major tasks of this period are to establish a niche in society, to anchor one's life more firmly, and to work in order to obtain this niche. Sara's migration acted against her developmental needs. Instead of settling down and creating a niche, she was destroying a previous life structure and was forced to create a new one in a foreign, strange territory. Hence, a cultural translocation crisis added to an adult developmental crisis.

Sara's translocation was aided by a friend, who provided crucial support. Nevertheless, the transition had an impact on her ethnic identity. During her Adlerian stage of disintegration, she married a West Indian and identified with another ethnic group. In contrast to Laura, who chose Black Americans as a reference group, Sara chose a group with whom she shared the common Caribbean background. Additionally, West Indians in the United States also experience cross-cultural translocation and subsequent culture shock and adjustment to the United States.

Discussion

In comparing both case examples, several differences emerge. Laura had suffered multiple translocations, which occurred during more vulnerable developmental periods. Consequently, her adjustment was harder and her dysfunctional behaviors were more extreme: unplanned pregnancy, alcohol abuse, and a suicide attempt. On the contrary, Sara's translocation occurred when she was an adult with a developmental task of "settling down." Although both clients suffered some identity confusion, Laura's case was more extreme, bordering on identity diffusion. Therapy helped Laura to formulate her identity, while it helped

Sara to reformulate and reintegrate her fragmented identity. For instance, while Laura was still struggling with her sense of identity, she chose to identify with a different ethnic minority group (Black Americans). Conversely, Sara had a previously developed ethnic self-concept, and she identified with another ethnic group that has more commonalities with island Puerto Ricans (West Indians). Thus, the different developmental stages in which the translocation occurred had distinct, different impacts on the two clients.

These clinical vignettes illustrate the interaction between developmental stages and cross-cultural translocation, as well as their clinical implication. Specific therapeutic interventions embedded in a cultural context can be used to alleviate symptoms and improve Puertorriqueñas' level of functioning, involvement in the transculturation process, and enrichment of the quality of their lives.

CONCLUSIONS

Migrant Puertorriqueñas comprise a paradox. They are a high-risk group and at the same time are resourceful and resilient. They observe traditional sex roles while exploring alternative, more egalitarian ones. Cross-cultural transition provides them with a transforming process. Cultural adjustment offers them the opportunity for regression, coupled with further development. As carriers of their cultural baggage, Puertorriqueñas actively shape the transculturation of their diaspora. Within this context, they are instrumental in the reformulation of their individual and collective ethnic identity.

REFERENCES

Acosta-Belén, E., and B. R. Sjostrom. 1979. "The educational and professional status of Puerto Rican women." In E. Acosta-Belén, ed., The Puerto Rican Woman, pp. 64-75. New York: Praeger.

Adler, P. S. 1975. "The transitional experience: An alternative view of culture shock." Journal of Humanistic Psychology 15, 4:13-23.

Akhtar, S. 1984. "The syndrome of identity diffusion." American Journal of Psychiatry 141, 11:1381-85.

Baskin, D., H. Bluestone, and M. Nelson. 1981. "Mental illness in minority women." Journal of Clinical Psychology 37, 3:491-98.

Bird, H. R. 1982. "The cultural dichotomy of colonial people." Journal of the American Academy of Psychoanalysis 10, 2:195-209.

Canino, G. 1982. "The Hispanic woman: Sociocultural influences on diagnoses and treatment." In R. Becerra, M. Karno, and J. Escobar, eds., Mental Health and Hispanic Americans, pp. 117-38. New York: Grune and Stratton.

Casté, C., J. Blodgett, and D. Rubinow. 1978. "Cross-cultural differences in presenting problems: Implication for service delivery and treatment modality." Unpublished paper. Yale University School of Medicine, Department of Psychiatry.

Christensen, E. 1975. "The Puerto Rican woman: The challenge of a changing society." Character Potential 7, 2:89-96.

Comas-Díaz, L. 1982. "Mental health needs of Puerto Rican women in the United States." In R. E. Zambrana, ed., Work, Family, and Health: Latina Women in Transition. New York: Hispanic Research Center, Fordham University.

_____. 1984. "Content themes in group treatment with Puerto Rican women." Social Work with Groups 7, 3: 75-84.

_____. 1985. "Cognitive and behavioral group therapy with Puerto Rican women: A comparison of content themes." Hispanic Journal of Behavioral Sciences 7, 3:273-83.

_____. 1986. "Puerto Rican alcoholic women: Treatment considerations." Alcoholism Treatment Quarterly 3, 1:47-57.

_____. 1988. "Mainland Puerto Rican women: A socio-cultural approach." Journal of Community Psychology 16, 1:21-31.

Comas-Díaz, L., and F. M. Jacobsen. 1987. "Ethnocultural identification in psychotherapy." Psychiatry 50, 3:232-41.

de Granda, G. 1968. Transculturación e interferencia lingüística en el Puerto Rico contemporáneo (Transculturation and linguistic interference in contemporary Puerto Rico). Bogotá, Colombia: Ediciones Bogotá.

Erickson, E. H. 1950. Childhood and Society. New York: Norton.

_____. 1959. Identity and the Life Cycle. New York: University Press, Inc.

_____. 1968. Identity, Youth and Crisis. New York: Norton.

Espín, O. M. 1986. "Cultural and historical influences on sexuality in Hispanic/Latin women." In J. Cole, ed., All American Women, pp. 272-84. New York: Free Press.

Fanon, F. 1965. The Wretched of the Earth. New York: Grove Press.

Fitzpatrick, J. P. 1971. Puerto Rican Americans: The meaning of migration to the mainland. Englewood Cliffs, N.J.: Prentice-Hall.

Garrison, V. 1978. "Support systems of schizophrenic and nonschizophrenic Puerto Rican migrant women in New York City." Schizophrenic Bulletin 4, 4:561-96.

Gómez, A. M. 1982. "Puerto Rican Americans." In A. Gaw, ed., Cross-Cultural Psychiatry, pp. 109-36. Littleton, Mass.: John Wright.

Jacobsen, F. M. 1988. "Ethnocultural assessment." In L. Comas-Díaz and E. H. Griffith, eds., Clinical Guidelines in Cross-Cultural Mental Health, pp. 134-41. New York: John Wiley.

Jorge, A. 1979. "The Black Puerto Rican woman in contemporary American society." In E. Acosta-Belén, ed., The Puerto Rican Woman, pp. 134-41. New York: Praeger.

Laosa, L. 1975. "Bilingualism in three limited state Hispanic groups: Contextual use of language by children and adults in their families." Journal of Educational Psychology 67:617-27.

Levinson, D. J. 1978. The Seasons of a Man's Life. New York: Ballantine.

Longres, J. F. 1974. "Racism and its effect on Puerto Rican continental." Social Casework 55, 2:67-75.

Maduro, R. 1983. "Curanderismo and Latino views of disease and curing." The Western Journal of Medicine 139, 6:868-74.

Malzberg, B. 1965. Mental Disease among the Puerto Rican Population of New York State, 1960-1961. Albany, N.Y.: Research Foundation for Mental Hygiene, Inc.

Mejía, D. 1983. "The development of Mexican-American children." In G. J. Powell, ed., The Psychosocial Development of Minority Group Children, pp. 77-114. New York: Brunner/Mazel.

O'Reilly, J. 1985. "Adapting to a different role." Time 126, 1:82-83.

Pacheco, M. A., S. Wapner, and N. Lucca. 1979. "La migración como una transición crítica para la persona en su ambiente: Una interpretación organísmico evolutiva" (Migration as a critical transition for the person in his or her environment: An evolutionary organic interpretation). Revista de Ciencias Sociales 21, 1-2:123-55.

Piers, G., and M. W. Piers. 1982. "On becoming a newcomer." The Annual of Psychoanalysis 10, 4:369-78.

Rendon, M. 1974. "Transcultural aspects of Puerto Rican mental illness in New York." International Journal of Social Psychiatry 20, 1-2:18-24.

Rivera Romero, E., and V. Bernal y del Río. 1983. "Mental health needs and Puerto Rican children." In G. J. Powell, ed., The Psychosocial Development of Minority Group Children, pp. 330-43. New York: Brunner/Mazel.

Sanchez-Korrol, V. 1980. "Survival of Puerto Rican women in New York before World War II." In C. E. Rodríguez, ed., The Puerto Rican Struggle. New York: The Puerto Rican Migration Research Consortium.

Senour, M. N. 1977. "Psychology of the Chicana." In J. L. Martinez, ed., Chicano Psychology, pp. 329-42. New York: Academic.

Simmons, R. G., F. Rosenberg, and M. Rosenberg. 1981. "Disturbances in the self image at adolescence." In L. D. Steinberg, ed., The Life Cycle: Readings in Human Development, pp. 199-208. New York: Columbia University Press.

Sluzki, C. E. 1979. "Migration and family conflict." Family Process 18, 4:379-90.

Somers, V. S. 1964. "The impact of dual membership on identity." Psychiatry 27, 4:332-44.

Steiner, S. 1974. The Islands: The Worlds of the Puerto Ricans. New York: Harper Calophen.

Torres-Matrullo, C. 1976. "Acculturation and psychopathology among Puerto Rican women in mainland United States." American Journal of Orthopsychiatry 46, 4:710-19.

_____. 1980. "Acculturation, sex-roles values and mental health among Puerto Ricans in the mainland United States." In A. M. Padilla, ed., Acculturation: Theory, Models and Some New Findings, pp. 120-32. Boulder: Westview.

United States Commission on Civil Rights. 1976. _Puerto Ricans in the Continental United States: An Uncertain Future_. Washington, D.C.: U.S. Government Printing Office.

8

Dual Discipline Role of the Single Puerto Rican Woman Head of Household

Vickie A. Borrás, Ph.D.

INTRODUCTION

The latest reports from the U.S. Bureau of Census (1985) present staggering statistics on the proportion of Puerto Rican households that are headed by a single woman and emphatically underline the importance of focusing social science research on the special issues that confront this type of family. As of 1985 as much as 44.0 percent of all Puerto Rican families in the United States were headed by single women. When data for Puerto Rican families below the poverty level are examined, the figures climb to an astonishing 77.4 percent. Given this high incidence, it is important to examine the women's adaptation to this situation, including concomitant changes in their role expectations.

One of the key areas in which adaptation to this family situation has become problematic is in child discipline (Borrás 1978). The single mother is forced to assume the dual role of mother and father in disciplining children. This duality of roles is truly alien for the migrant single mothers, given traditional Puerto Rican culture. Coupled with the family's migration to a foreign milieu, this has led to a problem of inconsistent child discipline.

This chapter examines the dual child discipline role played by single Puerto Rican mothers in the United States and presents a clinical model for counseling such mothers through the process of assuming the complex role. It will review the most relevant issues in the literature regarding the roles of the mother and of the father among Puerto Rican families, examining particularly the cultural expectations stemming from the culture of origin around childbearing and child discipline. The impact of migration on such cultural patterns will also be considered. While the chapter makes reference to aspects of the Puerto Rican family, in general, our discussion of post-migratory family life will focus particularly on low-income Puerto Ricans, among whom single parent family arrangements are most prevalent. Such are the families most often referred to mental health and social service agencies. The analysis will be illustrated with two case vignettes from families of this socioeconomic level. Clinical recommendations are provided at the end of the chapter.

CULTURAL EXPECTATIONS ON CHILDREARING AND CHILD DISCIPLINE

Since its origin in an agricultural society, Puerto Rican families have been defined as patriarchal (Steward 1956; Buitrago-Ortiz 1973; García-Preto 1982). Recently, in light of the high incidence of female-headed families, both in Puerto Rico and in the United States, the question of a change toward matrifocality has been raised (Morris 1979; Pelto, Román, and Liriano 1982). This issue will be further discussed in this chapter.

Traditionally among Puerto Ricans, child-rearing in general and child discipline specifically is ordinarily based on the simultaneous coordination of the actions of the complementary three elements that compose the nuclear family: the father, the mother, and the children. The extended family supplements the system. The role of each of these members of the family is distinct and is clearly defined by the tradition (Steward 1956; Buitrago-Ortiz 1973; Christensen 1975; García-Preto 1982).

The father has the ultimate authority in all family matters, including the discipline of children. Given this authority, he has the dual role of being both the definitive legislator and the definitive enforcer of the rules that govern the children's behavior. His additional role of economic provider of the family, under normal circumstances, keeps him away from the home and at work for a good part of the day. Therefore, it is not expected of him to deal with the discipline of children on a day-to-day basis. Even when at home, he gets involved in such matters rather infrequently. And yet it is the father, and only he, who intervenes when serious transgressions of the child discipline rules arise (cf. Buitrago-Ortiz 1973, 83; Wolf 1956, 220; García-Preto 1982, 172). In enforcing the rules, the father is expected to display justice, but above all, firmness.

The mother also plays a central part in the child discipline system. However, her roles as a legislator and rule enforcer are subordinate to and rest upon the father. She may and actually does develop rules regarding the children's behavior with the understanding that in so doing she does not go against the wishes of the father. As the children's primary caretaker, she holds no jobs outside the home and functions as the day-to-day enforcer. And yet, even while the father is away at work, the mother often makes use of his authority in enforcing discipline by reminding the children of a rule established or supported by the father, and also by threatening to report to him that a serious violation of the code has taken place (Buitrago-Ortiz 1973; García-Preto 1982).

The mother's role as the provider of love and affection in the family is by far more significant than her role as a discipline enforcer. As a direct consequence of this, and in contrast to the father, she is typically bland in enforcing discipline and relatively more tolerant than the father with rule infringements. Children know very well that they can get away with more when she is around than when the father is at home. Children find in her their best ally in defending against an overreacting father and in acting as an intermediary, even in instances when the father enforces obedience at her request (cf. Leavitt 1974; García-Preto 1982). Mothers tend to feel very close to their children, and many times seem more concerned with their children than with their husbands (Christensen 1975). Regarding the relationship between the mother and her children, Christensen (1975) made the following observation: "The mother-child relationship in Puerto Rico at times borders on hysteria, and mothers often seem to encourage a dependent relationship with their children" (p. 93).

A variety of rewards and punishments are utilized by parents as part of the discipline system. Verbal praise, and even more, verbal criticism are the most employed modes. Corporal punishment is seldom used in the typical agricultural family. Mothers usually warn their children repeatedly, but the punishment is not always carried out. In general, severe types of corporal punishment are rare among typical families and usually follow only the most serious transgressions. This and all other strong forms of punishment are usually administered by the father (Mintz 1956; Wolf 1952; Buitrago-Ortiz 1973).

The children, for their part, are expected to show respeto (respect) and to be obedient and submissive to both their parents (García-Preto 1982). Respect is one of the core themes in the lives of the Puerto Ricans and as such guides the relationship with all human beings (cf. Díaz-Royo 1975).

Cultural notions on sex role differences also have a bearing on the issue of the discipline of children (cf. Christensen 1975, 91; Mintz 1956, 384-85). The boy is characterized as desinquieto (active, restless), and atrevido (daring), and with his parents' complacency may more easily get away with disobedient acts. The girl is seen as quiet, submissive, nondaring, and is expected to be more obedient than her male counterpart.

It should be noted, however, that although boys are more frequently allowed violations of the code, the harsher forms of punishment, especially physical punishment, are also reserved for them. This practice seems also to be related to sex stereotypes; boys are considered stronger and thus capable of withstanding, as well as in need of, stronger disciplinary measures. The belief that males are "stronger" than females leads families to conclude that boys are harder to discipline than girls. The task is particularly difficult for the mother who, as a female herself, is expected to be weak and bland. Consequently, the father typically plays a relatively more active role in the discipline of their sons as opposed to their daughters who, "weak" themselves, are left to the "weak" mother.

The Puerto Rican culture has an elaborate back-up system for dealing with families in which the father is absent by separation, divorce, or death. With respect to the child discipline problem, the aim is basically to provide one or several male substitutes to fill the critically important father role. The substitute may simply be a new husband and father for the children, who is expected to become a full-fledged father (Wolf 1952), or they may be drawn from the men in the extended family and also from the father's compadres (godfathers) (Leavitt 1974; Minuchin et al. 1967). These two last terms, "extended family" and "compadre," require classification.

Regarding the extended family, Fitzpatrick's (1971) observations of this institution in the Puerto Rican culture are useful here:

> These are families in which there are strong bonds and frequent interaction among a wide range of natural or ritual kin. Grandparents, parents, and children may live in the same household or they may have separate households but visit frequently. The extended family is evident, regardless of the type of marriage (regularized or consensual), and it is a source of strength and support [p. 83].

For his part, the compadre is the baptismal godfather of one or more of the children. One becomes a compadre by undergoing a religious ritual. In the traditional culture he enjoys a very special relationship with the man who personally chose him for this greatly honored role. The compadre, in turn, is expected to oversee the successful overall development of his godson and particularly to fill the father's role, at least in part, when the father is absent (cf. Buitrago-Ortiz 1973, 135-40).

POST-MIGRATORY CHANGES IN FAMILY LIFE AND CHILD REARING PRACTICES

The social and economic conditions of Puerto Ricans in the United States have been proposed in the literature as an explanation for the high incidence of families headed by a single woman (García-Preto 1982; Pelto et al. 1982; Vázquez-Nuttall 1979). Especially, the high unemployment rate among Puerto Rican males and the ease with which the women get help from welfare and other governmental institutions in the United States are thought to be at the root of the issue. Notably, the same phenomena have been observed in Puerto Rico by Morris (1979).

For the Puerto Rican male, chronic unemployment challenges his self-image as breadwinner. Oftentimes, it is easier for women to find jobs, given their sewing and domestic skills. This situation can result in her having a job while the man remains without employment. This role reversal tends to diminish the male's authority and to lower his self-esteem. Consequently, marital conflicts and separations take place (Mizio 1974; García-Preto 1982). Consequently, the Puerto Rican woman, being the parent responsible for the care of the children, turns to welfare for financial support. Since the best financial support they can get from the welfare system requires a single parent household, many women present themselves as such even when there is the presence of a husband in the household. This situation creates very unstable marital ties. The male becomes publicly "illegitimate" and an intermittent husband who is expected to exercise his husband authority in some aspects.

Following migration, the conditions for dealing with single parenthood are different than the ones developed in the original cultural context. For instance, there are fewer alternative male figures available to the fatherless family. Geographical distance separates families from their respective extended family. Furthermore, the family bonds tend to be weakened by migration. Compadres might also have been left behind or are otherwise unavailable. Often, those who might be present are now unwilling to assume the responsibility of helping the single mother in disciplining her fatherless children.

After a separation, new husbands are sought. While they are first usually considered only as companions, ultimately, the Puerto Rican female ambivalently expects the new companion to fulfill the functions of a father, especially the disciplinary role. But in the new U.S. environment, the societal expectations that a new husband is a full-fledged father to the woman's children do not exist and the man does not feel an obligation to respond to such demands (García-Preto 1982).

Consequently, the woman is forced by default to carry out this dual role of mother and father under very stressful socioeconomic circumstances. In studying single-parent households in a small Puerto Rican community in Hartford, Pelto, Román, and Liriano (1982, 54) found that "a very considerable number of women as householders exhibit psychological strains, which they refer to as 'nervios,' that can be related to the compounding of economic, social, and cultural problems they face in a harsh environment."

The issue of matrifocality has been raised in studies of low-income Puerto Rican female heads of household here in the United States as well as in Puerto Rico (Pelto et al. 1982; Morris 1979). The question of whether these families have changed from patriarchal (father-dominated) to matrifocal (mother-dominated) remains unanswered. This is partly due to differences in the existing definitions, and partly to generalizations of this phenomenon to all low-income ethnic groups. The view of matrifocality has evolved from a pathologic (Frazier 1966) to a successful and positive adaptation to conditions of unemployment and migration (González 1970; Stack 1974). Advocates of the positive adaptation explain that the single mother family is financially secure through welfare and receives emotional and other material support from kinship networks. But, as Pelto et al. (1982) point out, low-income Puerto Rican families in the United States do not always have their kinship networks available. Furthermore, Morris (1979) observed that among female-headed families in Puerto Rico, the home still revolves around a male figure, even if absent, who can still make significant contributions and holds authority on many family matters. Perhaps these are remnants of a strong patriarchal family organization.

ANALYSIS OF THE DUAL-ROLE SITUATION

The socialization process in Puerto Rican culture is not aimed at preparing women for the child discipline role, a function reserved for the father/men. The task is beyond the behavioral repertoire provided to her by her culture. Consequently, many mothers are at a loss when, following migration, they find themselves at the helm of a fatherless family and solely responsible for their children's discipline.

The most salient feature that characterizes the discipline pattern of mothers in single families is inconsistency. This seems related to the mother's ambivalence, hesitation, and inability to assume the father's strong, strict disciplinarian role, who is able to firmly cope with the most difficult of discipline tasks. Furthermore, it certainly contradicts the mother's perception of herself as a giver of love and affection much more than a giver of sanctions. Consequently, she might feel that if she is too strict she could lose the children's affection for her.

This inconsistency is manifested in the frequent and seemingly arbitrary changes not only of the pattern of enforcement of the child discipline rules, but also of the set of rules themselves. Unaccustomed and ill-prepared to deal with all aspects of her children's discipline, the mother, at times unpredictably, overreacts to events that in her eyes and in her child's eyes are not so serious while choosing to "look the other way" in cases of serious breaches of clearly laid down rules. Additionally, the child finds that what was strictly prohibited yesterday is freely permissible today. In some instances, these mothers seem unable to adapt their discipline style to the new fatherless situation in the event of a major offense by one of their children, and they persist in threatening the child with telling the father, in spite of the fact that the father might have lived outside the home for many years. At the same time, the child is very much aware that this is a threat that cannot be enforced.

While parenting styles among Puerto Ricans have evolved through the years, the pattern currently transmitted to the Puerto Rican female is that parenting is conceived of almost exclusively in the context of a marital union. Significant changes in the marital union as well as in the support systems of the family or the marriage can create serious difficulties in successfully carrying out the parenting role. When the Puerto Rican woman is confronted with being a single head of household, she is faced with the dual role of being a mother and a father for her children. This is generally a conflictive situation to find herself in because these roles have been culturally transmitted to her as mutually exclusive, rather than as roles that can be integrated. The cultural expectations of her generation render her ill-prepared to integrate the father's role as disciplinarian in addition to her own role as nurturer and as an intermediary.

A major area in which this situation seems to create significant conflicts is in enforcement of child discipline. Her role as provider of love and affection in the family is by far more acceptable than the role of discipline enforcer. In fact, she is afraid to lose her children's affection if she becomes the strict enforcer of rules. The Puerto Rican female is not usually prepared for those tasks typically assigned to males. She does not believe herself capable of disciplining without a husband.

Under nonmigratory conditions, the cultural system where she comes from directs its efforts to assuring the presence of a substitute father through remarriage or by supplying male figures from the relatives and compadres of the extended family.

The following section will explain the model of intervention to be applied to the problem of conflicting dual roles among Puerto Rican single mothers.

MODEL OF INTERVENTION

The intervention consists of a stepwise progression empowering the Puerto Rican woman to assume the dual role of mother and father. The assumption is that male figures realistically may or may not become available in the immediate future to many families in the old ways, that is, as an economic provider, given unemployment. Consequently, many Puerto Rican women need help in adequately confronting the reality of single parenthood. The goal is not to lead her toward a "super-mom" role. This would only add more stress to her situation. Instead, the focus is on the need to learn new skills and to modify her perception of the mothering role as it was culturally defined. It is a complicated problem with no easy solution. Nonetheless, she will need to assume these new tasks more effectively in light of the socioeconomic incentives of the family to continue fatherless (e.g., welfare payments). This situation makes it difficult for the woman to rely on a new spouse or father to share the discipline tasks.

A first step in the intervention program consists of an assessment using the sociocultural framework just described. Subsequently, this is then explained and discussed with the woman in counseling to promote insight. Through a variety of techniques in individual (e.g., role playing) and family sessions, the single parent is trained to perform both roles.

The main goal of the intervention with the mother, in cases where no alternative fathers are available, is to train her to consistently and effectively fill the traditionally male role in the discipline of her children. In other words, since she is the only one dealing with discipline at home, she has to learn to function as sole legislator and decisive enforcer of child discipline rules. Consequently, she will have to acquire some of the firmness in dealing with the children that is typically attributed to males. It should be clear to her and her counselor that in doing so she does not have to, and indeed should not, renounce her traditional female role in child discipline. This would create an imbalance and a void in the other direction. The aim is not to supplant the father with the mother. Rather, efforts should be geared at allowing her to simultaneously perform both roles in a more integrated manner. From the mother's cultural perspective, and using the language of present-day psychology of women analysts such as Sandra Bem (1976) and Alexandra Kaplan (1976), that task is truly androgynous.

The following case vignettes will help clarify some of the points presented above.

Case A: Mrs. Fernández was 29 years old. She had four children ages 13, 12, 11, and 8. This woman had lived with the father of her four children without ever marrying him. He deserted the home when the last child was born. The children had little contact with their father. She never married, nor did she have a common-law husband again. Her mother, also a single mother, lived nearby. She did not represent a significant source of support in the area of child discipline because she was too busy her-self raising other grandchildren. This mother had only negative criticism for Mrs. Fernández's mothering style. Mrs. Fernández had difficulties setting limits and being consistent with disciplining all of her children, but most especially her eight-year-old son, who was her only male child. Whenever she felt overwhelmed with the children's misbehavior, she would warn them about telling their father about it. Of course, this threat had little effect on them since they were well aware that the probabilities of their father knowing were slim. At the start of the counseling sessions, Mrs. Fernández presented herself as an immature woman with low self-esteem and extremely overwhelmed with the discipline of her children. She was skeptical about believing that she could make her children respond to her discipline. Her discipline style was inconsistent. She would laugh (therefore jeopardizing the seriousness of the matter) while implementing or warning the children about a consequence. She would also warn them about conse-quences that were unrealistic, like reporting to their father. The counseling sessions were filled with new al-ternatives for this mother to implement discipline. In ad-dition, role-playing with the mother on how to warn the children was practiced and general support to the mother on such a difficult task was offered. Furthermore, discussions on the implications of inconsistent discipline and on laughing at the children's misbehavior were held. The difficulties faced by single mothers to discipline firmly and the cultural expectations behind this were explored as well as the importance of gaining self-respect. It was a difficult process for Mrs. Fernández and although she dropped out of treatment prematurely (a frequent event among low-income families), there were concrete gains. She became more effective in her discipline methods, began a weight control program at her neighborhood clinic, and even enrolled in a secretarial training program, which she reported to enjoy very much. These were all signs of Mrs. Fernández gaining self-respect, self-confidence, and control.

Case B: Mrs. Suárez, a woman 25 years old, had three children ages 10, 7, and 5. She had separated from her husband four years prior to the intervention and for the past three years had a common-law husband. The children heard from their father about once a year through a phone call or perhaps a visit. This man lived in another state. Mrs. Suárez did not have relatives nearby. Her illiteracy seemed to play a significant role in her low self-esteem and a sense of insecurity about her own capabilities. Her common-law husband represented a weak source of support because he would not get too involved with the discipline of the children, and their marital relationship was not very stable—they frequently broke off the relationship and got back together again. The children, for their part, did not regard him as a father. Mrs. Suárez had great difficulties with disciplining her children, especially her seven-year-old daughter, who was a very active girl. Her discipline style was to scream at the children constantly and either implement drastic consequences for their misbehavior or none at all. In counseling, we analyzed her current family situation and her discipline style. It was important for Mrs. Suárez to realize that if she could not rely on her partner for the discipline of her children, then such a task was almost exclusively hers. Regarding her discipline style, we discussed the negative implications of her constant screaming at the children, what were the consequences proportionate to the children's misbehavior, and the importance of being consistent with her discipline. Over time, and despite her inconsistency in keeping her appointments, there were some gains. Mrs. Suárez developed better control over her children's behavior. She also became interested in enrolling in an adult literacy program.

One frequent source of conflict for the mothers is to consolidate the firmness that is required with the affection she has for her children. The counseling situation, thus, has to deal with the mother's fear of not being motherly and feminine, and of losing her children's affection if the new discipline plan is implemented.

The counseling process should proceed gradually, depending on the progress made. It is wise, though, to try to make it a habit of pointing out the palpable gains along the way. This is particularly true of the first counseling sessions. Otherwise the mother might not feel motivated to return.

The client-counselor relationship should be characterized by mutual respect. If the counselor is non-Puerto Rican, he/she should be aware of any ethnocentric values that might lead him/her to be disrespectful toward cultural differences. As noted above, respect is the central guiding concept of all interpersonal relationships among traditional Puerto Ricans (Díaz-Royo 1975).

Given this analysis, one may conclude that it is difficult, though not impossible, for the traditional Puerto Rican woman living in the United States to effectively parent her children as a single mother. Culturally sensitive counseling can be of considerable help in promoting personal development in these adult migrant women so that they may meet the challenges posed by the parenting tasks of their new environment.

REFERENCES

Bem, S. L. 1976. "Probing the promise of androgyny." In A. G. Kaplan and J. P. Bean, eds., Beyond Sex-Role Stereotypes: Reading Toward a Psychology of Androgyny, pp. 47-62. Boston: Little, Brown.

Borrás, V. A. 1978. "Child discipline modes among mothers in fatherless Puerto Rican families: From tradition to inconsistency." Paper presented at the 30th Annual Meeting of the American Association of Psychiatric Services for Children, Atlanta, Ga.

Buitrago-Ortiz, C. 1973. Esperanza: An Ethnological Study of a Peasant Community in Puerto Rico. Tucson: University of Arizona Press.

Christensen, E. W. 1975. "The Puerto Rican woman: The challenge of a changing society." Character Potential 7, 2:89-96.

Díaz-Royo, A. T. 1975. "Dignidad and respeto: Two core themes in the traditional Puerto Rican family culture." Paper presented at the 14th Seminar of the Committee on Family Research under the auspices of the International Sociological Association, Curacao, Netherland Antilles.

Fitzpatrick, J. P. 1971. Puerto Rican Americans: The Meaning of Migration to the Mainland. Englewood Cliffs, N.J.: Prentice-Hall.

Frazier, E. F. 1966. The Negro Family in the U.S. Chicago: University of Chicago Press.

García-Preto, N. 1982. "Puerto Rican families." In M. McGoldrick, J. K. Pearce, and J. Giordano, eds., Ethnicity and Family Therapy, pp. 164-86. New York: Guilford.

González, N. S. 1970. "Toward a definition of matrifocality." In N. E. Whitten and J. G. Szwed, eds., Afro-American Anthropology. New York: Macmillan.

Kaplan, A. G. 1976. "Androgyny as a model of mental health for women: From theory to therapy." In A. G. Kaplan and J. P. Bean, eds., Beyond Sex-role Stereotypes: Reading Toward a Psychology of Androgyny, pp. 352-62. Boston: Little, Brown.

Leavitt, R. R. 1974. The Puerto Ricans: Cultural Change and Language Deviance. Tucson: University of Arizona Press.

Mintz, S. W. 1956. "Cañaveral: The subculture of a rural sugar plantation proletariat." In J. H. Steward, ed., The People of Puerto Rico, pp. 314-17. Chicago: University of Illinois Press.

Minuchin, S., B. Montalvo, and B. R. Guerny. 1967. Families of the Slums: An Exploration of Their Treatment. New York: Basic Books.

Mizio, E. 1974. "Impact of external systems on the Puerto Rican family." Social Casework 55, 1:76-83.

Morris, L. 1979. "Women without men: Domestic organization and the welfare state as seen in a coastal community of Puerto Rico." British Journal of Sociology 30, 3:322-40.

Pelto, P. J., M. Román, and N. Liriano. 1982. "Family structures in an urban Puerto Rican community." Urban Anthropology 11, 1:39-58.

Stack, C. B. 1974. All Our Kin: Strategies for Survival in a Black Community. New York: Harper & Row.

Steward, J. H., ed. 1956. The People of Puerto Rico. Chicago: University of Illinois Press.

U.S. Bureau of the Census. 1985. Persons of Spanish Origin in the United States: March 1985 (Advance report). (Current Population Reports, Series P-20, No. 403). Washington, D.C.: U.S. Government Printing Office.

Vázquez-Nuttall, E. 1979. "The support system and coping patterns of the female Puerto Rican single parent." Journal of Non-White Concerns 7, 3:128-37.

Wolf, K. L. 1952. "Growing up and its price in three Puerto Rican subcultures." Psychiatry 15:401-33.

9

A Contradiction in Ties: Autonomy and Social Networks of Adult Puerto Rican Women

María de Lourdes Mattei, Ph.D.

INTRODUCTION

This chapter discusses the significance of autonomy and social networks in the lives of adult Puerto Rican women in the United States, emphasizing the importance of the relational context for self-determination. As Puerto Rican women emerge from "traditional" cultural expectations and patterns, one needs to look at the various dimensions that may enhance or inhibit developmental growth and adaptation. As Kegan (1982) so aptly stated it, "I am using the word 'adaptation' not in the sense of 'coping' or 'adjusting to things as they are,' but in the sense of an active process of increasingly organizing the relationship of the self to the environment" (p. 113, emphasis added). That is, "adaptation" becomes a developmental criterion powered by an active dynamic relation of self to others.

Puerto Rican Women in the United States:
A Transitional Context

During this century several migratory waves of Puerto Rican people have flown in and out of the United States under a variety of political and economic pressures—for example, high levels of unemployment, colonial policies, rapid industrialization (see History Task Force's 1979 analysis of the Puerto Rican labor migration experience). Most of the "Puerto Rican diaspora" has concentrated on the eastern seaboard (López 1974).

These historical and socioeconomic realities present new challenges for Puerto Rican women and their communities. These changes are often discussed in terms of their culturally genocidal and socially catastrophic consequences, for example, high divorce rates, child abuse, delinquency, domestic violence, alcoholism, and so forth. Although I do not want to underestimate the conflictive and confusing elements involved in changes in social structure, I intend to emphasize the new alternatives and options that manifest themselves in transitional and crisis situations. As women become adults in these "transitional contexts," what conditions enhance, facilitate, and/or impede their self-determination in relation to their families and communities?

Autonomy and Social Networks in Women's Development

One of this study's basic assumptions is the importance of autonomy, at the individual and collective level, as a necessary condition for a truly emancipatory sphere of social interaction. By autonomy I mean self-determination, in the abstract sense of the word. Operationally, I define autonomy in this study as a process of decision making with others.

A manifestation of the struggle for autonomy is the growing effort by women for self-determination in all social spheres (e.g., reproduction, labor force participation, equal rights). Given the historical and institutional legacy of male domination in most social areas, it is important to determine the meaning of autonomy for women in general, and for different women in particular. Addressing the dissimilarity in experience of autonomy for women, Miller (1977) points out:

> Since women have to face very different consequences, the word autonomy seems possibly dangerous; it is a word derived from men's development not women's. . . . There is a further sense in which the automatic transfer of a concept like autonomy as a goal for women can cause problems. Women are quite validly seeking something more complete than autonomy, as it is defined for men, a fuller not a lesser ability to encompass relationships to others,

> simultaneous with the fullest development of
> oneself [p. 95].

Without having to coin another word, I believe that women
can appropriate, that is, they can actively shape a meaning for the word "autonomy" that would more accurately
reflect their individual and collective struggles for self-
determination. Nevertheless, Miller's insight is analytical-
ly helpful: women experience autonomy differently.

For a woman, the process of separation–individuation
(i.e., the developmental process of psychological autonomy)
takes a specific "relational" character:

> core gender identity for a girl is not prob-
> lematic in the sense that it is for boys. It
> is built upon, and does not contradict her
> primary sense of oneness and identification
> with her mother and is assumed easily along
> with her developing sense of self. Girls grow
> up with a sense of continuity and similarity
> to their mothers, a relational connection to
> their social worlds [Chodorow 1978, 64].

More recently, Hare-Mustin and Marecek (1986) commented on the complexities of autonomy as it relates to
gender differences. Offering a critical perspective, the
authors frame autonomy and relatedness as transactional,
that is, a person emphasizes one or the other, depending
on their position (relative power and status) in society.
Thus, individuals belonging to groups who are less powerful tend to voice the need for affiliation, and the ones
with more status frequently claim rationality and rules in
interpersonal exchanges.

Another study that explores the dimensionality of
autonomy in women's lives suggests that the significance
of autonomy changes throughout the life span. Mellinger
and Erdwins (1985) found that older women placed more
emphasis on affiliation and less on personal autonomy than
younger women.

In order to determine the level of decision making
(autonomy) exercised by working-class, urban Puerto Rican
women living in the United States, this study assessed
their decision making in the area of birth control, and
explored the woman's relational context (her relationship
within her family and community) in terms of her social
network.

Women's Decision-Making Activities

A crucial area in the struggle for autonomy is women's control over their own bodies, that is, reproductive determination. The history of birth control in the twentieth century clearly illustrates how this struggle is determined by historical and socioeconomic conditions (Gordon 1977). What for some women (upper- and middle-class White women) meant reproductive choice, for other women (poor and Third World women) meant reproductive oppression (see Mamdani 1972 and Mass 1977 for lucid accounts of repressive population control policies in India and Puerto Rico, respectively).

González et al. (1980) concluded in their study of the impact of sterilization on Puerto Rican women in Hartford, Connecticut, that several factors contributed to a "push towards sterilization." These factors (limited English language ability, household size, women-centered households) place limits on the woman's "resources and support systems," greatly affecting her decision-making possibilities.

In another study of Puerto Rican women, López-Garriga (1978) found that efforts at self-affirmation varied by socioeconomic level. Working-class women in Puerto Rico reported less use of manipulation as an interpersonal strategy than middle-class women. Paradoxically--although with less educational and economic resources--working-class women showed higher levels of self-affirmation in their personal lives than their more affluent counterparts.

Addressing a different social context and its relation to autonomy, Sacks and Eisenstein (1979) conducted a year-long study on the decision-making activities of a group of 15 women participants. In their reports of the group experience, the authors found that group participation enhanced personal autonomy for the women.

In her research on working women's lives, Moore-West (1981) reported a relationship between the woman's social networks and her personality style. Women with looser ties were more autonomous than women embedded within a more densely knit web. Furthermore, she comments on work as an important factor impacting women's personality styles by its relaxing effect on their social networks.

Thus, the social context of women's lives is of utmost importance in the efforts at self-determination in decision making. The following section addresses the social context as reflected in women's social networks.

Women's Social Networks

If a mature, autonomous ego is developed through its relationships with others, what kind of relationships do Puerto Rican women have? How do these relationships affect the level of self-determination exercised in their families and communities? What are the theoretical and practical implications of social networks for women?

One of the analytical advantages of the social network concept for women, at a personal as well as a political level, is its potential for grasping women's reality beyond their domestic group. Feminist theorists (e.g., Rosaldo and Lamphere 1974) have pointed out the historical consequences of the split between the private/personal/ domestic sphere and the public/social sphere (see Zaretsky 1976): the decline of women's status in their communities. Once accepted, the seclusion of women in the domestic sphere--and their concomitant exclusion from political and economic life--significantly affects women's status and power. Nonetheless, this analytical distinction is often overemphasized; it obscures the important ways in which these two spheres have developed and continuously shape each other (see Donzelot 1979 for an historical account of this process in France). This social network paradigm has the analytical possibility of reaching beyond the woman's domestic domain (household/family) into her community.

In addition, this concept does not limit its analysis of networks to their supportive characteristics or kinship ties. Addressing the issue of support, Wellman (1981) makes this clarification:

> We all know intuitively that ties are not al-
> ways supportive: that support is transmitted
> in variable, often ambiguous ways; that people
> often participate in several social networks in
> different spheres of their lives. However,
> the "support system" concept negates this
> sound intuitive knowledge of the complexities
> of ties and networks by denoting a single sys-
> tem composed only of supportive social rela-
> tions. Its focus on a simple "support-non-
> support" dichotomy de-emphasizes the multi-
> faceted, often contradictory nature of social
> ties. . . . Its assumption that there are no
> conflicts of interest between "supporters"

invokes the false promise of a common good [p. 173, emphasis added].

The personal and political implications of the study of women's networks are multidimensional. Evidence suggests a strong relationship between mental health and social networks. Although mostly concerned with the support aspect of network systems, psychologists have begun to apply network analysis to mental health studies (e.g., Todd 1980; Walker et al. 1977).

Adding an insightful and critical perspective on the stress of social ties for low-income women, Belle's research (1982) questions the frequent automatic assumption of support implicit in the literature on social networks. In a study of poor women with young children, Belle found that the size or the degree of involvement with network members was not as critical in their mental health as the quality of support available within the network. In fact, since women are often called to be providers of support (rather than the recipients), extensive social commitments can be more a burden than a buffer against stressful life events. Cohler and Lieberman's findings (1980) suggest similar conclusions in their research on European ethnic middle-aged groups. In their study among women of the two groups they consider most ethnically dense or "embedded"—Italian and Polish—reports of numerous and available social ties were adversely related to mental health.

Hirsch's (1980) research on the natural support system (NSS) explores the relationship between support, network characteristics, and an individual's life situation. The study tries to identify NSSs that enhance dealing with major life changes. Hirsch's findings suggest that structural characteristics of NSS have a significant relationship to how a woman copes with major life changes. High-density networks were significantly associated with poorer support (his previous research with college students also supports these findings, 1979). Furthermore, Hirsch reports that a denser network was related to fewer multidimensional friendships and smaller network size based on his analysis of two prototypical NSSs. One model is what he calls the "extended family" system. This system is characterized by the homogeneous interactions among its members (lower dimensional associations), often relationships revolving around children (child-centered). According to Hirsch, this model represents a type of cultural ideal. In contrast, he found that a low-density, multidimensional NSS, although less of a cultural ideal, seemed more adaptive in certain life situations (e.g., widowhood, return to college at an older age).

Other research that emphasizes the importance of weak (less dense) networks is Granovetter's (1973) study of the ties of young, mobile professionals. He was interested in finding out how this group of people found new jobs. Granovetter reports that of the individuals who got new jobs through contacts, their contacts fell toward the lower (weaker) end of the continuum. Thus, he argues for "the strength of weak ties."

Another study that stresses the importance of social networks for women's mental health is Garrison's (1978) research on schizophrenic and nonschizophrenic Puerto Rican migrant women in New York City. In contrast to Hirsch's findings, Garrison reports that women with either no significant or mild emotional disturbance were characterized by the "ideal/modal" pattern in their support network. This network pattern was called ideal because its features are consistent with cultural (traditional) ideals, and modal because of the statistical representativeness of its characteristics. The pattern is characterized by a nuclear family household, marriage, and frequent interactions with kin living within proximity. The other groups--from moderate to severely disturbed women--exhibited deviations (variations) of this ideal/modal network pattern.

One of the major differences found between schizophrenic and nonschizophrenic women in Garrison's study is the dependency pattern on kin. Except for the inpatient schizophrenic (who showed an almost exclusive intergenerational dependency), the "ideal/modal," less disturbed group of women were more kin-oriented in their support core group. She found that "a progressive decrease in reliance upon kin ties is associated with a progressive increase in reliance on non-kin ties and a corresponding increase in the incidence and severity of emotional disturbance" (p. 591). Thus, women who deviated from the cultural, traditional pattern of relating to kin had higher levels of emotional distress. The socioeconomic level of the samples may account for the difference in the women's relationship to their social network. The women in Garrison's research came from a poor community, and their educational level was on the average lower than in Hirsch's sample.

Studies of networks of nonpsychiatric, middle-class populations (e.g., Brennan 1977) indicate that these groups of people have networks that are more friend- and less kin-oriented. Further, it has been noted (see Granovetter, above) for this segment of the population, weaker ties can prove to be more adaptive. Therefore, one can speculate that what may constitute an adaptive network pattern for one group may have serious consequences for another. A variation/deviation of the "ideal" (whether cultural or class) pattern of social relationships may imply different consequences for different women. In the case of working-class women, breaking with the kin-dependency pattern may be disadvantageous since reliance on kin is not only a matter of emotional support but of economic survival. The importance and contradictory nature of family ties for women will be discussed further later. Nonetheless, given the historical and social "transitional context" of Puerto Rican women in the United States, a diverse and heterogeneous network composition can provide a more flexible and dynamic environment.

Once again, it should be emphasized that social ties are complex and often of an ambiguous and contradictory nature (see Wellman, above; Granovetter 1973; and Fischer 1980 for similar analyses of the complexities of social ties). The working-class Puerto Rican woman's contradictory position in her family and community clearly illustrates this point. The remainder of this section will address briefly some of the contradictions that face Puerto Rican women's attempts at self-determination.

In their families, most women are still expected to be primary caretakers of children, while at the same time, economic pressures force them into a discriminatory labor market. On the one hand, a woman's access to economic resources undermines patriarchal authority within the family; on the other, it has doubled women's labor (inside and outside the household).

Increasing attention is being focused on the important supportive functions the family fulfills for working-class women (e.g., Humphries 1977). But as Sen (1980) insightfully notes,

> The claim that the working-class family has beneficial aspects for women does not contradict the view that women are indeed subordinate to men within that same family. What is

> contradictory is not the analysis, but rather
> the position of women itself. . . . The
> mother whose private interests are always
> secondary, the daughter whose aspirations
> must give way to the son, know the contra-
> dictory nature of their membership in the
> family only too well [pp. 84-85].

For Puerto Rican women, these contradictions express themselves in ways specific to their families and communities. Their families, in an analogous situation to other low-income families in the United States, encountering limited access to economic resources and faced with brutal sociopolitical discrimination, perform vital survival functions for their members (Stack 1974; Humphries 1977; García-Bahne 1977). In particular, families in minority communities throughout the United States affirm and maintain the cultural continuity of their people: The woman in these families is often seen as the transmitter of that culture.

In an analysis of the situation faced by most Chicanas, García-Bahne (1977) comments on the relationship between family and community solidarity and autonomous behavior:

> All factors in and outside the family, situa-
> tional and historical, must be examined for
> developmental growth to take place. The
> Chicano family can thus be seen as a vehicle
> which incorporates these strengthening quali-
> ties that are necessary for social units to
> survive under exploitative conditions and
> paradoxically embodies those values which
> mitigate against the development and exercise
> of self-determination [p. 43].

A social analysis that portrays the Puerto Rican woman, her family, and community in simplistic ways can lead to mystifying and romantic visions of Puerto Rican culture. While the preservation of the cultural heritage is a necessary aspect of the Puerto Rican people's struggle for self-determination, an acceptance of traditional patterns—such as a patriarchal family organization—goes against the empowerment and development of autonomy for Puerto Rican women and thus for society as a whole. New sociocultural and personal expectations, patterns, and structures that integrate both autonomy and solidarity need to be shaped. A static (nondynamic) vision of culture militates against the struggle for self-determination at all levels, for all Puerto Rican people.

STATEMENT OF THE PROBLEM

In order to explore the relationship between the Puerto Rican woman's level of autonomy and the structure of her social network, the following areas were assessed: (a) decision making in the area of birth control, (b) size, strength of ties, density, diversity, and geographical dispersion of network membership, and (c) demographic background information.

This study addresses two central questions: What is the relationship between autonomy and social ties? And, what kind of social networks do working-class Puerto Rican women have?

The major hypothesis emphasizes the assumption that possibilities for autonomous behavior(s) are enhanced in a more diverse and loosely knit social network than in a homogeneous, dense social structure. Thus, social networks with these significant structural characteristics can offer a more functionally adaptive social and interpersonal context for adult women in transitional life situations such as Puerto Rican women who have migrated to the United States.

METHODOLOGY

Sample

In this study, 40 Puerto Rican women employed in an urban area were interviewed. The participants' characteristics were controlled for education (no graduate training) and occupation (service-related work). Factors influencing stability of network, such as recent migration and parenting, were accounted for by requiring that the participant reside for a minimum of one year in the area, and that she have at least one child under the age of 16 living at home.

In the group studied, 88 percent (35) of the women were born in Puerto Rico. Mean age was 32 1/2 years (ranging between 19 and 44 years of age). The average length of stay in the United States was 17 years, with a mean of 11 years in the Boston area. Seventy-three percent (29) of the women participating were married (either legally or consensually) at the time of the interview. A fourth of the group was either divorced or separated, and only one participant reported being single.

Most women had a high school degree and/or a few years of college (only six of the participants reported not having completed high school). With the exception of eight respondents, all other women were employed full time.

The language preference of the group was Spanish (65 percent) while 10 percent chose English and 25 percent stated no language preference for the interview.

Procedure

A structured interview was conducted in the participant's language of preference (Spanish, English, or both). The interview consisted of three main parts.

Part I—Background Information. The first section of the interview gathered important background demographic information. These characteristics included information such as marital status, length of residence in Boston and the United States, and household composition.

Part II—Autonomy Questionnaire. Autonomy or autonomous behavior was operationally defined as the degree of decision making in the area of birth control. Information about the participant's history of birth control was gathered. This section was an adaptation of a questionnaire designed by Darity, Turner, and Thiebaux (1971) and Borrás (1981). Part of the questionnaire required the woman to rate on a scale from 1 to 5 her contribution to decision making in birth control. These questions required that the women specify whether the decisions were made alone or shared (and with whom). Another section addressed additional information such as the woman's level of birth control knowledge and her expectations and conflicts in this area.

Decisions reported as shared were given the same weight as decisions made alone as long as the woman claimed equal contribution to decision making. If the woman indicated not having participated in the decision she was given the lowest score on the scale (i.e., it was considered that she contributed little or nothing to the decision-making process). The scaled weights were combined to give the participant's decision-making rating on birth control.

Part III—Social Network Mapping. The third component of the interview was designed to determine several structural characteristics of the participant's social network. Using a network map designed by Todd (1980), the participant was initially asked to name and/or write the names of the people with whom she kept regular contact (face-to-face, telephone, or letter contact). Once the list of network members was completed, the woman determined the degree of closeness of each member according to the three levels on the map. The inner circle (C1) reflects the zone of intimacy; the middle ring, the intermediate zone (C2); and the outer ring (C3), the zone of acquaintance. After each network member was placed on the map, the interviewer inquired about the nature of the relationship to each member (homogeneity/heterogeneity), where each member lived (dispersion), and degree of membership interconnectedness (density). Subsequently, these structural characteristics were measured as follows:

1. Size of network: sum of the number of people with whom the participant reported having regular contact.[1]

2. Strength of ties: the degree of relatedness and/or intimacy of the members was measured as the sum of the number of network members in Circles 1 and 2, minus the sum of network members in Circles 2 and 3:

$$\Sigma (C1 + C2) - (C2 + C3) = (C1 - C3).$$

3. Density of the network: how many people in the woman's network related to one another (i.e., knew each other); a density matrix (Rands 1980) was used to determine member interconnectedness.[2]

4. Homogeneity/heterogeneity of membership: the types of relationships in the participant's social network (e.g., kin, friend, workmate, etc.).

5. Dispersion of membership: the geographical location of members. IN—sum of number of network members living in Massachusetts; OUT—sum of number of network members living outside of Massachusetts.

RESULTS

Autonomy

The women in this study scored relatively high in the autonomy measure based on the participants' decision-making ratings on birth control. The mean score (average based on the sum of scores in terms of proportion) was .80. That is, out of a maximum score of 15, women on the average obtained 12 points (SD of 4.2). Thus, as a group, the women in this sample reported relatively autonomous behavior when making birth control decisions. At the same time, additional information gathered suggests that, although well-informed, these women consider birth control a conflictive area of decision making.

In order to assess the relationship between the autonomy measure and the social network variables, correlation coefficients were computed and are presented in Table 9.1.

Table 9.1

Pearson Correlation Coefficients for Autonomy
Measure and Social Network Variables

Autonomy measure	Social network variables					
	Size	In	Out	Density	HET	Strength
N = 20	.22	.22	.04	.21	.27	.33*

*p < .05

There was a significant relation between the woman's level of autonomy and the strength of her social ties (r = .33, p < .05). That is, the greater the proportion of close network members, the higher the levels of autonomy reported. The types of relationships reported in Circle 1 are summarized in Table 9.2. As can be observed in this table, most of the women's intimate network members consist of family, friends, and workmate-friends, in order of frequency. The circle of intimates included people who are not kin-related. This finding is consistent with previous research (e.g., Moore-West 1981) highlighting the impact of employment as a loosening factor in women's networks.

Table 9.2

Composition of Social Network Membership
in the Intimate Circle (C1)

Type of relationship	Number of participants reporting in this category	Percentage
Kin	30	77%
Friend	26	67%
Acquaintance	0	0%
Workmate-friend	14	36%
Workmate	3	8%
Other	5	13%

No other measures of the participants' social network were of statistical importance. Similarly, no significant relationships were found between the autonomy measure and demographic factors such as age or years in the city and in the United States.

Social Networks

The analysis of social network data gathered in the structured interview revealed both surprising and predictable results. The network characteristics assessed were: size, dispersion (number of network members living IN Massachusetts and number of members residing OUT of state), density ($\underline{D}$, interconnectedness of members), heterogeneity of relationships (HET, types of member composition), and the strength of the participants' social ties (STRE, relative number of intimate members). Table 9.3 summarizes the mean and standard deviation for each of the network variables. In addition, Table 9.4 presents the correlation coefficients calculated for all the network characteristics.

Table 9.3

Means and Standard Deviations for Social
Network Structural Characteristics

Social Network Characteristic	Mean	SD
Size	15	17
n - 39		
Dispersion		
In	14	16
n - 39		
Out	1	2
n - 39		
Heterogeneity	3	1
n - 40	.78	.27
Strength of ties	6	10
n - 39		

Table 9.4

Pearson Correlation Coefficients Matrix for
Social Network Structural Characteristics

(Size (s), Dispersion (IN, OUT), Heterogeneity (HRT),

Density (DEN), and Strength of Ties (STRE)

	Size	IN	OUT	HET	DEN	STRE
Size		.99***	.23	.59***	.22	.75***
IN			.11	.50***	.28	.73***
OUT				.08	-.40*	.32*
HET					-.14	.45**
DEN						.16
STRE						

*p < .05

**p < .01

***p < .001

228

Two structural features--heterogeneity and strength
of social ties--were found to have the most significant relationships with other network variables. Strength of ties,
the relative number and degree of closeness of the woman's
network ties, was positively related to the participant's
network size and diversity. This characteristic was also
associated with geographical dispersion of members. Thus,
participants with the strongest intimate circle tended to
have a larger, more diverse network composition with more
members residing both in and out of state.

Heterogeneity of network membership was another
structural feature of importance. As expected, the diversity of ties is significantly related to the network's size,
that is, larger networks had a more varied composition.
Furthermore, membership variety is strongly associated
with the number of members living close to the participant.
Thus, women with a more diverse member composition identified their ties as living in close geographical proximity
(in state).

Other significant correlations included the positive
relationship between network size and number of ties living
in-state (see Table 9.4). Thus the participant's network
size is comprised mostly of ties with those who reside in
close geographical proximity versus having members of a
large network dispersed geographically. These findings
would support Garrison's (1978) observations that Puerto
Rican women who migrate recreate in the new environment
social relationships that are strikingly similar to the network of their place of origin.

Contrary to expectations, the membership density or
interconnectedness was not found to relate significantly to
size or heterogeneity. Nonetheless, it was inversely associated with number of members living out-of-state. Therefore, the degree of membership connectedness had less
relation to size or diversity than to geographical location.
Unsurprisingly, denser networks had fewer members residing
at a distance.[3]

In order to analyze the possible associations between
demographic data and the social network characteristics of
the participants, Pearson correlation coefficients were computed for the variables of chronological age, years in the
United States, years in Boston, and network characteristics.
This analysis revealed a significant inverse relationship
between the woman's age and the heterogeneity of her network ties.[4] The findings presented in Table 9.5 suggest

Table 9.5

Pearson Correlation Coefficients Matrix for
Social Network Characteristics and Age,
Years in the United States, and Years in Boston

		Demographic characteristics	
Social network variable	Age	Years in U.S.	Years in Boston
Size	.01	-.16	.13
IN	-.01	-.14	.16
OUT	.12	-.18	-.28
HET	-.39**	-.29	-.02
Density	-.01	.15	.25
Strength	.03	-.14	.03

**p < .01

Table 9.6

Comparison of Network Heterogeneity
and Birthplace

	Birthplace	
	Puerto Rico	United States
Homogeneous network	24	1
Heterogeneous network	11	4

$x^2 = 4.40$, df = 1, p < .05

that younger participants had a more diverse network composition than older Puerto Rican women. Women who are older and born in Puerto Rico reported less variety in social ties. In addition, membership variety was related to the participant's birthplace. As results in Table 9.6 indicate, island-born women tended to have a relatively homogeneous network.[5]

DISCUSSION

The present study explores the relationship between women's level of autonomy and their social networks. This relationship is considered particularly relevant to women in their efforts at self-determination in their families and communities. It is argued that women must appropriate and transform the meaning of autonomy in order for the word to more accurately reflect their experience. Women's psychosocial development is characterized by its embeddedness in relationships. Feminism as well as some psychological theories (e.g., object relations theory) emphasize the importance of the relational context in the development of autonomy. Thus, this investigation examines the autonomous behavior of working Puerto Rican women in the context of their social networks.

Autonomous behavior was operationally defined in this study as the women's contribution to decision making in the area of birth control practices. Autonomy in birth control is considered a necessary (although not sufficient) condition for women's self-determination.

Traditionally, women have not been expected, and are often actively prevented from, behaving in an autonomous manner (these expectations vary according to the woman's class, culture, and race). Therefore the exercise of self-determination is a dynamic and continuous struggle for women. This struggle is carried out in the specific historical context of women's relationships within their families and communities. Looking at women's relational networks can help us understand as well as promote this struggle.

This investigation assumes that certain network characteristics can maximize the possibilities for exercising autonomous behavior in adult life. These characteristics may be conducive to a variety of alternatives and options that can support women in their struggle, and consequently help them transcend their often contradictory position in their respective communities. One of the characteristics that was considered important in facilitating women's autonomy in relationships was the diversity of network membership versus the density of interconnections.

Research on social networks has identified certain social network characteristics important in stressful situations. Hirsch (1980) found that women in life crisis circumstances reported less satisfaction with emotional support received in dense social networks. Denser social networks were also characterized by fewer multidimensional friendships as well as smaller overall network size. Studying the effects of marital break-up in the social networks of women, Rands (1980) reported larger networks for women who expressed greater desire for autonomy.

Analysis of the present data obtained from interviewing a group of Puerto Rican working women living in an urban setting in the United States revealed no significant relationships between autonomy and their networks' size, density, and heterogeneity. Nonetheless, there is a significant relationship between autonomy in birth control practices and the strength of a woman's network ties.

Women's Autonomy and the Significance
of Close Ties

This study strongly suggests a significant relationship between a participant's level of autonomy in decision making in birth control and the relative concentration of intimate ties (strength of woman's ties) in her network. High levels of autonomous decision making were found to correlate positively with a greater concentration of close ties in the woman's network. This association emphasizes the importance to women of emotional closeness in social ties and autonomy.

The literature's focus on density stresses the importance of the interconnectedness of network membership; that is, density refers to the degrees of integration in a person's community, not their "emotional connectedness." A commonly held assumption is that a fragmented network, characteristic of urban life, leads to social decay (see Wellman's 1979 argument on the "Community Question" in sociology). This study's findings indicate that the prevalence of emotionally close ties seems to be a critical variable in the urban web of social relationships. For adult women, the relevance of the significant relationship between autonomy and strength of ties in urban social networks gives weight to our initial argument: The relational context--in this case, the concentration of emotional ties in the social network--is a critical factor in women's efforts at self-determination.

Although network size and heterogeneity were not found to interrelate significantly with the autonomy measure, these structural characteristics correlated with the strength of ties in the women's networks. Higher levels of autonomy are associated with greater concentration of close links. Concomitantly, the prevalence of intimate relationships is significantly related to a larger network size and a more heterogeneous membership. Thus, women with networks characterized by more intimates also tend to have bigger as well as more diverse network ties.

Research on the birth control patterns of Puerto Rican communities in the United States established the importance of women's social links in decision making in this area. In their study of the effects of sterilization on Puerto Rican women in a community in Hartford, Connecticut, González et al. (1980) concluded that "at the present time, the most important source of information and support for the sterilization decision comes from family and friends" (p. 36). Borrás (1982) observed that women tend to discuss birth control issues with people perceived as supportive of the decision. If a woman's choice or decision goes against the traditional values and expectations of her community, one could assume that a larger, more diverse network tie could maximize the possibilities for self-determination in the control of her fertility.

From a different but related perspective, one can elaborate on the significance of close ties by exploring the quality of emotional closeness. As Garrison (1978) points out (see Introduction), certain types of closeness, for example, almost exclusive intergenerational dependence, can be associated with severe psychological disturbance. Family therapists often emphasize the pathological effects of "enmeshment" (fused or undifferentiated relationships between people). Although exploring the psychological dimensions of different social networks was beyond the scope of this study, the results of this investigation indicate possible connections between important structural features and psychological correlates for autonomy. For example,

a prevalence of intimate ties in a large and diverse social
network may be related to important psychological dimensions for autonomy and be indicative of a woman with
mature interdependence, that is, with close and differentiated interpersonal relationships.

Social Networks

One of the main objectives of this study was to begin
exploring the social ties of adult Puerto Rican women in
the United States. This investigation measured five structural characteristics of the social networks of working
Puerto Rican women living in a metropolitan area: size,
strength of ties, density, heterogeneity of members, and
their dispersion.

These women's social networks were characterized by
an average network size of 15 members. Most network
members resided in geographical proximity; that is, they
lived in Massachusetts. In fact, the larger the social
network, the greater number of network members lived
within the state. These social relationships featured an
average of three different types of social links. Thus,
women usually had more than family and friends in their
networks.

The average participant had a relatively dense social network (.78). Furthermore, 13 (32 percent) of the
women described networks typical of other working-class
communities (Cubbitt 1973). These social networks reveal
considerable overlap in their relationships: kin, friends,
and workmates consist of the same group of people.

In this study, density did not prove to be a significant factor when related to network size and diversity.
Rands (1980) observed that research on the relationship
between density and size shows inconsistent findings. In
addition, different measurement methods for these variables
further confound conclusive comparison and decisive inter-
pretations.

Strength of network ties was the most critical structural network feature in this study's analysis; it was the
one significant social network characteristic that most frequently related with other variables in this study. Similarly, Wellman's (1979) findings suggest an analogous
analysis: Density seemed to be a less central dimension
than was closeness of intimates in mobilizing help in the
social networks of a community in Toronto.

Another interesting finding was the relationship between strength of the woman's ties and the network's membership dispersion. Networks with a large concentration of intimates tend to have greater numbers of members residing in as well as outside of Massachusetts. These findings point to the fluidity of networks in the urban context.

In their study of rural-urban migration networks in Kenya, Ross and Weisner (1977) stress the importance of considering the migrants' place of origin and the city in which they settle as interdependent social systems. Much like African migrant populations, Puerto Ricans harbor and sustain the hope of returning eventually to the island. This hope is kept alive by the constant flow of resources and travel between Puerto Rico and the United States. Thus, maintaining strong ties with geographically distant network members is emotionally as well as economically important.

Finally, the second most important network characteristic in the analysis at hand was the heterogeneity of network members. Psychologists have often emphasized the importance of diversity in social relations, utilizing several methods in order to analyze the complexity and variety of relational contexts in a person's social world. For example, Hirsch (1979, 1980) looks at a relationship's dimensionality. Hirsch's research highlights multidimensional relationships as a strong predictor of students' satisfaction with their support networks. Interpreting the advantages of this characteristic in the support networks of women undergoing major life changes, he suggests that women require natural support systems that extend beyond the family sphere.

Demographically, the participant's age tends to relate inversely to the diversity of her network composition. Younger women tend to have a more heterogeneous group of ties. It seems that as women's relational worlds expand with changing socioeconomic conditions (e.g., participation in the labor force), especially in the case of younger generations, so do their networks.

Birthplace of the participants was another demographic characteristic significantly associated with the woman's network heterogeneity. More homogeneous network ties were related to the group of women born in Puerto Rico. The predominance of island-born women in this sample (88 percent) precludes any definite conclusions about the implications of these results. Nonetheless, these findings may help delineate important factors in future research with this community.

Conclusions and Implications for
Further Research

The findings of this exploratory study highlight the importance of social relationships in the exercise of autonomous decision making. Initially the exploration led to identifying structural network characteristics (e.g., density, size) that might facilitate and/or deter autonomy. Unforeseen, but in hindsight to be expected, was the significance of the relational closeness in the woman's social network. In contrast to commonly held (i.e., male-based) assumptions about autonomy, close ties can enhance rather than impede or "burden" self-determination. For urban, working-class (employed) women with children, autonomous decision making in birth control is associated with a higher concentration of intimates in a social network further characterized by its larger size and member diversity. These results are presented with the purpose of generating debate and continued discussion, rather than as conclusive data on Puerto Rican women's experience. The research was conducted in an effort to contribute to the sparse fund of knowledge and information about Puerto Rican women and, as such, it affirms as well as raises a variety of questions to be considered for further inquiry.

In light of the above findings and the researcher's experience conducting this exploration of autonomy and social networks of Puerto Rican women, the following areas for future research are suggested:

1. Life Cycle/Developmental Stage: How does autonomy vary through the woman's life cycle? Are there specific social network characteristics that facilitate and/or thwart a woman's decision making at different stages in her development?

2. Class and Race: How do women of different classes and/or racial backgrounds compare in the various components of autonomy? If working-class women are more dependent on their extended families (as opposed to relying on one male provider) for economic survival, how is their decision making different from that of middle-class women? Are middle-class women less autonomous in decision making

about financial matters but are more autonomous in decisions about their fertility? What other components are important in measuring autonomy for women? How does racial discrimination affect the social networks of various Puerto Rican women?

3. Employment and Migration: Although the Puerto Rican experience of migration has been studied from a variety of perspectives (in literature, economy, politics), there is a noteworthy absence of information about this experience as it touches women. How do the social networks of migrant Puerto Rican women compare to those of women who remained on the island? How do second- and third-generation women's networks in various parts of the United States compare, both with one another and with those in Puerto Rico? The effects of employment--or lack of employment--needs to be further analyzed. As mentioned previously, what are other important aspects of autonomy for women who hold employment? Furthermore, one may speculate about the effects of different kinds of employment (e.g., factory work, professional practice) in women's autonomy and social networks.

Other related areas of interest include investigating women with nontraditional lifestyles such as lesbian women and women who are childless. In several cases in this sample, the women reported having carried out decision making with their own mothers. The mother-daughter relationship appears as an important dimension in the study of autonomy for women.

It is hoped that the areas identified here for future investigation stimulate discussion and future research relevant to Puerto Rican women as well as other people's struggles for self-determination.

NOTES

1. In cases where the participant was unclear or unsure about the number of network members in any particular category, for example, precise number of workmates, church friends, and so forth, an average number was calculated based on the number of network members of a type given in the total sample.

2. Density was calculated only for participants who clearly met the computational (scoring) criteria. If the participants comprised eight members or less, the density

matrix was used to calculate the proportion of number of actual linkages ($\underline{a}$) by number of possible linkages ($\underline{p}$) among network members $\underline{p}\frac{a}{}$. Density measures were computed for only 27 of the participants.

3. The network density results must be understood with caution since scoring difficulties limited the number of networks for which this measure was calculated, probably inflating the density measure. Nevertheless, this measure gives us an initial density baseline from which to speculate both in this study and in future research in the Puerto Rican community.

4. Since the effects of age and number of years spent in the United States were not found to be independent, further statistical analysis was conducted. A partial correlation coefficient revealed that the relationship between age and network heterogeneity almost reaches significance ($\underline{r} = -.30$, $\underline{p} = .06$, trend) even when the effect of years in the United States was controlled.

5. It must be noted that the validity of the chi-square presented in this section may be in question due to the relatively small size of the sample. Nevertheless, these statistics have descriptive qualities that will be elaborated on in the discussion section.

REFERENCES

Belle, D., ed. 1982. Lives in Stress: Women and Depression. Beverly Hills: Sage.

Borrás, V. A. 1981. "Family planning among mainland Puerto Ricans: An analysis of the decision-making process." Master's Thesis, University of Massachusetts, Amherst.

_____. 1982. "Opting for sterilization in the U.S. and Puerto Rico: An overview." Comprehensive examination paper, University of Massachusetts, Amherst.

Brennan, G. T. 1977. "Work/life segmentation and human service professionals: A social network approach." Ph.D. doctoral dissertation, University of Massachusetts, Amherst.

Chodorow, N. 1978. The Reproduction of Mothering, Psychoanalysis and the Sociology of Gender. Berkeley: University of California Press.

Cohler, B., and M. Lieberman. 1980. "Social relations and mental health among three ethnic groups." Research on Aging 2, 4:445-69.

Cubbitt, T. 1973. "Network density among urban families." In J. Boissevain and J. Claude Mitchell, eds., Network Analysis Studies in Human Interaction, pp. 67-82. Paris: Mouton.

Darity, W. A., C. B. Turner, and H. J. Thiebaux. 1971. "An exploratory study of barriers to family planning: Race consciousness and fears of Black genocide as a basis." In A. J. Sobrero and R. M. Harvey, eds., Advances in Planned Parenthood, vol. 3, pp. 20-32. Amsterdam: ICS 246, Excepta Medica.

Donzelot, J. 1979. The Politics of Families. New York: Random House.

Fischer, C. S. 1980. "The effects of urbanism on social networks and mental health: Final report." Connections 3, 2:23-26.

García-Bahne, B. 1977. "La Chicana and the Chicano family." In R. Sánchez and R. Martínez Cruz, eds., Essay on La Mujer, Anthropology, No. 1, pp. 30-47. Los Angeles: Chicano Studies Center Publications.

Garrison, V. 1978. "Support systems of schizophrenic and nonschizophrenic Puerto Rican migrant women in New York City." Schizophrenic Bulletin 4, 4:561-95.

González, M., V. Barrera, P. Guarnaccia, and S. L. Schensul. 1980. "The impact of sterilization of Puerto Rican women, their families and the community." Paper presented at the Hispanic Women's Conference, Hispanic Research Center, Fordham University, New York.

Gordon, L. 1977. Woman's Body, Woman's Right. New York: Penguin.

Granovetter, M. S. 1973. "The strength of weak ties." American Journal of Sociology 78, 6:1360–80.

Haren-Mustin, R. T., and J. Marecek. 1986. "Autonomy and gender: Some questions for therapists." Psychotherapy 23, 2:205–66.

Hirsch, B. J. 1979. "Psychological dimensions of social networks: A multidimensional analysis." American Journal of Community Psychology 7, 3:263–77.

_____. 1980. "Natural support systems and coping with major life changes." American Journal of Community Psychology 8, 2:159–66.

History Task Force, Centro De Estudios Puertorriqueños. 1979. Labor Migration Under Capitalism: The Puerto Rican Experience. New York: Monthly Review Press.

Humphries, J. 1977. "The working class family, women's liberation and class struggles: The case of nineteenth century British history." Review of Radical Political Economics 9, 3:25–41.

Kegan, R. 1982. The Evolving Self. Problem and Process in Human Development. Cambridge, Mass.: Harvard University Press.

López, A. 1974. "The Puerto Rican diaspora: A survey." In A. López and J. Petras, eds., Puerto Rico and Puerto Ricans: Studies in History and Society, pp. 316–46. Cambridge, Mass.: Schenkmann.

López-Garriga, M. 1978. "Estrategias de Auto-afirmación en Mujeres Puertorriqueñas." Revista de Ciencias Sociales 1, 3–4:257–85.

Mamdani, M. 1972. The Myth of Population Control. New York: Monthly Review Press.

Mass, B. 1977. "Puerto Rico: A case study of population control." Latin American Perspectives 4, 4:66–82.

Mellinger, J. C., and C. J. Erdwins. 1985. "Personality correlates of age and life roles in adult women." Psychology of Women Quarterly 9:503–14.

Miller, J. B. 1977. Toward a New Psychology of Women. Boston: Beacon.

Moore-West, M. L. 1981. "Family, friends and partners: The search for intimacy and autonomy." Dissertation Abstracts International 41 (12-A, Pt. 1), 5259.

Rands, M. 1980. "Social networks before and after marital separation: A study of recently divorced persons." Doctoral dissertation, University of Massachusetts, Amherst.

Rosaldo, M. Z., and L. Lamphere, eds. 1974. Woman, Culture and Society. Stanford: Stanford University Press.

Ross, M. H., and T. S. Weisner. 1977. "The rural-urban migrant network in Kenya: Some general implications." American Ethnologist 4:359-75.

Sacks, S. R., and H. Eisenstein. 1979. "Feminism and psychological autonomy: A study in decision making." Personnel and Guidance Journal 57, 8:419-23.

Sen, G. 1980. "The sexual division of labor and the working class family: Towards a conceptual synthesis of class relations and the subordination of women." Review of Radical Political Economics 12, 2:76-86.

Stack, C. B. 1974. All Our Kin: Strategies for Survival in a Black Community. New York: Harper & Row.

Todd, D. 1980. "Social networks, psychosocial adaptation, and preventive/developments interventions: The support development workshop." Paper presented at a meeting of the American Psychological Association, Montreal, Canada, September (Erie Report Microfilm No. ED 198420).

Walker, K. N., A. MacBride, and M. L. S. Vachon. 1977. "Social support networks and the crisis of bereavement." Social Science and Medicine 44:35-44.

Wellman, B. 1979. "The community question: The intimate networks of East Yonkers." American Journal of Sociology 84, 5:1201-31.

_____. 1981. "The application of network analysis to the study of support." In B. Gottlieb, ed., Social Networks and Social Support in Community Mental Health. Beverly Hills: Sage.

Zaretsky, E. 1976. Capitalism, the Family and Personal Life. New York: Harper & Row.

10

Elderly Puerto Rican Women in the Continental United States

Rita E. Mahard, Ph.D.

INTRODUCTION

Despite considerable growth in research on ethnicity and aging over the last several decades, very little is known about the Puerto Rican elderly (Markides and Mindel 1987). Given the general lack of research on this population, it is not surprising to find a corresponding lack of attention to the variations among the Puerto Rican elderly with regard to gender, acculturative level, educational attainment, or other factors. Women constitute 59 percent of the Puerto Rican elderly residing in the continental United States (New York City Department of City Planning 1982) and, from a research standpoint, they are a particularly neglected population.

Because so little is known, description as a research task has an important role to play in moving our understanding of this group forward. In this chapter, we report some early descriptive results from a recent large-scale household survey of a representative sample of elderly Puerto Ricans residing in the New York metropolitan area. The availability of a large probability sample, coupled with the fact that over half of the Puerto Rican elderly in the continental United States live in the New York metropolitan area (New York City Department of City Planning 1982), means that it is possible for the first time to describe this population in detail as well as to attend to the considerable within-group diversity that characterizes it.

Our descriptive efforts focus on two broad classes of variables: demographic characteristics, which are important determinants of the life experience of any older population; and characteristics of the migration experience and the acculturation process, which reflect the more culturally specific experience of older Puerto Ricans in the New York area. Beyond its descriptive interest, information of this type can provide insight into the kinds of problems older Puerto Ricans face and this, in turn, can be useful for policy and planning purposes.

While our primary concern is with the older woman, we also wish to understand the older woman's experience in a context. Hence we present our data for both women and men and note points of similarity and dissimilarity. Before presenting our results, however, we turn to a brief overview of the existing survey literature on New York area Puerto Rican elderly.

Data from the 1980 census suggest that poverty is one of the major problems facing the Puerto Rican population as a whole and that this is the case for the elderly as well. For example, at the time of the census, 49 percent of elderly Puerto Rican households in New York City were headed by females, a statistic suggestive of considerable economic hardship (New York City Department of City Planning 1982).

Two interview studies conducted in the New York area involved samples of elderly Puerto Ricans, and these provide additional insights into the problems and strengths of this group. Cantor's 1979 study surveyed 1,500 Puerto Rican, Black, and non-Hispanic White elderly from New York's inner city. The 200 elderly Puerto Ricans in Cantor's study were found to have significantly greater physical disability as measured by the Townsend Index of Functional Status than either the Black or the non-Hispanic White samples (Cantor and Mayer 1976). A more subjective physical health measure showed a similar, although less pronounced, pattern. Elderly Puerto Ricans also had the lowest current and past incomes, and multivariate analyses indicated that income was the strongest predictor of race/ethnic differences in physical health.

A more recent study by Mahard (1988), involving intensive interviews with 30 psychiatric outpatient elderly and 30 nonpatient community residents, underscores the importance of both the migration experience and the acculturation process. Homesickness for absent loved ones in

Puerto Rico, one consequence of migration, and acculturative difficulties, particularly problems with the English
language, were common among the older people interviewed,
and both of these factors were found to be significantly
correlated with the experience of depressive symptoms.

A number of researchers have noted the strength of
familistic ties among Hispanics and have suggested that
the extended family is an important resource for older
people (Dowd and Bengtson 1978; Valle and Mendoza 1978).
The Cantor study found that familistic ties were indeed
strongest among Puerto Ricans (Cantor 1979). Older Puerto
Ricans had more children, more frequent contact with children, and received a greater variety and amount of assistance from children than older Blacks or non-Hispanic
Whites.

Both the Cantor and the Mahard studies involved
relatively small and select samples of older Puerto Ricans,
which may limit the generalizability of their results.
These studies, taken together with the 1980 census data,
suggest that poverty, health, and acculturative difficulties
need to be considered in research on the elderly Puerto
Rican population, and the census data suggest that poverty, in particular, may disproportionately affect the older
Puerto Rican woman.

One other finding from the census data also deserves
comment, and that is the relative youth of the Puerto Rican
population. In New York City, the Puerto Rican population
is younger than the total city population by an average of
8.9 years; the median age for Puerto Ricans is 23.7 compared to a city median of 32.6 years (New York City Department of City Planning 1982). The census data suggest
further that age-linked life events such as child-bearing
and the "emptying of the nest" also occur earlier for
Puerto Rican families than for all New York City families
(New York City Department of Planning 1982). Other data
suggest that elderly Puerto Ricans may retire well before
age 65 and earlier even than other Hispanic groups
(Lacayo 1980).

These data fit well with theoretical evidence of
"quicker timing" of the life cycle for minority than for
majority group persons (Bengtson et al. 1977; Newton 1980).
They also suggest that a conventional definition of elderly
as aged 65 or older is probably not appropriate for the
New York area Puerto Rican population. Our decision to
interview persons beginning at age 55 stems from these

considerations. We turn now to a description of the larger study from which our data are drawn.

METHODS

The data are drawn from personal interviews with a representative cross-section of 1,002 New York area Puerto Ricans aged 55 and over. The sample design and field work for the survey were carried out in 1986 by Temple University's Institute for Survey Research under contract to the Hispanic Research Center at Fordham University. The design involved a disproportionate, stratified multistage area probability sample of Puerto Ricans 55 years of age and over residing in households in the New York metropolitan area. To minimize the great screening costs that are involved in identifying eligible respondents of this rare population (less than 1 percent of the total population), the study utilized the household sampling frames from several recently completed household surveys conducted by the Institute for Survey Research. The sampling frames from these previous studies identified Hispanic households that were then again screened to determine whether they contained an individual eligible for the Puerto Rican elderly study. In order to address possible problems of sample obsolescence, fresh, previously unscreened households were added to the sample. Ninety-eight percent of the households in the final sampling frame were successfully screened, yielding 1,161 eligible respondents of whom 1,002 (86 percent) were interviewed. Most of the 14 percent nonresponse was due to refusals.

Interviewing for the study took place from July 1986 through February 1987. Interviews were conducted by trained bilingual interviewers and averaged two hours in length. Respondents were offered the choice of language of interview, and 97 percent chose to be interviewed in Spanish. At the completion of the interview, respondents were given $10 as a token of appreciation for their time.

The data reported in this chapter are weighted. The weighting reflects probabilities of selection, adjusts for nonresponse, and brings our data into alignment with the 1980 census data on the age, sex, and geographical distributions of the Puerto Rican elderly in the New York metropolitan area.

Table 10.1

Demographic Characteristics of Elderly Puerto Ricans for Total Sample and by Sex*

	WOMEN	MEN	TOTAL	x^2	df	p
AGE (YEARS)						
55 – 59	32 %	36 %	33 %			
60 – 64	23	25	24			
65 – 69	18	18	18			
70 or more	27	21	24	5.15	3	.161
MARITAL STATUS						
Currently married	26 %	60 %	40%			
Not currently married	74	40	60	115.76	1	.001
EDUCATION (YEARS COMPLETED)						
0 – 2	21 %	17%	20%			
3 – 4	25	22	24			
5 – 7	25	22	24			
8 or more	29	38	33	8.50	3	.037
INCOME						
less than $5,000	40 %	23 %	33 %			
$5,000 – $8,999	36	35	35			
$9,000 or more	25	42	32	41.28	2	.001
SOURCES OF INCOME (3 items) % YES:						
Social Security	50 %	47 %	49 %	.89	1	.346
Supplemental security	47	26	38	44.01	1	.001
Food stamps	48	34	42	17.73	1	.001

[1]Total weighted N = 1002; N for women = 586; N for men = 416

RESULTS

Demographic Characteristics

Table 10.1 shows selected demographic characteristics of the Puerto Rican elderly for the total sample and separately by sex. As the table indicates, the Puerto Rican elderly are a relatively young population overall. Fifty-seven percent are between the ages of 55 and 64, while roughly one-quarter are age 70 or greater. While women are slightly more likely than men to be represented in the oldest age category and slightly less likely to be represented in the youngest age category, the overall distribution on age does not differ significantly by sex ($\underline{X}^2 = 5.15$, df = 3, $\underline{p}$ = .16).

The data on marital status show a striking sex difference, with women being considerably less likely than men to be currently married ($\underline{X}^2 = 115.76$, df = 1, $\underline{p} < .001$). Only 26 percent of women are currently married compared to 60 percent of men. Widowhood and separation or divorce make up roughly equal proportions of unmarried women. Relatively few of the women have never been married.

The data on education indicate a low level of formal schooling, with 44 percent of the sample having completed four years of schooling or less. Only one-third have completed as much as eight years of schooling. In the total sample, the percentage completing high school or beyond (not shown in the table) is only 12 percent. Women and men differ significantly in terms of education, with proportionately fewer women having completed eight or more years of schooling and proportionately more women being in the lower education categories ($\underline{X}^2 = 8.50$, df = 3, $\underline{p}$ = .04).

The data on income show that one-third of all respondents reported a 1985 pre-tax annual income for self (and spouse) of less than \$5,000. Income distributions show a pronounced sex difference ($\underline{X}^2 = 41.28$, df = 2, $\underline{p} < .001$).[1] Women are considerably more likely than men to be represented in the lowest income category. The major source of income for these older people is Social Security, with men and women being about equally likely to receive income from this source. In addition to being overrepresented in the lowest income category, women are also more likely than men to receive income from public assistance programs such as Supplemental Security Income and food stamps.

Table 10.2

Current Work Status and Major Lifetime Occupations
of Puerto Rican Elderly for Total Sample
(Ns in parentheses)

WORK STATUS	
Currently working for pay	17 %
Not currently working for pay	71
Never worked for pay	12
	(1002)

MAJOR LIFETIME OCCUPATION[1]	
Managerial, Professional, Technical or Sales	11 %
Service	21
Precision Production	15
Operators, Fabricators, Laborers	51
Other	2
	(863)

[1]Excludes those who have never worked for pay

Table 10.2 shows the current work status and the
major lifetime occupations of the Puerto Rican elderly.
These data are presented for the total sample only; restricted variability in the percentage currently working for
pay and in the percentage never having worked for pay
precludes detailed analyses of these categories by sex.
Nevertheless, the data for the total sample are instructive.
The table shows that only 17 percent of these older people
are currently working for pay. The great majority are not
currently working, but have worked for pay at some point
in the past (71 percent). The remainder—12 percent—have
never worked for pay. Virtually all of those who have
never worked for pay are women, with the great majority
indicating responsibilities as housewife or mother as their
primary reason for not working outside of the home. Data
on major lifetime occupations were classified according to
the categories used in the 1980 census (U.S. Bureau of the
Census 1982). If we examine the major lifetime occupations

of those who are either currently working or who have
worked for pay in the past, it is evident that the majority
of these older people have worked in low-status occupations.
Only 11 percent report major lifetime occupations in the
managerial/professional or technical/sales categories.
Roughly three-quarters of the ever-employed can be found
in two major occupational categories: operators, fabricators and laborers, and service occupations. Men and women
are equally likely to be represented in the service category,
with launderers, cooks, nursing aides, orderlies, and jani-
tors being the most common service occupations. Ten percent of those who ever worked for pay had these particular
service jobs as their major lifetime occupations.

The majority of those who have worked did so as
operators, fabricators, and laborers, with women being
more likely to be represented in this category than men
(60 versus 41 percent; $\underline{X}^2$ = 31.37, df = 1, $\underline{p} < .001$).
Most of these persons worked as machine operators. Twenty-
seven percent of all ever-employed women worked in a
single occupation: textile sewing machine operator.

Given the relative youth of this population, the fact
that the great majority are no longer working is perhaps
surprising. This finding can be understood better in the
context of the occupations that these older people have
held. The data suggest that the difficult working conditions and the level of physical demand associated with
service and laborer occupations have taken a toll on the
health of this group and resulted in an earlier age for
leaving work than would otherwise have been expected.
Table 10.3 addresses these issues.

The table shows that almost one-third of past workers
stopped work between the ages of 47 and 57. Women are,
of course, more likely to have stopped work before age 47
due to family and child care responsibilities, but 29 percent of women who have worked left the labor force between
the ages of 47 and 57. For each age group, health is
most frequently cited as the primary reason for stopping
work, more frequently cited than child care and housewife
responsibilities in the lowest age category and more frequently cited than retirement per se in the oldest age
category.

Men are significantly more likely than women to report health as their primary reason for stopping work (58
percent), but half (49 percent) of the women who have
worked also cite health as their primary reason ($\underline{X}^2$ = 5.56,

Table 10.3

Age at Last Paid Employment for Those Not Currently Working
Who Have Worked for Pay in Past, and Percentage of Each
Age Group Citing Health as Primary Reason for Stopping Work

| | Persons Not Currently Working Who Have Worked for Pay in Past | | | |
	WOMEN (n=395)	MEN (n=309)	TOTAL (n=704)	% OF EACH AGE GROUP WHO STOPPED WORK PRIMARILY FOR HEALTH REASONS
Age When Last Worked for Pay				
age 46 or less	45 %	21 %	34 %	50 %
between ages 47 and 57	29	36	32	69
age 58 or more	26	43	33	41

FOR SEX DIFFERENCE IN AGE AT LAST PAID EMPLOYMENT

$X^2 = 46.12$, df = 2, p < .001

df = 1, p = .02). The second most frequently mentioned reason for women was child care and housewife responsibilities (cited by 20 percent of past women workers), whereas for men it was having reached the age of retirement (cited by 23 percent of past men workers).

The data that we have examined thus far give a broad outline of the Puerto Rican elderly population in terms of demographic composition and provide a sense of how women and men differ along these dimensions. Data on education, occupation, and income point to low socio-economic status in this population overall. Two characteristics in particular, probably interrelated, distinguish women from men: They show a considerable income disadvantage relative to men and they are much less likely than men to be currently married.

Because the Puerto Rican elderly are a culturally distinctive population, however, demographic characteristics alone do not tell the full story. An adequate description of this population also requires attention to the migration experience and the acculturation process, and it is to these aspects of the lives of older Puerto Ricans that we now turn.

Migration and Acculturation

Virtually all of the older people in this study (97 percent) were born in Puerto Rico and migrated to the continental United States as part of a large wave of Puerto Rican migration that followed World War II (New York City Department of City Planning 1982). We asked our respondents what year they came to the United States with the intention of taking up permanent residence. The mean year of arrival in the total sample was 1951 (SD = 11 years), with men arriving about two years earlier on the average than women (for men $\bar{X}$ = 1950, SD = 11 years; for women, $\bar{X}$ = 1952, SD = 11 years; difference significant at $p < .001$, $\underline{t}(979)$ = 3.15). Fifty-seven percent of the sample arrived in the period between 1945 and 1955. At the time of our study, the median length of residence in the United States was 36 years, with only 6 percent of the sample having taken up permanent residence in the last 15 years.

Despite a relatively long period in the United States, elderly Puerto Ricans are largely unacculturated, although there is some slight variation, depending on which aspect of acculturation is being considered. Within this population, the women are less acculturated than the men.

Acculturation is often defined empirically in terms of language preference and usage, with many of the more widely used survey measures of acculturation containing language questions as core items (Cuellar et al. 1980; Szapocznik et al. 1978). One clear measure of language preference is the language in which the respondent chose to be interviewed. Since this was overwhelmingly Spanish in our study (97 percent of all interviews), this measure was not useful in helping distinguish respondents who varied in degree of acculturation.

We asked respondents a series of questions about language usage in different settings that offered five response alternatives ranging from "Spanish all of the time" to "English all of the time." Table 10.4 shows the percentage reporting exclusive use of Spanish in four different settings. The data show Spanish to be the language of choice for conversations at home and with friends, with greater percentages of women than men reporting exclusive use of Spanish.

There is some departure from this pattern for language of television programs. Only 37 percent of the total sample watch Spanish language television exclusively. There is a sizeable sex difference, however, with women being significantly more likely than men to watch Spanish television only (44 versus 27 percent; $X^2 = 28.21$; df $= 1$, $p < .001$). Language of radio programs is much more likely to be exclusively Spanish than language of television programs, probably because English-language radio, lacking the visual cues provided by television, is more difficult for these older people to understand.

We also asked respondents how they thought of themselves in terms of ethnic identity. Given the importance of language to culture, it is not surprising that we find that these older people have retained a strong Puerto Rican identity. As the table shows, 48 percent of all respondents said they considered themselves "more Puerto Rican than American." The two other alternatives to this question, "equally Puerto Rican and American" and "more American than Puerto Rican," were chosen by 44 percent and 8 percent of these elderly, respectively (data not shown). Women are significantly more likely than men to define themselves as more Puerto Rican than American (52 percent versus 42 percent; $X^2 = 11.01$, df $= 1$, $p < .001$).

Table 10.4

Migration and Acculturation Characteristics of Puerto Rican Elderly for Total Sample and by Sex*

	WOMEN	MEN	TOTAL	X^2 (df=1)	p
LANGUAGE USAGE (% Spanish all the time)					
at home	77 %	63 %	71 %	21.47	.001
with friends	67	51	60	25.86	.001
television programs	44	27	37	28.21	.001
radio programs	68	49	60	35.45	.001
SUBJECTIVE IDENTIFICATION					
% more Puerto Rican than American	52 %	42 %	48 %	11.01	.001
TIES TO THE ISLAND HOME (% YES)					
visited Puerto Rico since arrival	87 %	88 %	87 %	.44	.508
would like to return permanently	46	42	44	1.33	.249
plans to return permanently	24	26	25	.33	.564
life would be better in Puerto Rico	20	24	22	1.57	.210
MIGRATION STRESS (% very or fairly often)					
miss relatives and friends	67 %	50 %	60 %	23.44	.001
homesick for island	52	45	50	4.78	.029
ACCULTURATIVE DIFFICULTIES					
% many problems speaking English	42 %	29 %	37 %	18.42	.001
% many problems understanding English	42	26	35	29.18	.001
% need translator with bureaucracies	48	28	40	36.91	.001

[1]Total weighted N = 1002; N for women = 586; N for men = 416

Of the aspects of acculturation examined in Table 10.4, the sexes are most alike in terms of their ties to the island home of Puerto Rico. Contact with Puerto Rico is the rule rather than the exception, with the great majority of both sexes (87 percent) having traveled to Puerto Rico since taking up residence in the United States. Not shown in the table is the fact that over half (58 percent) of those who had taken trips to Puerto Rico had done so within the five years preceding the interview, with women being significantly more likely than men to have traveled to Puerto Rico in the last five years (61 versus 53 percent; X^2 = 5.49, df = 1, $\underline{p}$ = .02).

A substantial proportion of elderly Puerto Ricans say they would like to return to Puerto Rico on a permanent basis (44 percent), although relatively few (25 percent) currently have plans to do so. Most respondents said they thought their lives were better in the United States than they would be in Puerto Rico. The percentage saying life would be better in Puerto Rico is roughly the same as the percentage with plans to return permanently and, as would be expected, there is significant overlap between these groups ($\underline{X}^2$ = 217.04, df = 1, $\underline{p}$ < .001).

Both migration and the experience of living in a culture that differs from their culture of origin have been important sources of chronic stress for elderly Puerto Ricans. Although the migration experience occurred in the relatively distant past for most of these older people, some of its consequences continue to be felt in the present. Chief among these, and particularly important for the women in our sample, is the physical separation from loved ones in Puerto Rico. Virtually all of the people we interviewed reported that they had family members or friends on the island, and homesickness for these absent loved ones is common. Sixty percent of the sample indicated that during a typical week they thought about absent relatives and friends very often or fairly often, with women being considerably more likely than men to report such frequent thoughts (67 versus 50 percent; X^2 = 23.44, df = 1, $\underline{p}$ < .001). Many of these older people also feel considerable nostalgia for the island home of Puerto Rico, with these feelings being more common among the women as well.

Acculturative difficulties, particularly problems with the English language, also affect a substantial proportion of these older people. Slightly over one-third of all respondents indicated that they had "many" problems (as opposed to "some" or "no" problems) making themselves

understood in English, and approximately the same proportion indicated "many" problems understanding spoken
English. (Both of these figures include persons who speak
no English at all.) Since an additional 25 percent indicate "some" problems on each of these two items (data not
shown), we can see that difficulties with the English language affect the great majority of these older people.
Given the sex difference observed earlier with respect to
language usage, it is not surprising that women are significantly more likely than men to report having "many"
English problems.

As part of a series of questions on language difficulties, we also asked respondents if they ever brought someone with them to serve as a translator when they had to
deal with bureaucracies such as hospitals, clinics, or
government agencies. A large percentage (40 percent) of
the sample indicated that they did, with women being significantly more likely to report bringing a translator than
men (48 versus 28 percent; $\underline{X}^2$ = 36.91; df = 1, $\underline{p} < .001$).

DISCUSSION

This chapter has reported some early descriptive results from a recent probability survey of older Puerto
Ricans living in the New York metropolitan area. Our descriptive efforts have focused on selected demographic
characteristics of this population as well as on their migration history and the acculturation process as it affects
these elderly.

Data on education, occupation, and income provide a
broad outline of the socioeconomic status of older Puerto
Ricans. Education, an important determinant of occupational position and earning power over the life course, is
seen to be very low, with two-thirds of the sample having
completed less than an eighth grade education. We see
also a difficult labor history. Despite their relative
youth, the great majority of these elderly are not currently working for pay, although they have done so in the
past. Health is cited most frequently as the primary reason for leaving the labor force, perhaps an expected consequence of the fact that almost three-quarters of the ever-
employed have had low-level service and laboring occupations as their major lifetime employment. Household incomes are correspondingly low, and substantial proportions

of these elderly rely on income from public assistance programs such as food stamps.

Within the elderly Puerto Rican population, we see considerable evidence of the "feminization of poverty" (Minkler and Stone 1985; Pearce 1978). While the absolute level of income is extremely low for the population as a whole, women carry a disproportionate share of this burden. The income disadvantage of elderly Puerto Rican women is probably related to a second demographic factor that distinguishes the sexes: the considerably greater likelihood of women being separated, divorced, or widowed. These findings are of particular concern because both low income and disrupted marital status have been linked in the general literature to a greater likelihood of mental health problems (Dohrenwend and Dohrenwend 1969; Gove 1972; Guttentag et al. 1980). The data thus suggest that within a high-risk population, the older woman may be at particular risk for mental health problems.

The data on acculturation indicate that, despite a relatively lengthy period of residence in the United States, the elderly Puerto Rican population is largely unacculturated and that this lack of acculturation is more pronounced among the women. The great majority of the sample reports at least some difficulty with the English language, and fully 40 percent indicate that they bring someone with them to act as a translator when they need to deal with bureaucracies.

This finding of high reliance on translators, and level of English problems more generally, is of considerable interest. While the importance of having someone to help negotiate bureaucratic encounters has been documented for older people generally (Shanas and Sussman 1981; Sussman 1976), our data suggest that for the Puerto Rican elderly the usual difficulties older people have with bureaucracies are compounded by language barriers.

More generally, the data are of interest in that they point to a type of dependency that one does not usually think about with respect to old age. Analyses that are currently underway indicate that roughly one-quarter of our sample has English problems that are so severe that they interfere with the older person's ability to carry out routine environmental transactions such as using public transportation, shopping, or going to the doctor. These persons, the majority of whom are women, have higher levels of depressive symptoms than do persons with less severe English problems. They also have higher levels of dependency in a number of activities of daily living that gerontologists have found to be important determinants of the older person's ability to remain independently in the community (e.g., dressing, bathing, climbing stairs, or going outdoors). We are also finding that most of the persons who serve as translators for these older people are adult daughters, which suggests further that acculturative difficulties on the part of the older generation are not limited in their effect to the older people themselves, but affect the succeeding generation as well.

ACKNOWLEDGMENTS

This research was supported by National Institute of Mental Health Grant numbers MH40881 from the Mental Disorders of the Aging Research Branch to the author and MH30569 from the Minority Research Resources Branch to the Hispanic Research Center. Gerald Gurin and Robert Malgady offered helpful comments on the manuscript.

NOTE

1. This difference is to be expected because household income is correlated with marital status, and the women in our sample are much less likely to be currently married than the men.

REFERENCES

Bengtson, V. L., P. L. Kasschau, and P. K. Ragan. 1977. "The impact of social structure on aging individuals." In J. E. Birren and K. W. Schaie, eds., Handbook of the Psychology of Aging, pp. 327-53. New York: Van Nostrand Reinhold.

Cantor, M. 1979. "The informal support system of New York's inner city elderly: Is ethnicity a factor?" In D. E. Gelfand and A. J. Kutzik, eds., Ethnicity and Aging, pp. 153-74. New York: Springer.

Cantor, M., and M. Mayer. 1976. "Health and the inner city elderly." The Gerontologist 16, Pt. 1:17–25.

Cuellar, I., L. C. Harris, and R. Jasso. 1980. "An acculturation scale for Mexican–American normal and clinical populations." Hispanic Journal of Behavioral Sciences 3:199–217.

Dowd, J. J., and V. L. Bengtson. 1978. "Aging in minority populations: An examination of the double jeopardy hypothesis." Journal of Gerontology 33:427–36.

Dohrenwend, B. P., and B. S. Dohrenwend. 1969. Social Status and Psychological Disorder. New York: Wiley.

Gove, W. 1972. "The relationship between sex roles, mental illness and marital status." Social Forces 51: 34–44.

Guttentag, M., S. Salasin, and D. Belle. 1980. The Mental Health of Women. New York: Academic.

Lacayo, C. G. 1980. A national study to assess the service needs of the Hispanic elderly. Final report to the Administration on Aging. Los Angeles: Asociacion nacional pro personas mayores.

Mahard, R. E. 1988. "The CES–D as a measure of depressive mood in the elderly Puerto Rican population." Journal of Gerontology: Psychological Sciences 43:24–25.

Markides, K. S., and C. H. Mindel. 1987. Aging and Ethnicity. Newbury Park, Calif.: Sage.

Minkler, M., and R. Stone. 1985. "The feminization of poverty and older women." The Gerontologist 25:351–57.

Newton, F. C. 1980. "Issues in research and service delivery among Mexican–American elderly: A concise statement with recommendations." The Gerontologist 20: 208–13.

New York City Department of City Planning. 1982. The Puerto Rican New Yorkers: A Recent History of Their Distribution and Population and Household Characteristics. New York: Author.

Pearce, D. 1978. "The feminization of poverty: Women, work and welfare." Urban and Social Change Review 11:28-36.

Shanas, E., and M. B. Sussman. 1981. "The family in later life:. Social structure and social policy." In R. W. Fogel, E. Hatfield, S. B. Kiesler, and E. Shanas, eds., Aging: Stability and Change in the Family, pp. 211-31. New York: Academic.

Sussman, M. B. 1976. "The family life of old people." In R. H. Binstock and E. Shanas, eds., Handbook of Aging and the Social Sciences, pp. 218-43. New York: Van Nostrand Reinhold.

Szapocznik, J., M. A. Scopetta, and W. Kurtines. 1978. "Theory and measurement of acculturation." Interamerican Journal of Psychology 12:113-30.

U.S. Bureau of the Census. 1982. 1980 Census of Population: Alphabetic Index of Industries and Occupation. PHC80-R3. Washington, D.C.: U.S. Government Printing Office.

Valle, R., and L. Mendoza. 1978. The Elder Latino. San Diego: Campanile Press, San Diego State University.

Index

About the Contributors

Cynthia T. García Coll, Ph.D., was born and raised in Río Piedras, Puerto Rico. She obtained a bachelor's degree at the University of Puerto Rico. She then moved to the United States to pursue graduate education. She obtained a Master's degree in Developmental Psychology at the University of Florida and a Ph.D. in Development and Personality Psychology at Harvard University. Dr. García Coll has been a faculty member at Brown University since 1981 in the Pediatrics and Psychology Departments. Since 1983 she also holds an honorary appointment at the Department of Pediatrics at the University of Puerto Rico Medical School, where she has been conducting research since 1982. Dr. García Coll's main research interests are on the interplay between biology and sociocultural influences on human development.

María de Lourdes-Mattei, Ph.D., obtained her doctoral degree in Developmental and Clinical Psychology at the University of Massachusetts, Amherst, following her undergraduate studies at the University of Puerto Rico. She has been associated with the Gándara Mental Health Center since 1983. Dr. Mattei is an Associate faculty member at Antioch/New England School of Professional Psychology and lectures at the School of Social Work at Smith College. In addition, she is a psychologist and consultant in private practice in western Massachusetts. Dr. Mattei's main area of interest is the psychodynamic and sociocultural aspects of mental health, with special focus on Puerto Rican women.

Vickie A. Borrás, Ph.D., is a clinical psychologist of Puerto Rican background who has specialized in the field of child psychotherapy. She obtained her doctoral degree at the University of Massachusetts, Amherst, in 1984. She trained at Judge Baker/Children's Hospital in Boston during her pre-doctoral internship. Dr. Borrás was director of the Hispanic Program at the Worcester Youth Guidance Center where her research on single Puerto Rican women began. Subsequently, she was director of the Parent and Child Development Program at Brookside Community

Health Center, Brigham and Women's Hospital, Boston. During this time she was also instructor of psychology at the Department of Psychiatry, Harvard University. Recently, Dr. Borrás migrated to Miami, Florida, where she is in private practice.

Pedro Cebollero, M.S., obtained his Bachelor of Science degree in Biology at the University of Puerto Rico in 1973. In 1986 he finished his Master of Science degree in Psychology at Brown University, where he did his graduate research on social cognition. He currently works at the Child and Family Psychiatry Department of Rhode Island Hospital, where he does research on children's knowledge of, and attitudes toward, acquired immunodeficiency syndrome (AIDS).

Lillian Comas-Díaz, Ph.D., completed her Bachelor of Arts and Master of Arts degrees at the University of Puerto Rico. She finished a Ph.D. in Clinical Psychology at the University of Massachusetts. Dr. Comas-Díaz was a faculty member at the Department of Psychiatry School of Medicine Yale University. She also directed the Hispanic Clinic at the Yale University School of Medicine. Dr. Comas-Díaz directed the American Psychological Association Office of Ethnic Minority Affairs. In 1986 she co-founded the Transcultural Mental Health Institute, where she acts as its Executive Director. She also maintains a private practice in Washington, D.C. Dr. Comas-Díaz has published extensively on the topics of cross-cultural mental health, gender, and ethnicity in psychotherapy, and mental health needs of Puerto Rican women. Since 1983 she has been listed as a member of Who's Who of American Women. She is a fellow of the American Psychological Association Division of Psychology of Women and the Society for the Psychological Study of Ethnic Minority Issues.

Maribel Escobar, B.A., was born in Fajardo, Puerto Rico, and grew up and studied in Naguabo, Puerto Rico until the twelfth grade. She graduated with a Bachelor of Science degree in Nursing in 1983 from the University of Puerto Rico. Her work experience includes: Hospital Universitario de Adultos (1983-1985), and the Hospital Pediátrico Universitario (1985-1987), where she coordinated a study of adolescent pregnancy and childbearing and a study of feeding intervention in babies suffering intrauterine growth retardation. She moved to Boston, Massachusetts

in April 1987 to pursue a Master's degree. At present,
she is working at Martha Eliot Health Center in Boston as
a Pediatric Clinic Nurse.

Rita E. Mahard, Ph.D., is a research associate at
the Hispanic Research Center at Fordham University. Dr.
Mahard received her Ph.D. in Sociology from the University
of Michigan in 1983, and also holds a Bachelor's degree
in Spanish from Bates College. She is currently principal
investigator of a large survey study of Puerto Rican elderly residing in the New York metropolitan area. Dr.
Mahard's research is supported by the Mental Disorders of
the Aging Research Branch of the National Institute of
Mental Health.

Maria T. Margarida Juliá, Psy.D., obtained a Master's degree in Counseling Psychology at Harvard University in 1980, and a Psy.D. in Clinical Psychology at
Massachusetts School of Professional Psychology in 1986.
She completed a Post-Doctoral Internship in child neuropsychology at the Children's Hospital, Boston, Massachusetts. Her professional experience includes clinical work
at several community mental health centers and university
settings in the Boston area such as Harvard University
Law School Counseling Center. She is presently an associate professor at the Caribbean Center for Advanced
Graduate Studies and associate in private practice with
the Collective of Psychological Services, San Juan, Puerto
Rico. Her areas of special interest include women's development and feminist psychotherapy, family therapy, and
clinical neuropsychology.

Marya Muñoz Vázquez, Ph.D., obtained her Bachelor's
and Master's degrees from the University of Puerto Rico
and her Ph.D. in Counseling Psychology from the University of Missouri. She is currently an associate professor
of psychology at the Psychology Department, University of
Puerto Rico, Río Piedras, Puerto Rico. She is the author
of the book, El Divorcio en la Sociedad Puertorriqueña,
and has published on issues related to women's work and
health, sexual harassment, and community organization.

Ivonne Romero-García, M.Ed., is a doctoral candidate
in the School Psychology program at the University of
Massachusetts, Amherst. She completed her undergraduate

education at the University of Puerto Rico-Mayagüez Campus and moved to the United States in order to pursue graduate studies. She obtained her Master's and certificate of advanced educational studies at Boston College. During her stay in Massachusetts she has worked with Latino populations, both as a school psychologist and family therapist. She is currently the coordinator of the Assessment and Research Training Unit at the University of Massachusetts and, together with Dr. Vázquez-Nuttall, is in the process of editing a book on preschool assessment.

María del Carmen Santos-Ortiz, M.A., MPHE, is a doctoral candidate in School Psychology at Temple University, Philadelphia. At present she works as an instructor in the Graduate Health Education Program, School of Public Health, University of Puerto Rico. She worked previously as director of educational services at the Latin American Center of Sexually Transmitted Diseases. Santos-Ortiz holds two Master's degrees, one in Public Health Education and one in Clinical Psychology at the University of Puerto Rico. She is a member of the following professional associations: the International Society for AIDS Education; the Puerto Rican Association of Sex Educators, Counselors, and Therapists; Puerto Rico Health Educators Association; American Psychologists Association; and the Puerto Rican Association for the Study of Immunodeficiencies, Inc. She is currently conducting research in sex education and sexual behavior among adolescents and educational programs for asthmatic children and their families.

Marta Valcárcel, M.D., born in Puerto Rico, became the first woman to chair the Department of Pediatrics of the University of Puerto Rico School of Medicine in 1977, a position that she still occupies. She had obtained a Bachelor of Science degree in 1951 and a Doctor of Medicine degree in 1955 from the University of Puerto Rico. After pediatric training in New York at Kings County Hospital, she returned to Puerto Rico. She was director of Maternal and Infant Care Clinics and participated in newborn care in the University Hospital. This experience sparked her interest in neonatology and led her to return to New York for a fellowship in neonatal perinatal medicine at Columbia Presbyterian Medical Center. On her return to Puerto Rico, she resumed her activity in the medical school as director of the Newborn Service of the University District

Hospital (1967-1977), and chief of the Perinatal-Neonatal Section of the University of Puerto Rico School of Medicine. In 1978 she was instrumental in the conversion of the pediatric facilities of the University Hospital, under her direction as executive director, into a Pediatric Hospital. She resigned from this position in 1986. Her main interest in research has been on maternal and infant interaction of high-risk infants.

Ena Vázquez-Nuttall, Ed.D., is associate professor of School and Counseling Psychology at the University of Massachusetts, Amherst and at Northeastern University, Boston, Massachusetts. Dr. Vázquez-Nuttall completed her undergraduate education at the University of Puerto Rico and migrated to the United States where she completed degrees at Radcliffe (Harvard University) and at Boston University. She is presently on the editorial board of the Journal of Counseling and Development and is in the process of editing a book on preschool assessment. She has published widely in the areas of assessment, evaluation, and research, cross-cultural issues in counseling and testing, families, substance abuse, educational achievement, and Hispanic women.

Diana L. Vélez, Ph.D., got her Bachelor of Arts degree at City College of New York, her Master of Arts and Master of Philosophy degrees, and Ph.D. at Columbia University. She is an associate professor of Spanish at the University of Iowa, where she teaches Latin American, Chicano, and Puerto Rican literature (especially women's writing), translation, and bilingualism. She is interested in gender issues and issues of national identity. Her book of translation, Reclaiming Medusa: Short Stories by Contemporary Puerto Rican Women, was published by Spinsters/Aunt Lute in 1988.

Iris Zavala-Martínez, Ph.D., born in Puerto Rico in the 1940s, is a Puerto Rican feminist clinical community psychologist and mother to an adolescent. She obtained her Bachelor of Arts degree from the Universidad Interamericana, moved to the United States in 1975, and mistakenly got two Master's degrees: one in psychiatric rehabilitation from Boston University and one in clinical psychology. Her doctorate is in clinical psychology from the University of Massachusetts. She has been chief psychologist at a mental health center in Lowell, Massachusetts, director of a Latino mental health program in Worcester, Massachusetts, and deputy of Mental Health Services at the Executive Office of Human Services for the State of Massachusetts. She also pursued independent projects and was clinical instructor of psychology at Cambridge Hospital, Harvard Medical School. She has published various articles on critical aspects of mental health and presented at conferences and workshops. She is interested in discovering the emancipatory potential and limits of therapeutic practice and in developing relevant and creative mental health programs. She returned in the spring of 1988 to her patria and is currently Director of San Juan Mental Health Division.